"**Mother Loyola's name** is becoming one that in itself is an endorsement of every book over which it appears...A careful use of Mother Loyola's work will be productive of the best results." --Rosary Magazine, November 1901

About Mother Mary Loyola:

Most Catholics today who have heard the name Mother Mary Loyola know her as the author of *The King of the Golden City*, which has enjoyed a resurgence in popularity in recent years. But few know that she wrote over two dozen works, and that she was once a household name among Catholics of her era. What made her unique among Catholic authors was her ability to draw in her listeners with story after story—and not just any stories, but ones that incorporated current events and brand new inventions of the time. Despite the fact that those events are no longer current, and those inventions no longer brand new, her books scintillate with the appeal of an active mind that could find a moral in the most unusual places. And while the printed word lacks the animated facial expressions and vocal inflections which reveal a gifted storyteller, hers convey her enthusiasm so capably that the reader can easily imagine sitting at the feet of this wise old nun.

About *Jesus of Nazareth*:

James Cardinal Gibbons was Archbishop of Baltimore when he asked Mother Loyola to write this story of the Life of our Lord. As a revered author himself, and considering the number of such stories available even then, we can only imagine the admiration he must have held for Mother Loyola's rare talent for narrative. She does not disappoint in this story, for as always, she brings to life the most vivid images of our Lord, such that the children who read it will feel almost as if they were following the dusty paths our Saviour trod. Now enhanced with an abundance of contemporary engravings and lithographs, this volume is an invaluable means of impressing upon the minds of young children the reality of our God become Man.

To learn more about Mother Mary Loyola, visit our website at
www.staugustineacademypress.com.

With the Children

"My delights were to be with the children of men."

(Proverbs 8:31)

Jesus of Nazareth

The Story of His Life
Written for Children

BY

Mother Mary Loyola
OF THE BAR CONVENT, YORK

EDITED BY

Rev. Herbert Thurston, S.J.

2014
St. Augustine Academy Press
Lisle, Illinois

This book is newly typeset based on the tenth edition published in 1907 by Benziger Brothers. All editing strictly limited to the correction of errors in the original text and minor clarifications in punctuation or phrasing. Any remaining oddities of spelling or phrasing are as found in the original.

Nihil Obstat
    REMIGIUS LAFORT, S.T.L.
    Censor

Imprimatur
    JOHN M. FARLEY
    Archbishop of New York

New York, June 24, 1906.

This book was originally published in 1906 by Benziger Brothers. This edition ©2014 by St. Augustine Academy Press. Editing by Theresa Kleck and Lisa Bergman.

ISBN: 978-1-936639-26-7
Library of Congress Control Number: 2014937906

Unless otherwise noted, all illustrations in this book, including the cover, are either the original illustrations as found in the book, or are public domain images.

to
The Children of America

THIS STORY OF HIM

WHO LOVES THEM

AND DIED FOR THEM

AND INVITES THEM

TO SPEND WITH HIM

A HAPPY ETERNITY

IS AFFECTIONATELY DEDICATED.

Editor's Note

I have endeavored in this new edition of Mother Mary Loyola's *Jesus of Nazareth* to be as faithful as possible to the original text as printed in the 1907 edition by Benziger Brothers. However, I have, in a few cases, judiciously corrected punctuation and spelling, and in a handful of instances, I added or changed a word to improve the grammar or the clarity of a passage.

The greatest change has been to greatly increase the number of illustrations included, and to place them where they are relevant to the text. Where possible, I have retained the original illustrations, especially the beautiful lithographs by Heinrich Hofmann. Others have been added from various artists contemporary to the time in which this book was published.

Lastly, I would point out that all Scriptural references found in this book are from the Catholic Douay-Rheims version, and thus they often do not align in chapter and verse with modern bibles, which conform more closely to the chapter and verse structure of the Protestant King James Version.

In Christ,
Lisa Bergman
St. Augustine Academy Press
April 2014

Contents

I. "Who Art Thou, Lord?"	1
II. On Trial	7
III. The Promised One	15
IV. A Joyful Surprise	31
V. Holy Mary	34
VI. Holy Mother of God	41
VII. Mary's Song	45
VIII. The First Christmas Night	50
IX. In the Temple	61
X. The Star in the East	69
XI. Jesus of Nazareth	78
XII. In the Temple Again	84
XIII. The Hidden Life	93
XIV. Palestine and its People	105
XV. The Banks of Jordan	113
XVI. In the Desert	120
XVII. The First Disciples	128
XVIII. Galilee	136
XIX. The Court of the Gentiles	144
XX. At Jacob's Well	154
XXI. A Sabbath at Nazareth	163

XXII. His Own City	171
XXIII. "We have seen wonderful things today"	179
XXIV. The Twelve	190
XXV. The Sermon on the Mount	204
XXVI. "Who went about doing Good"	213
XXVII. "Never spake like this Man".	225
XXVIII. "Talitha Cumi".	232
XXIX. A Holiday	246
XXX. "Will you also go away?"	256
XXXI. "Lord, Help me!"	263
XXXII. At Cæsarea Philippi	271
XXXIII. With the Children.	282
XXXIV. With the Twelve	288
XXXV. With His Friends	304
XXXVI. The Beginning of the End	316
XXXVII. "Jerusalem! Jerusalem!"	327
XXXVIII. The Night in which He was Betrayed.	348
XXXVIII. "It is Finished."	374
XL. "Jesus Christ Yesterday, Today, and the Same For Ever.".	411
XLI. "This Jesus shall so come as you have seen Him going into Heaven."	438

Prefatory Note

THE pressure of an earnest invitation sent me from America must be my excuse for venturing to add another Life of Christ for the Young to the excellent ones already existing.

The aim proposed is to strengthen faith in our Lord's Divinity, and to draw the hearts of children to Him by a personal love. To do this within the limits assigned, it has seemed better to omit a certain amount of matter rather than sacrifice detailed descriptions of leading facts, which by impressing the imagination leave a vivid picture in the mind.

Where different views, as to chronology, etc., prevail, I have adopted the one supported by the greater number of Catholic authors. To the following books of reference in particular I desire to acknowledge my indebtedness:

La Sainte Bible, by M. l'Abbé L. C. Fillion.
The Christ the Son of God, by the Abbé Fouard.
Jesus Christ, by Père Didon, O. P.
Life of Jesus Christ, by Fr. Maas, S. J.

Life of Our Life, by Fr. Coleridge, S. J.
The Passion, by Père Ollivier, O. P.
Dictionnaire de la S. Bible, by the Abbé F. Vigouroux.
Cambridge Companion to the Bible.
Helps to the Study of the Bible.
St. Luke, by the Right Rev. Mgr. Ward.
Jesus the Messiah, by Dr. Edersheim.
Sketches of Jewish Social Life, by Dr. Edersheim.
The Resurrection of Christ, by G.W.B. Marsh, B.A.
Holy Gospel According to St. John, by the Very Rev. J. MacIntyre.

Should this little book help even a few children of the great Catholic Church of America, so free, vigorous, and expanding, to withstand the infidelity of the day, and lead them to a tender, personal love of Jesus Christ, it will have happily attained its end.

M. Loyola.

FOREWORD
from Cardinal Gibbons

WE all realize that the children form the most precious portion of the flock committed to our care. The little ones were very dear to the heart of our Blessed Lord: "*Suffer the little children to come unto me, and forbid them not; for of such is the kingdom of God.*" (Mark 10:14) Hence we are all willing with St. Paul "*to spend ourselves, and be spent*" in a special manner for the sake of the dear children. In their turn the children are destined to be the people; and we know that impressions are the more abiding when made in the time of youth: "*A young man according to his way, even when he is old he will not depart from it.*" (Prov. 22:6) Whoever contributes toward implanting the seeds of piety and virtue in the minds of children, has a special claim to the promise of the Holy Ghost: "*They that instruct many to justice, shall shine as stars for all eternity.*" (Dan. 12:3) The most efficient way of forming the youthful heart to virtue and piety is to cause the love of God to predominate over the fear of God: "*Be ye followers of God, as most dear children; and walk in love,* as Christ also hath loved us, and hath delivered Himself for us, an oblation and a sacrifice to God for an odour of sweetness." (Eph. 5:1) Again the Beloved Disciple tells us: "*Every one that loveth is born of God, and knoweth God. He that loveth not, knoweth not God; for God is charity. Fear is not in charity; but perfect charity casteth out fear, because fear hath pain. And he that feareth is not perfected in charity. Let us therefore love God, because God first hath loved us.*" (1 John 4)

The beautiful life-story of Our Blessed Lord, when well told, is a most powerful means of inflaming the hearts of youth with love for God. This love, in turn, will help the children to keep God's commandments: "*And this is charity that we walk according to His commandments.*" (2 John 1:6)

My heart was delighted on reading the proof-sheets of *Jesus of Nazareth: The Story of His Life, Written for Children* by Mother Mary Loyola. The book is eminently practical, simple, unctuous, and interesting. It will make a powerful impression on the minds of the children. In fact no one can read it without loving God more, and therefore becoming better. The Author evidently realizes the wants of the child-mind, and, at the same time, comforts every soul in its longing for something higher and better.

This gifted Religious has contributed much toward the salvation of souls in the many beautiful and useful works that she has written. These books are silently, yet surely, doing their work in the family circle, in the schools, and in the work shops. The remarkable success of the Author of these works is evidently to be attributed to her genuine piety, her life of prayer and union with God, and her knowledge of the Sacred Scriptures and the Fathers. The learned Father Thurston, S. J., carefully supervises her works. Her attractive suggestions, and her enlightening doctrines are put so simply, and applied so well, that a person would almost wonder why he did not think of expressing his thoughts in that way himself.

Parents, teachers and instructors will find Mother Loyola's works very useful in the difficult task of forming the minds of children to a life of virtue. We would be glad to see a copy of *Jesus of Nazareth, Written for Children* in every household in the land. We wish it God-speed in going out on its great mission.

J. Card. Gibbons
Baltimore, March 25, 1906

I.
"Who Art Thou, Lord?"
(Acts 9:5)

Nineteen hundred years ago there came into this world a Man whose Life of thirty-three years is the chief event in the world's history, and—whether we think of it or not—the chief event in the history here and hereafter of every one of us.

He was promised four thousand years before He came. The race, the tribe, the family, the time of His coming, the chief events of His Life were known. So that in the reign of the Roman Emperor, Augustus Cæsar, when the time foretold by the prophets had come, there was a widespread expectation of a great Deliverer, and many eyes were turned to the little country of Palestine where He was to appear. And there, in Bethlehem, in a stable, on a winter's night, He came. Angels sang in the heavens and sent shepherds to His crib. A star shining out in the eastern sky brought wise men to His feet. Then the marvels around Him ceased, and whilst men were still expecting, and wondering why the promised One delayed so long, He was growing up from youth to manhood, and working at a carpenter's trade in the despised village of Nazareth.

Jesus of Nazareth

At the age of thirty He left His cottage home and began to show Himself to men. The majesty and grace of His Person, His winning ways, the power and the sweetness of His words, and His marvellous works, soon carried His fame far beyond the limits of His own land. His feet trod the stormy waves. His voice stilled the tempests, cast out devils, and brought peace to the souls of men. The touch of His hand gave sight to the blind, hearing to the deaf, speech to the dumb, life to the dead.

Multitudes followed wherever He went, through the crowded streets, up the hillsides, into the desert. When He preached on the seashore, the people so thronged Him that He had to step into a boat and push off from the land, His eager hearers pressing down to the water's edge to catch His every word. No man had ever spoken like this Man. His words not only fell upon their ears, but sank into their souls, stirring them to higher thoughts and desires, to a sorrow for their sins which brought them peace, to a love of Him which drew them near to God. Wounds of body and of soul too sore for other handling His light touch healed. The poor, the ignorant, those of whom the world makes little account, went after Him in thousands, heedless of food and shelter, of everything—save the Face and the Voice of Jesus of Nazareth.

Multitudes flocked after Him. But there was no multitude to Him. Each soul stood out before Him clear and distinct, with its needs, its troubles, its sins, its desires for better things. The little child, the widow, the eager youth, the trembling sinner, felt that He read them through and through, understood them, loved them, cared for their love, wanted to help them, to make them happy—and could do it.

Gradually there gathered round Him a band of disciples. From among these He chose twelve men to be His intimate companions and friends. He kept them constantly with Him, He carefully taught and trained them, He let them into His secrets, He shared with them His miraculous powers, so that like Him they cast out devils, and cured the sick. He called them Apostles, that is, messengers sent, because they were to take His place and carry on His work when He should leave the earth. They were fishermen, most of them, rough and ignorant, but with simple, devoted hearts. Father, mother, home, everything they had in this world, they left for their Master's sake, ready to follow Him everywhere, even to prison and to death.

For not all men revered Him for His holiness and wonderful works, and loved Him for His goodness. He had fierce enemies, men who were jealous of Him and hated Him for His teaching, His warnings, His miracles. During three years they slandered and persecuted Him. And at last they laid hands on Him, scourged Him as a slave, crowned Him with thorns as a mock king, nailed Him to a cross between thieves, and watched Him die in lingering agony. He was buried. His grave was sealed, and guards were set to watch.

Then His enemies thought the world was rid of Him, and that they would hear His Name no more. But three days after His Crucifixion He rose from the tomb as He had foretold, and showed Himself to His friends. For forty days He went in and out among them, eating with them, letting them touch His wounded hands and feet, giving them His last instructions. On the fortieth day after His Resurrection, He led His disciples to the top of Mount Olivet, and having blessed them, slowly rose above their heads into the heavens till a cloud received Him out of their sight. As they remained looking up into the sky, two Angels in white garments stood by them and said: "Ye men of Galilee, why stand you looking up to Heaven? This Jesus who is taken up from you into Heaven shall so come as you have seen Him going into Heaven."

"This Jesus." Who was this wonderful Man? Was He a true Man, and if so, was He more than Man? Pilate, the Roman Governor who condemned Him to death, was so struck by His calm majesty, His silence, and His patience in the midst of cruel injustice and pain, that he asked Him: "Whence art Thou?" He wanted to know if He was a mere man, or if there was any truth in the belief of many, that He was more than Man, that He was the Son of God.

Pilate's Prisoner made him no answer, because none was needed. He had been three and thirty years in the world, and the question: "Whence art Thou?" had been answered so plainly by the wonderful works He had done, that those only who were wilfully blind could help knowing who He was and whence He came.

Who art Thou, Lord?

About five years after the Ascension of Christ into Heaven, a young man was hastening to Damascus to seize and punish all he could find, men and women who believed in Jesus of Nazareth. Suddenly, a light from Heaven shone round about him, and, falling on the ground, he heard a Voice saying to him: "Saul, Saul, why persecutest thou Me?" And he said: "Who art Thou, Lord?" And the Voice made answer: "I am Jesus whom thou persecutest."[1]

That question and its answer changed the persecutor Saul into the great St. Paul. He came to know and love our Blessed Lord so well, that neither tribulation, nor danger, nor the sword, nor death, nor any creature, he said, could separate him from Him.

Now the question of Pilate and of Saul was of immense importance, not to themselves alone, but to every one of us. A more important question has never been asked; for, to know the truth about Jesus Christ, and to guide our lives by what we know, is the end for which we were sent into this world.

We did not see what the people of His own land saw every day; but we have the story of His Life written by those who knew Him intimately, and it ought to be familiar to us all. Every man and woman, every boy and girl should know it well. It is of more importance to us by far than anything else we have to learn. It was written, not for mankind in general, but for each of us, one by one, that we might study it and copy its lessons into our own lives.

---

1 Acts 9:5

These are days in which our belief in Jesus Christ must be firmly rooted if it is to be unshaken by the unbelief and indifference around us. We should try, then, to bring home to ourselves in every possible way the truth about Him—Who He is; what He came into this world to do; what we must do that He may not have come for us in vain. Let us ask, then, humbly and earnestly with St. Paul:

"Who art Thou, Lord?"

II.

On Trial

To find the answer to this question, we must go back a long way—before that time, nearly six thousand years ago, when human history began—right back to the Eternal Years.

From all eternity God had lived alone—alone, but not lonely—One God in Three Persons, Father, Son, and Holy Ghost. No sound broke the stillness of His Life; no events came, and went, and brought a change. He was infinitely happy; for in Himself He had all things. If there was to be life, beauty, joy, outside of Him, from Him it must come.

And God willed these things should be. He would not keep always to Himself the happiness He could share with others, but would pour it out upon creatures able to know and love and enjoy Him.

He created the Angels, noble and beautiful spirits, not made to be united to bodies.

He created man, a being in some respects more wonderful than the Angels, because of the union of an immortal spirit with a body formed of the dust of the earth. And because God saw it was not good for man to be alone, He gave him a companion worthy of him. We are now so spoilt by sin that we can form no idea of those beautiful creatures of God in their state of innocence. We have never seen anything so noble and so lovely as Adam and Eve; and what was hidden within was nobler and lovelier still. There was no darkness, nor ignorance, nor weakness. They understood the laws by which this world is governed, the secrets of Nature which men are puzzling out now bit by bit. They had no evil passions, no liking for what is wrong. Their hearts were pure and loving; their wills were strong and right.

They were perfect, then, in their human nature; but God was not yet satisfied. He loved them so much that He enriched them with a gift altogether above their nature, with a supernatural gift called sanctifying grace, which made their souls beautiful in another and far higher way, and gave them a right to see Him face to face one day. They were to pass from a fair home on earth to the one prepared for them in Heaven, not by sickness and through the gate of death, but gently and painlessly as a child is carried in its father's arms from one room to another.

Meantime He placed them in "the paradise of pleasure," a garden stored with everything that could serve them for use or enjoyment. No plants or flowers, no birds or beasts that we have ever seen can compare with those of that garden of theirs. The animals great and small reverenced and obeyed them, came at their call, gambolled about them, ate from their hand. All was

On Trial

in order there. The irrational creatures were subject to Adam and Eve, and they themselves were subject with joy and gratitude to the God who had given them all.

Here, then, in "the paradise of pleasure," the father and mother of us all were placed on trial.

Yes, on trial. For it was the Will of God that both Angels and men should have the happiness which was prepared for them increased by meriting or deserving it. Therefore He gave them free will, or the power to choose good or evil. He loves a cheerful, loving service, and He determined that by an act of obedience His reasonable creatures should win their everlasting reward. What the trial of the Angels was we do not know. All we know is that one-third of them were unfaithful to God, and, with full knowledge of the wickedness of their act, rebelled against Him and were lost forever.

Like Adam and Eve, the Angels were created in a state of sanctifying grace. They were very dear and precious in the sight of God. But sin is so hateful to Him, that for that one deliberate act of rebellion against Him He took from them that priceless gift of grace, and drove them from the brightness of His Presence into everlasting darkness.

But He did not take from them their natural gifts, their clear intellect, their strong will. And these they now determined to use against Him by leading into their own rebellion those favoured children of His in Paradise. Thus it was more hatred of God than envy of these heirs of Heaven that led Satan to plan the destruction of Adam and Eve. It would never do to tempt them openly, for sin had made him so ugly that they would have been frightened of him. So he disguised himself, and fitly took the form of a serpent.

See Eve in her beauty and innocence walking alone through the garden. She is supremely happy. She is the dear child of God; she has all she can desire. Suddenly she comes upon the serpent coiled round the foot of a tree, "the tree of the knowledge of good and evil." It is a mysterious name and reminds the owners of this fair garden that God who has given it to them is Master still. For He has said:

"Of every tree of Paradise thou shalt eat. But of the tree of knowledge of good and evil, thou shalt not eat. For in what day soever thou shalt eat of it, thou shalt die the death."

A simple command, but a very solemn one. Disobedience to it would make them lose the grace and favour of God, and deserve His most dreadful punishments in this world and in the next. They know, then, all that depends on that tree, and never pass it without a feeling of awe.

Eve is surprised to see the serpent there and stops to look at him. The serpent begins to talk and she listens:

"Why do you not eat of the fruit of this tree?" he asks.

Notice how he begins his first temptation as he has begun so many since, by trying to make God appear hard.

A little Spanish girl who heard this story for the

first time said: "Eve should not have listened; she should have made the sign of the Cross and gone down another walk." But Eve did listen. She looked up shyly and wistfully at the tree and said:

"God hath commanded us that we should not eat, lest perhaps we die."

"Die!" answered the tempter, "no, you shall not die."

And then he makes a show of trusting her with a secret. There is always something fascinating about a secret. Eve is curious and draws nearer.

"God doth know," he goes on, "that in what day soever you shall eat thereof your eyes shall be opened and you shall be as Gods."

This was what enticed her. It was not gluttony, but curiosity and ambition that were her ruin. To see what would happen; to be as Gods, this was what she wanted; as to the punishment, she would risk it. She stretched out her hand, plucked the fruit, and ate it. Oh, what a change came over her in that moment! When Adam saw her a minute later, the blush of guilt was on her face, her peace and happiness were gone.

She told him what she had done, and at first he was shocked and terrified. At first—and then came his temptation, but in a different form from hers. She was his tempter. She used her influence with him, and his love for her to make him fall. She tempted him even with the appearance of good. "God has given us to each other; we have been so happy together; we must go together now. We must perish—if it is a case of perishing—together."

And she gave him the fruit, and he ate it. In that instant Adam fell from grace and the whole human race fell with him. Had he remained faithful, we should all have come into the world with souls beautiful and pleasing in the sight of God. We should have had our trial, but had we fallen no one would have been ruined but ourselves. Had Eve alone fallen, her sin would not have harmed us. It is because Adam is the father and the origin or head of the race that his fall has hurt us, that we are all born into this world without grace, in *disgrace* until by Baptism this original sin is taken away.

This is soon said, but it would need Adam and Eve themselves to tell us what it means, to make us understand how miserably unhappy they were after their sin. God used to come and walk with them in Paradise in the cool afternoon air, and they rushed forward to meet Him. Now they trembled when they heard His voice calling them. When people agree together to do wrong, they turn upon one another when the wrong is found out and they are called to account. Adam laid the blame upon Eve; Eve upon the serpent. Then came God's terrible words of punishment:

"In the sweat of thy face shalt thou eat bread till thou return to the earth out of which thou wast taken: for dust thou art and unto dust thou shalt return."

Innocence, happiness, freedom from pain and death, the possession of the paradise of pleasure—all lost and lost forever: suffering and death, and all the evils of this life let in upon the earth through them; the gates of Heaven closed, and those of Hell opened by their hands—this was what came of that one sin. For the punishment they deserved was not only the death of the body but the everlasting death of the soul. They had shared the rebellion of the bad angels; it was just they should share their condemnation.

But God had pity on them and on us. Their sin, though great and inexcusable, was less than that of the angels. They had indeed risen up in rebellion against the Infinite God, yet not with such clear knowledge; and they had been tempted. Moreover, each of the fallen angels had himself done the evil for which he was justly punished. But Adam's unhappy children had lost all by an act that was not their own.

Perhaps it was for these reasons that God determined to save the race of man. He could have done this by granting a free pardon to us. But to show the hatefulness of sin, and still more His exceeding love for us, He willed that we should be redeemed; that is, bought back; and that our Redeemer should be no other than His own Eternal Son, the Second Person of the Holy Trinity, equal to the Father in all things. It was decreed by the Three Divine Persons, Father, Son, and Holy Ghost, that a full and perfect satisfaction or compensation for the evil done should be offered to God. Now, for this two things were necessary. He who was to make the satisfaction must be equal to God, or it would not be infinite and enough; and He must be man, too, because man who had sinned must satisfy for sin.

No Angel, however high, nor all Angels and men together, could make this sufficient atonement. God himself must do it if it was to be done. And God was ready. Not counting the cost, thinking only of our misery and of His own love, the Second Person offered Himself to satisfy fully for our sins—for the first or original sin, which was not our own act, but his who was the origin and father of us all, and for those sins, too, which are our own free act.

All this load of sin which men have heaped up from the beginning against the Majesty of God, which we have each of us helped to increase, the Son of God took upon Himself, to suffer for in our stead, and thus reopen for us the gates of Heaven, which otherwise would have been closed against us forever. In place of Adam who had ruined us, another Head was given us in our dear Lord Jesus Christ. He was to put all right. He was to come and live amongst us a hard, suffering Life, and then to die upon the Cross for each of us one by one. Well may the Church cry out:

"O happy fault that has had such a Redeemer!"

III.

The Promised One

Some people ask: "Why did God put our first parents to this trial when He knew they would fall under it, and knew the terrible consequence to themselves and to all their children?"

The first and chief reason is because He is Lord and Master. He can do what He wills, and all that He does is not only right and good, but the best, as we shall see some day.

Another reason is this: Though God can never will what is evil, He can and does continually bring good out of evil. The fall of Adam and Eve, and with them of the whole human family, was a frightful evil, but out of this harm God has brought the greatest good.

By coming amongst us and becoming one of us, in order to put right again what was so wrong, He has done more than put all right. He has given us much more than we had lost. And His best gift to us is—Himself. Since the Incarnation we no longer think of Him as far away in Heaven, where we can scarcely reach Him even by thought, but as one of ourselves—a Man who could be seen, and heard, and handled, a Man with a country and a family, with ancestors good and bad, with a Mother and a home; a Man with friends and enemies; a Man with a certain character and ways, with His likes and dislikes, with His sorrows and His joys. This Man is our God, the God whom we have to adore and love. Can we not do this easily now, when He has come so near to us that we may study Him and know Him almost as we know a neighbour of next door? Truly God knows how to draw good out of evil!

We must notice, for they are very important, the words in which the Redeemer was promised by God Himself.

As soon as Adam and Eve had sinned, they, for the first time, were afraid of God. "And when they heard the voice of the Lord God walking in Paradise at the afternoon air, Adam and his wife hid themselves amidst the trees of Paradise.

And the Lord God called Adam, and said to him: Where art thou?

And he said: I heard Thy voice, and I was afraid, and I hid myself.

And He said to him: Thou hast eaten of the tree whereof I commanded thee that thou shouldst not eat.

And Adam said: The woman whom Thou gavest me to be my companion gave me of the tree and I did eat.

And the Lord God said to the woman: Why hast thou done this?

And she answered: The serpent deceived me, and I did eat.

And the Lord God said to the serpent: Because thou hast done this thing, thou art cursed among all beasts of the earth. I will put enmities between thee and the woman, and thy seed and her seed: she shall crush thy head, and thou shalt lie in wait for her heel."

Thus from the beginning, and in the words of God Himself, are the Redeemer and His Mother placed together, just as we see them in our pictures and statues. There is to be enmity, that is, hatred and warfare, between her and her Divine Child on one side, and all the brood of the serpent, the wicked angels, on the other. She through her Son is to crush the serpent's head, and the serpent in revenge will lie in wait for her other children, all those of whom her Son has made Himself the Brother.

As the Redeemer has His types or figures all through the long years when the world was waiting for Him, so has His Mother hers. And when at last He came, the word of God again places together the Mother and her Child. Those who seek Him find "the Child with Mary His Mother." In sorrow and in joy they are side by side. "Take the Child and His Mother," is the order when the Babe has to fly for His life. At a marriage feast "the Mother of Jesus was there, and Jesus also was invited." She followed Him about during His preaching. And when at last He redeemed the world with His Blood, "there stood by the Cross of Jesus His Mother." We must never separate what God Himself has thus joined together.

The Promise of Salvation

"She shall crush thy head, and thou shalt lie in wait for her heel."
(Genesis 3:15)

The Promised One

How hard the life of Adam and Eve must have been during their nine hundred years of penance! Could those who had known the paradise of pleasure ever get used to the world outside! "Cursed is the earth in thy work," God had said to Adam; "with labour and toil shalt thou eat thereof all the days of thy life. Thorns and thistles shall it bring forth to thee. In the sweat of thy face shalt thou eat bread till thou return to the earth out of which thou wast taken: for dust thou art and into dust thou shalt return."

But hard labour was only a small part of their penance. What must it have been to see on every side, as time went on, the evil fruits of their sin; not only disease and death, but death in its most frightful form—to see their first child a murderer, and the murderer of his brother! We can picture them sitting sadly hand in hand after Abel's death, recalling the time when wickedness and pain and sorrow were things unknown.

One comfort alone was left to them—the Promise, that Promise which had brightened their last moments in Paradise, and now shed its cheering light on the dark world outside. How far they understood what it meant, we cannot tell. But they built all their hopes on it, and handed it on to their children and children's children to be guarded as their most precious bequest. And when at last they left this world and went to that place of rest called Limbo, where the souls of the just were detained till the gates of Heaven should be reopened, it was to wait with eager expectation for His Coming who was to undo and more than undo all the harm their sin had done.

Century after century went by, and still He did not come. But the Promise became fuller and clearer, as a river, small at its source, broadens by the streams that flow into it. The race, the tribe, the family, and at last the time of His Coming, were made known. The kind of man He would be, His work, His sufferings, His death, were foretold vaguely indeed, here and there, yet with sufficient clearness to enable man to recognize Him when He came. The life of other men is written after their death. But God, who knows all things and who had arranged even the smallest circumstances of the Life of His Divine Son, would have the main events of His history written long before His Birth.

He was to save men not only after His Coming but before. His Precious Blood flows backward as well as forward, and by It, all those who will ever reach Heaven, from Adam and Eve downwards, will enter there.

Therefore, even before He came, God would have men know something of Him to whom the whole human family owes all the happiness it has in this life as well as all it hopes for in the next. They could not know Him as fully as we do who have the story of His Life in our hands and can study it every day if we will. But it is wonderful how much God did tell men by means of His prophets. These were holy men to whom He showed now this event, now that in the Life of Him who was to come. Were we to put together all that the prophets told of Him, we should find His Life was written hundreds of years before He came.

The Promised One

Men knew He was to be of the race of Abraham, therefore a Jew, of the Tribe of Judah, of the family of David.

His Mother was to be a Virgin:

"Behold a virgin shall conceive and bear a Son, and His name shall be called Emmanuel, which being interpreted, is God with us."[1]

He was to be born in Bethlehem:

"And thou, Bethlehem, art a little one among the thousands of Juda; out of thee shall He come forth unto Me that is to be the Ruler in Israel."[2]

He would be meek and humble of Heart, compassionate and forgiving:

"I will seek that which was lost, and I will bind up that which was broken, and I will strengthen that which was weak."[3]

He would go about doing good:

"Then shall the eyes of the blind be opened, and the ears of the deaf unstopped. Then shall the lame man leap as a hart, and the tongue of the dumb shall be free."[4]

In spite of His wonderful works and His miracles of mercy, He would be hated and rejected by His own people:

"Despised and the most abject of men, a man of sorrows and acquainted with infirmity."[5]

One of His chosen friends would sell Him to His enemies:

"And they weighed for My wages thirty pieces of silver."[6]

---

1 Isaias 7, Matt 1.   2 Micheas 5.   3 Ezechiel 34.
4 Isaias 35.   5 Isaias 53.   6 Zachary 11.

He would be scourged and spit upon, and buffeted, and crucified:

"*I have given my body to the strikers and my cheeks to them that plucked them; I have not turned away my face from them that rebuked me and spat upon me.*"[1]

"*They have dug my hands and feet. They have numbered all my bones. They have parted my garments among them, and upon my vesture they cast lots.*"[2]

After death He was to rise again:

"*For Thou wilt not leave my soul in hell, nor suffer Thy Holy One to see corruption.*"[3]

These prophecies belonged to God's chosen people the Jews, who guarded them jealously, and studied them with diligence and delight, those especially that told of the Messiah's greatness and power:

"*I will make Him higher than the kings of the earth.*"[4]

"*Sit thou at My right hand until I make thine enemies thy footstool.*"[5]

They took these words to mean that He was to be a great king of this world who would make their nation the grandest of the earth, and give them in abundance honours, riches and all the pleasant things of this life. But other prophecies quite as clear which described Him as "*a Man of sorrows, a Leper, One struck by God and afflicted,*" they passed by unnoticed. And when He came poor and lowly, a King indeed not of this world, they would not own Him for the Messiah of the prophets, but persecuted Him and put Him to death.

---

1   Isaias 1.   2   Ps. 21.   3   Ps. 16.
4   Ps. 89.   5   Ps. 110.

The Promised One

There was another way by which the world was prepared for the coming Redeemer. As He was foretold in prophecy, so He was foreshadowed in *types* or *figures*, by which we mean certain persons or things in the Old Law representing persons or things in the New.

We all know that there is nothing like a picture for giving right notions and correcting wrong ones. A teacher who has anything difficult to explain—the structure of a flower, the plan of a battle, the family of a king—turns at once to the blackboard, and with a few strokes of chalk shows easily what many words would never have made clear.

God taught His people by examples as well as by words. In a number of types He sketched before their eyes the character of the Messiah and the main lines of the work He was to do. The likeness fell far short of the perfect beauty of our Lord's character, but it was a likeness still.

- Innocent **Abel**, slain through jealousy by his brother, was a figure of Christ put to death through the hatred and envy of His brethren, the Jews:
- **Noe** who built an ark, one only, to save all who entered therein, prefigured our Lord, the Founder of one Church for the salvation of men:
- **Isaac**, the beloved son of his father, willingly submitting to death, and carrying the wood on which he was to be sacrificed, represented the well beloved Son of God led without resistance to the slaughter, and bearing His own cross on the way to Calvary.

We can all see how the following were types of our Lord:
- **Joseph**, sold for twenty pieces of silver, thrown into prison with two criminals, then raised to honour and becoming the saviour of his people:
- **Moses**, saved from death in his infancy; sent by God to deliver his people from a cruel bondage, and lead them safely through the desert to the land of promise; fasting forty days; giving the Law to the people of God; feeding them with bread from Heaven; delivering them from their enemies; working miracles for them again and again, yet saddened by their murmuring and ingratitude:
- **David**, born in Bethlehem; rebelled against by his subjects; insulted in his affliction; followed by a faithful few; gentle, merciful, and patient.

These in their character reflect our Lord's beautiful virtues.

Others, such as Josue, Samson, Jonas, Solomon, in their actions foreshadow His. In many of their acts we may see but little resemblance to our Lord's, and in some, what is very unlike. But this does not prevent their being types of Him. All such types, and others, such as the Paschal Lamb, the Brazen Serpent, the Manna, are like little bits of mosaic that have to be pieced together to make up a beautiful and perfect picture. The Son of God was not coming on earth in blinding light and majesty, as men might have imagined, but in poverty and humility. It was to help them to recognize Him as God without the glory of God about Him that such an abundance of type and prophecy was provided.

MOSES

*"Say to the children of Israel: I am the Lord
who will bring you out from the work prison of the Egyptians."*
(Exodus 6:6)

Time went on. Nearly four thousand years had passed since the Great Promise was made in Paradise. One Empire had followed another, conquering and conquered in its turn. And now the whole world was in peace, for mighty Rome had crushed every rival. But peace did not mean that men were happy. Never had they been more miserable. The worship of false gods had brought them so low, that animals, trees, stones, wicked things even—theft, rebellion against parents, cruelty, murder, bad passions of every kind—nay, the very devils themselves, were adored as gods.

The strong cruelly oppressed the weak. Men and women were so given up to the pleasure of soft, self-indulgent lives, that their hearts were hardened against the sight of pain and misery. The weak and the helpless—children, slaves, the poor, the old, the sick, were treated with a barbarity that only the most frightful selfishness can explain.

Truly the world needed its Saviour!

The Jewish prophecies were known far and wide, and all over the East there was the expectation of a Deliverer who was to appear in Judea. No man knew exactly what He was to do, but He would reform the world in some way, set right all that was wrong, and bring a golden age to the earth.

Among the Jews themselves there was naturally a more eager waiting and watching. They knew the prophecies by heart. They could tell better than the heathen what the work of the Messiah was to be.

And now that the time was at hand, the best among them were earnestly praying for the speedy coming of those Promised Ones, the Woman who was to be the serpent's enemy, and her Child who was to redeem the world.

Jesus of Nazareth

*"Honor thy father and mother,
that thou mayest be long lived uopn the land."*
(Ex. 20:12)

The Childhood
and
The Hidden Life

GABRIEL VISITS ZACHARY

*"thy wife Elizabeth shall bear thee a son,
and thou shalt call his name John"*
(Luke 1:13)

IV.
A Joyful Surprise

Before our Lord came, the holiest place in the world was the Temple of Jerusalem. Only there would God allow sacrifice to be offered, and there twice a day it was offered—a little lamb was slain, and the smoke of sweet-smelling incense rose from the golden altar in the Holy Place. At the hour of incense the people assembled in their part of the Temple, the open Courts, and prayed silently, in union with the priest who was within.

One day there was a great stir among them. A priest whose name was Zachary had been a long time in the Holy Place, and when he came out he was trembling—and dumb. What had happened? They crowded round him to ask, but he made signs to show he could not speak. The news spread fast that Zachary had seen something wonderful, and that he looked as if he had heard good news.

Good news! Indeed he had; he was dumb because he had thought it too good to be true. For many years he and his wife Elizabeth had longed to have a child, in the hope that the Messiah, now so near, might be of their family. But God had not seen good to hear their prayer, and when all expectation was gone, they had made His Will their own, and encouraged one another to bear their disappointment bravely.

Now, on this day, just as Zachary was going to pour the incense upon the flame, he saw a glorious vision—an Angel of the Lord standing on the right side of the altar. And seeing him he was troubled, and fear fell upon him. But the Angel said to him:

"Fear not, Zachary, for thy prayer is heard."

Then he went on to tell him that Elizabeth should have a son who should bring gladness to many. Even as a little child he would be great before God, and when he was grown up he would convert many of his people and prepare them for the coming of the Messiah.

Bewildered by such a joyful surprise, Zachary asked how he should know all this was true.

"I am Gabriel, who stand before God," was the answer, "and am sent to speak to thee, and to bring thee these good tidings. And, behold, thou shalt be dumb, and shalt not be able to speak until the day wherein these things shall come to pass, because thou hast not believed my words which shall be fulfilled in their time." So Zachary had the sign he asked, though it was a punishment too because of his unbelief.

Good news, as well as bad, travels fast, and when a week later he returned to his home at Ain-Karim, in the hill country of Judea, he found that Elizabeth had heard all that people knew about the vision in the Temple. She came out to meet him, anxious, yet, somehow, full of joyful expectation. He laid his finger on his lips,

A Joyful Surprise

sent for his writing tablets, and, with a trembling hand, wrote down all that had passed. Then they rejoiced together, and thanked God for His goodness to them, and waited in quiet happiness for the fulfilment of His promise.

Weeks passed by, and months. Priest after priest went by turn into the Holy Place to offer incense, and Zachary's vision came to be forgotten. But not by all. Not by those who noted every sign of the Messiah being at hand. There was an old man in Jerusalem who had a promise from God that he should not die till he had seen the Christ of the Lord. There was an aged woman who departed not from the Temple, serving night and day lest she should miss the Lord at His Coming. Such as these did not forget. And all over the world, wherever Jews were to be found, were eager hearts praying Him to come quickly.

Where was the most eager? Was it in Jerusalem among the doctors of the Law, whose life was spent in the study of the prophecies? Was it the High Priest's, or that holy old man's, or the aged woman's, or Zachary's, or Elizabeth's?

No. Not in Jerusalem, nor among the learned, nor those who had grown old in the service of God. Where then?

V.
Holy Mary

Have you ever watched the clouds on a wild day hiding the sun? They move along, a dark, heavy mass, as if determined to keep his light from the waiting world. At times, through the rifts, you catch a glimpse of him; or there is a golden border which shows he is somewhere near. You think he must be coming soon. But no, it is all too dark for him yet. Suddenly, in the midst of the gloom appears a little white cloud. It grows bright, brighter and brighter as he fills it with his glory. Yes, surely he is there; only his splendour could make it shine like that. A few moments at most and he must show himself; a few moments and he will scatter the darkness and flood the earth with light.

Hidden among the mountains of Galilee, amid a profusion of wild flowers, lies the village of Nazareth, the houses, small, low, with flat roofs, looking like little white boxes set on the slope of the hill. That one, half cottage, half rock, the lowest in the steep street, is the home of Joseph, the carpenter of the place. All things are in quiet silence. Night is in the midst of her course.

Holy Mary

No light anywhere, except the stars overhead, and they shine out brightly in the clear, frosty air, for it is the month of March. Yes! a lamp is burning in that last house. Who can be the watcher there when all the village is asleep? Let us go in noiselessly and see.

Alone in her little room kneels a girl of fourteen. What a wonderful face! so grave and yet so sweet, so childlike and innocent, and still so full of dignity. She must be very near to God. A great reverence comes over us as we gaze upon her, and we fall on our knees. This can be no ordinary child. Let us go back fourteen years and learn what we can about her.

Her name is Miriam, or Mary, which means "Lady," and also "Star of the Sea." Her holy parents, Joachim and Anne, had prayed long and earnestly for a child to gladden their old age before this blessed child was given them. Who shall ever tell what she was to them! They were never tired of watching her at prayer or play, and when she thought herself alone; and they soon found out that she knew more about God and holy things than they could tell her. It seemed to them that God Himself was her Teacher, and they reverenced her as one very precious in His sight. What would have been their awe and their joy had they known that she was to be the Mother of His only Son! Yes, she was to be the woman promised long ago in Paradise who was to crush the serpent's head, the Mother of Him who was to redeem the world, the Mother of God. And God was getting her ready for this. Think what a preparation it must have been.

Solomon's Temple was many years building because everything in it had to be of such costly material—marbles, and sweet-scented, incorruptible cedar, and precious stones, all "artfully wrought and carved. The floor of the house was overlaid with gold within and without, and there was nothing in the Temple that was not gold or covered with gold—the altar of gold, and the table of gold, and the golden candlesticks of pure gold, and flowers like lilies, and the lamps over them of gold, and golden snuffers, and censers of most pure gold, and the hinges for the doors of the inner house of the Holy of Holies gold, pure gold, most pure gold."[1] Why? Because everything about this house of God must be as far as possible worthy of Him. Yet the Temple of Jerusalem, with its Holy of Holies, its Ark of the Covenant, and its Tables of the Law, what was it compared with that Blessed One whom He had chosen to be His Mother? What must He do to make her worthy, as far as she could be worthy, to have God for her Son?

First of all there must be no sin. When we are going to embroider richly on white satin, we take care to see that it is spotless. It would be wasting our silk and our gold thread to lay them on what is soiled, or ever has been soiled. God prizes spotlessness more than we do. He was going to enrich His Mother with His best gifts, and the first must be a perfect purity. No stain of sin must so much as come near her. She must be more dazzling in her whiteness than the Angels who come nearest His throne.

---

1   3 Kings 6, 7.

Holy Mary

But what about original sin? Was not Mary a child of Adam? Yes; and she would have been stained with Adam's sin had not God kept her free because of her nearness to Himself. She was not cleansed from original sin as babies are when they have been baptized, for no sin of any kind ever touched her.

Some people cannot understand why Mary should have had this perfect freedom from sin which we call the Immaculate Conception. It would be clear as day to them if they would think who Mary is. A Protestant lady, who had this difficulty, was asked:

"Do you believe that Jesus Christ the Son of Mary is truly God?"

"I do," she answered reverently.

"And is there anything God could do for His Mother that He would not for His own sake be bound to do?"

She was silent for a moment, and then said: "I do not think there is."

It was the Precious Blood that even before our Lord came saved Mary so grandly, and preserved her from the sin that has spoilt everyone else: "My spirit hath rejoiced in God my Saviour," she says. "For He that is mighty hath done great things to me."

Imagine a burning mountain throwing up flames and volumes of smoke; the burning lava pouring down the sides, destroying fields, vineyards, cottages, cattle. Down it rushes, leaving everything a black ruin behind it. Down, down, till it is suddenly checked before a fair garden that lies in its way; checked and turned aside,

The Presentation
of the Blessed Virgin Mary

so that no harm is done, and the trees and flowers and fruit look all the more lovely for the desolation around.

So was the torrent of original sin stayed when it came to Mary.

When the little Mary was three years old, she was carried by her parents to the Temple to be solemnly offered to God. She understood quite well what she was going to do. She knew that God had done great things for her, and she wanted to give herself entirely to Him, that He might do just as He liked with her always, whether it was what she liked or not. With her hands joined, her face bright with holy joy, she went up alone the fifteen steps, her parents looking on with admiration and gladness. And with sorrow, too. For they were going to leave her in the Temple to be brought up with other Jewish girls, and they thought how sad and lonely they would be without her.

As she grew older Mary spent her time in prayer, in working for the Temple, and in studying the holy Scriptures. The parts she liked best were the prophecies which told of the promised Redeemer. She knew His time was come. Perhaps He was even now upon earth. Perhaps His Mother might be in want of a little servant. Oh, how happy she would be to wait upon them both!

When she was about fourteen years old, she left her home in the Temple to be espoused to Joseph, a carpenter, and to take care of a little home of her own at Nazareth. Her life was different now. No more glorious services morning and evening, but a life of work, and of very humble work. But she was content, more than content; she was quite happy, and she made Joseph happy by her brightness, her tenderness, her sweet, unselfish ways. As he came to know her more and more, he was filled with the deepest reverence for her, child though she was. And he was worthy of her, for he came next to her in holiness and nearness to God. He was trusted with the greatest treasure God had on earth, and he was about to be trusted with One more precious still.

VI.
Holy Mother of God

Let us go back now to that night in March and see Mary kneeling in her little room in prayer. Her heart is full, fuller to-night than ever with the thought that fills it always. When, when will He come? Why does He delay so long? Oh, that He would rend the heavens and come down!

Her lamp burns low as she prays on. How reverent she is, how still. Her strong prayer is moving God Himself.

See! See! in the midst of a dazzling light, not of this world, an Angel stands before her. He comes near, and, kneeling, salutes her:

"Hail, full of grace, the Lord is with thee: blessed art thou amongst women!"

What glorious praise, and from one so high and holy! For this is Gabriel, one of the seven who stand before God. How will she answer him?

There is no answer. A blush, a troubled look is on her beautiful face as she thinks within herself what manner of salutation this may be. She knows we cannot always trust those who speak to us in words of praise, and surely such words as these are not for her. Is this a messenger from God? She will be silent till he speaks again.

The Angel sees her trouble and says:

"Fear not, Mary, for thou hast found grace with God. Behold, thou shalt bring forth a Son, and thou shalt call His name Jesus. He shall be great and shall be called the Son of the Most High, and the Lord God shall give unto Him the throne of David His father, and He shall reign in the house of Jacob forever, and of His kingdom there shall be no end."

See her listening, coming to understand that she, the little handmaid of the Lord, is to be the Mother of the Messiah. Does she break forth into words of thanksgiving and praise? No, she has a question to ask, for she is not sure yet what God wants. Long ago she promised to belong only to Him, to be His little handmaid or servant all her life. She does not know if she can do this and be the Mother of the Messiah as well, and she will not break her promise to God for anything. She is quite calm and mistress of herself. Gabriel has told her that her Son shall be the Son of the Most High, that of His Kingdom there shall be no end—and she is not excited or overjoyed. She knows from the prophecies that the Messiah is to be a Man of Sorrows, and that His Mother will have to share His pains—and she is not frightened. All she wants is to know the Will of God.

The great Archangel beholds her with profoundest admiration. There is no holiness in heaven to equal

The Annunciation

*"And the Angel being come in, said unto her:
Hail, full of grace, the Lord is with thee."*
(Luke 1:28)

this. He thought he knew how far the love of God and forgetfulness of self can go, but the little Maiden of Nazareth has taken him by surprise. He understands now the full meaning of those reverent words which God Himself put upon his lips: "Hail, full of grace!" He bows lower before her—see how low! This is he who in words of majesty rebuked the aged priest of the Temple. But in Mary's presence, what a difference! He speaks to her as to one far above him; he waits while she ponders what he has said; he solves her doubts; he waits for her reply.

When at length she is satisfied that it is God's Will she should be the Mother of the Messiah, and that He wants her consent, thinking neither of the dignity nor of the pain this will bring upon her, she bows her head and says:

"Behold the handmaid of the Lord, be it done unto me according to thy word."

And the Word was made Flesh and dwelt amongst us.

And the Angel returned to God who sent him; and all Heaven was made glad that night.

VII.
Mary's Song

God often tells His secrets to His friends. He bade Gabriel tell Mary of the happiness his good news had brought to Zachary and Elizabeth, and now He Himself tells Elizabeth of the dignity that had come to Mary. The two were cousins, and Mary thought it would be kind to go to Ain-Karim to visit her relatives and make herself useful in the house. She would much rather have stayed at home just now, but she did not listen to likes and dislikes; when God put a good thought into her mind, or wanted a service of her, she obeyed at once. And so, without considering it beneath her to serve others, or lay her hands to household work, she set off in haste on her long journey.

No one, not even Joseph whom she loved so tenderly, had been told of Gabriel's visit, for Mary disliked notice as much as some young girls seek it, and she was afraid of honour and praise. One of the prophets had said: "My secret to myself, my secret to myself." This was Mary's rule all her life through.

We are not told whether she went alone, but it is most unlikely. If Joseph did not go with her, she probably joined some of her relatives who were on their way to the Holy City. At last she came upon the rising ground of Judea, and, climbing the rugged side of a mountain, found herself at the door of Zachary's home.

Elizabeth was standing on the threshold as if expecting someone. Mary hastened towards her, and saluted her with loving words. But what was her surprise when the aged woman, instead of returning her embrace, sank on her knees and cried out:

"Blessed art thou amongst women, and blessed is the fruit of thy womb. And whence is this to me that the Mother of my Lord should come to me?"

Her secret, then, was known. God, Himself, must have told Elizabeth. Mary's heart was full—full to overflowing. She could not keep back its burst of joy and praise:

"My soul doth magnify the Lord," she said, "and my spirit hath rejoiced in God my Saviour. Because He hath regarded the humility of His handmaid; for behold from henceforth all generations shall call me blessed. Because He that is mighty hath done great things to me, and holy is His name. And His mercy is from generation unto generations to them that fear Him. He hath shewed might in His arm; He hath scattered the proud in the conceit of their heart. He hath put down the mighty from their seat and hath exalted the humble. He hath filled the hungry with good things, and the rich He hath sent empty away. He hath received Israel His servant, being mindful of His mercy, As He spoke to our fathers, to Abraham and to his seed for ever."

The Visitation

*"Blessed art thou amongst women,
and blessed is the fruit of thy womb."*
(Luke 1:42)

Elizabeth listened in silence and in awe. She knew by heart the triumphant hymns of God's servants in the past, but there was not one like this. Mary's song was the sweetest earth had ever heard. It sank into the heart of the aged saint. It sounds through the Church for ever. Every day it is on the lips of thousands of her children. It teaches us many lessons, and among them this—that it is not proud and wrong to know that we have gifts of God entrusted to us, gifts of fortune, gifts of body or of mind. There is no harm in knowing we are well off, or good-looking, or clever, or kind-hearted. Harm comes in when we forget that whatever good we have is the gift of God and that we shall have to account to Him for it, and that in the meantime we have to use it in His service who gave it.

Mary understood as no other will ever do what "great things" God had done for her, things so great that all generations should call her blessed. But all the glory was His. Of herself she was nothing, and had nothing. She rejoiced in God her Saviour as we do, only more, because He had done more for her. She magnified the Lord as we should do, because He had looked down on the humility, that is, the littleness of His handmaid.

It is no humility, then, to pretend not to know what God has done for us. The really humble, like the grateful poor, are quick to acknowledge kindness and to show themselves thankful. Gratitude and humility go hand in hand. There is no better shield against vanity and self-conceit than Mary's words: "He who is mighty hath done great things for me;" and when our hearts are stirred to praise God for His goodness to us, we shall find none more fitting than those of her beautiful *Magnificat*.

For three months Mary stayed with her cousin, and all that time God's richest blessings were poured out upon the family of Zachary, because of her presence there. At the first sound of her voice the Holy Ghost had so inspired Elizabeth that she reechoed Gabriel's words: "Blessed art thou among women," adding to them the praise of Mary's Son: "Blessed is the fruit of thy womb." When we repeat these words in the Hail Mary, it will help us to remember the reverence with which they were said by an Archangel and a saint at the feet of her whom Elizabeth called "the Mother of my Lord."

VIII.
The First Christmas Night

At last the time came when Joseph too was to know what the Angel of the Lord had declared unto Mary. An Angel, perhaps Gabriel again, came to tell him who she was that swept and washed and cooked in his little cottage, and went about her daily work as the simplest and lowliest of the women around. He told him, too, that her Child was to be called JESUS, because He would save His people from their sins.

Think with what new veneration Joseph looked upon Mary now, and what quiet, deep talks they had together. They pondered the words of holy Scripture; they studied the types; they put prophecy by the side of prophecy. Because their hearts were so pure, they saw better than the learned doctors of the Law the meaning of these types and prophecies, and they wondered more and more that they should have been chosen to be so near to Jesus when He came. That blessed Name at which St. Paul says every knee should bow, each had first heard from an Angel's lips. How reverently they pronounced it. To the world outside, the Promised One all were expecting was "the Messiah," or "the Christ;" to Mary and Joseph alone He was "JESUS."

The First Christmas Night

Mary and Joseph knew from the prophecy of Micheas that Bethlehem, six miles south of Jerusalem, was to be the birthplace of the Messiah. This was four or five days' journey from Nazareth. When were they to go? And what reason could they give to their neighbours for suddenly quitting their home? And were they to quit it for good? The answer to these questions was: "Let us leave all to God; He is watching and guiding everything; He has come to our help always in the past." And so they waited in peaceful trust for a sign of His Will.

One day there was great excitement in the marketplace of Nazareth. A decree had gone out from Rome for the whole world to be enrolled. Augustus Cæsar, the Roman Emperor, who ruled over the greater part of the known world, wanted to find out how many people he governed that he might know the extent of his power, and how much he could tax his subjects. The Jews, who were subject to him, were to go to the city or town which was the home of their ancestors, and there give in their names and take an oath of fidelity to Cæsar.

Now the townsfolk of Nazareth were a rough, quarrelsome set of people, easily moved to deeds of violence. They had such a bad name among their countrymen that it was an insult to call anyone a Nazarene. This decree of Cæsar filled them with indignation. "Why should all men be disturbed and set on foot for his foolish whim?" they cried. "O, that the Messiah would come quickly to free His people from the yoke of the wicked empire, and make all His enemies His footstool as David said!"

However, they had to make the best of a command which they dared not disobey. A Roman official went the round of the town, came to the little house at the bottom of the street, found that Joseph was one of the family of David, and ordered him off to Bethlehem, David's city.

Here was the sign for which Mary and Joseph were waiting. What matter if the order were roughly given, if in going to Bethlehem they seemed to be doing Cæsar's bidding only; God was arranging all things for them. Their preparations were soon made; the few things absolutely necessary put together; Mary seated on the ass; the door of the little house fastened behind them; and then Joseph took the bridle in one hand and his staff in the other, and they set out.

It was the worst season of the year, the road was bad, the weather cold, and they had no conveniences for the journey. Again and again Joseph led the ass into the ruts by the wayside to make room for some of David's wealthier descendants, well clad and well mounted, and, like their poor relations, bound for Bethlehem. Not many words were spoken. There was much for both to ponder, and there was much to suffer. Each day's halt brought fresh anxiety to Joseph, for there were no inns on the road, and the caravansaries, or *khans*, were devoid of every comfort. They were merely enclosed spaces surrounded by sheds; four bare walls and a mat

The First Christmas Night

were all the accommodation provided; food, cooking utensils and bedding, travellers had to bring with them, or do without.

The two journeyed slowly, and the evening of the fifth day was closing in, when, grey and dim on the hillside, the walls of Bethlehem came in sight. Party after party overtook them on the road, all hastening forward to reach shelter before nightfall. Joseph looked at Mary and urged on the tired beast. What could he do if the place should be full? At last they reached the *khan*, situated on the hill, a little way below the town. A glance round showed them they were too late. Every place was taken. Beasts and baggage crowded up the central square. On every side was shouting, disputing, the bustle and confusion of a crowd of travellers who had everything to do for themselves.

No one had time to attend to any business but his own, and Joseph's questions were roughly answered. He went back to Mary, whom he had left outside, and taking the bridle turned towards the city.

Night was falling as they passed within the walls, but there was light enough to see that it was full—full to overflowing. The better sort had long ago secured all that was to be had in the way of lodging. Poor people like themselves had little chance. Joseph searched diligently everywhere, but to no purpose. Wherever he saw a door open he hastened towards it; he pointed to Mary and held out his hand with the few coins he had left. But all in vain; everywhere the same answer: "No room."

Up and down the streets they wandered that bitter night. No one would take her in. Joseph's tearful eyes looked up into her face. She was utterly worn out, but the smile on her lips told of a peace within that no trouble of this world could disturb. What was he to do? It was no use trying any more. He brushed his sleeve across his eyes and led the ass carefully down the hill again.

It was quite dark now, and he had to hold his lantern low to keep a safe footing. A little way out of Bethlehem a cave in a chalk hill opened upon the road. He said to Mary: "Let us go in here." The cave narrowed into an inner and smaller one, which seemed to be used as a stable, for an ox was there standing over a manger. They went in. Mary dismounted and knelt down in a corner to pray. Joseph hung up his lantern on the damp wall. Its flickering light showed the moisture trickling down on every side, and all the foulness of a neglected Eastern stable. This was the place which from all eternity God had chosen for the birthplace of His only Son. And here at midnight the Son of God was born; *the Word was made Flesh and dwelt amongst us.*

Mary bowed herself down to adore. Here was the Messiah she had so longed to see. Here was Jesus who by bitter pain was to save His people from their sins; Oh, how soon He had begun His work, she thought, as she looked upon the tiny limbs that lay trembling on the straw. Yes, this was He who, Gabriel said, should be great and should be called the Son of the Most High. A Roman judge, struck by His meek majesty, will say

The Holy Night

"This day is born to you a Saviour, who is Christ the Lord, in the city of David."

(Luke 2:11)

to Him one day: "Whence art Thou?" All through the first Christmas night His Mother is asking Him this question, not because she does not know, but because she cannot get used to the wonderfulness of the answer. She knows He has come from the highest heaven, from the right hand of the Father to whom He is equal in all things. And still He is her very own Babe, crying for her, nestling to her like any other helpless child.

She adores Him as her God. And then she takes Him up in her arms, wraps Him up in swathing bands, and lays Him in the manger on a handful of straw, the best that Joseph can find about. She is grateful to the two animals which share it with Him and stand over Him warming Him a little with their breath. The words of Isaias come to her mind: "The ox knoweth his owner and the ass his master's crib, but Israel hath not known Me, and My people hath not understood."[1] No one ever understood and pondered the Scriptures as she did, and the words of prophecy come to her one by one as she worships there. This tiny Child is the Leader of God's people whom Micheas said was to come out of Bethlehem; whom Isaias called "the Hidden God," of whom David said: "God shall come manifestly, our God shall come."[2] She and Joseph kneel beside Him, and look, and look, and wonder at the great God become so small, and at the love that has brought Him—to this.

About a mile from Bethlehem and lying at the foot of the hill on which the little city stands is a field into which the shepherds of the neighbourhood led their

---

1   Isaias 1.   2   Ps. 49.

The First Christmas Night

flocks at evening. All day the sheep roamed in safety on the hills, but as night drew on, when wild beasts prowled about, they were brought down here. Eastern shepherds belong to the very lowest and poorest class of the people; their lives are hard, for they must guard their flocks all day and in all weathers, and lie out with them on the wet grass in the bleak nights of winter.

A company of shepherds was watching in this field when Mary and Joseph took refuge in the cave. And at midnight "behold an Angel of the Lord stood by them, and the brightness of God shone round about them, and they feared with a great fear. And the Angel said to them:

"Fear not, for behold I bring you good tidings of great joy that shall be to all the people. For this day is born to you a Saviour who is Christ the Lord in the city of David. And this shall be a sign unto you. You shall find the Infant wrapped in swaddling clothes and laid in a manger.

"And suddenly there was with the Angel a multitude of the heavenly army praising God and saying:

"Glory to God in the highest, and on earth peace to men of good will.

"And it came to pass after the Angels departed from them into heaven, the shepherds said one to another:

"Let us go over to Bethlehem and let us see this word that is come to pass which the Lord hath showed to us.

"And they came with haste; and they found Mary and Joseph and the Infant lying in the manger. And all

Apparition to the Shepherds

"Glory to God in the highest; and on earth peace to men of good will."
(Luke 2:14)

that heard wondered, and at those things that were told them by the shepherds."[1]

Why were these men called before all others to worship the new-born Child? Because they were simple and docile, and patient under the many hardships of their rough lives. And because the Holy Child would teach us from the first this important lesson—that poverty is not a thing to be despised or to be ashamed of. It is a very painful thing, because it puts out of our reach the comforts, conveniences and amusements which make life pleasant. We care far too much for these things. An apple was too great a temptation for Adam and Eve, and nice things in the shape of food, dress, scents, bodily enjoyment of every kind, are often and often too much for us, their children. Not that pleasant things always lead us into sin. But a life of ease and self-indulgence, in which such things abound, is always a dangerous life, because the body never says: "It is enough." It is always ready to indulge itself at the expense of the soul, and to get what it wants it will not stop at sin. We have to distrust it and to be on the watch always. This is why the poor are safer by far than the rich if only they bear their privations patiently.

Our Lord came on earth to show us the safest way to heaven, and to show us in the best of ways, by example. It cost Him a great deal to teach us in this way all His life, but He never thought of cost when He could help us by it. And so He began at once, the very night He was born, to teach us the value of poverty, and

---
[1] Luke 2.

to comfort the poor. How easily, after that midnight visit to the cave, the shepherds would bear cold, hunger, weariness, the want of nice, pretty, comfortable things such as the rich can get. "The little Babe Messiah had nothing of this kind," they would say to one another; "surely, then, we can do without."

And we who have comfortable homes, and pleasures in plenty, what lesson has the poor Babe of Bethlehem for us? This at least, that we must learn to honour the poor, who are most like Him, and to deny ourselves at times that we may have something to give to them in their need. We ought to be glad to serve them and work for them with our own hands, because they represent our Blessed Lord who will take as done to Himself whatever kindness or unkindness we show them.

See now why the shepherds were called first to the cave on the first Christmas night.

IX.

In the Temple

Eight days after His birth the Holy Child shed His Blood for the first time, and received at His Circumcision the Name of JESUS, that Name which St. Bernard says is "honey in the mouth, music in the ear, joy in the heart;" so sweet to us, but costing Him so dear who took it for our sakes. Other children do not know what name is given them or why it is given. He knew perfectly all that He took upon Himself to do and to suffer that He might be our Jesus, our Saviour. He was afraid, for He was a true child, and shrank like every child from all that hurts. But He loved us so dearly that He offered Himself bravely for us in spite of the pain.

A month passed away, and then Mary and Joseph prepared to go up to Jerusalem for the double ceremony of Purification and Presentation required by the Jewish Law. Our Lord was Himself the Lawgiver, and, therefore, not bound by the Law; but He wanted to be like us as far as possible that He might help us more and be our Model in all things. He came to teach us all, and to teach Mary first, who was to profit most by His lessons. No one has ever imitated Him as she did, because no one has ever studied Him so closely. From the first we are told that she pondered in her heart all that happened to Him and all that He said and did. And then she tried to copy Him. When she saw Him submitting to laws to which He was not obliged, she joyfully did the same, and on the day of her Purification went up to the Temple to offer a sin-offering for herself and her Divine Child. The sacrifice of the rich was a lamb and a turtle-dove or young pigeon. Those who could not afford a lamb took two doves. Mary was poor and made the offering of the poor. But she made a rich Offering too, richer than that gorgeous Temple had ever seen.

The Law required the eldest son of each Jewish family to be presented to God and consecrated to Him. The babe was put into the arms of the priest and solemnly lifted up towards Heaven. Then it was bought back by the parents for five silver shekels, about four dollars in our money.

On the fortieth day, then, after His birth, Mary took the Holy Child in her arms, and folding her veil closely round herself and Him, set out for Jerusalem. Joseph carried the doves in a wicker basket, and the silver shekels.

Solomon's Temple was the most glorious building the world has ever seen. It was destroyed when the Jews were taken into captivity by Nabuchodonosor the Great. The Second Temple was built on their return from captivity, and, at the time of our Lord, it had been

In the Temple

restored by the Herod whom history calls "the Great." He was a selfish, wicked man, whose one thought was to keep the throne of Judea which the Romans had given him, and to put to death anyone and everyone who might be a possible rival. His people feared and hated him, and it was to turn away their attention from his cruelty that he restored the Second Temple on so magnificent a scale, that in some respects at least it equalled or even surpassed the First.

Four Courts, open to the sky, rose one above the other on Mount Moriah. The lowest and largest was called the Court of the Gentiles, because it was open even to pagans. But no Gentile, under pain of death, might pass beyond; the rest of the Temple was reserved for the people of God. Fourteen steps led to the Court of the Women, so called because women might not go further except when they went with an offering for sacrifice into the Court of Israel. Highest of all was the Court of the Priests. In this enclosure stood the altar of holocausts, the brazen laver, and a building of snowy marble roofed with gold. It consisted of two rooms; one called the Holy Place contained the altar of shewbread, the altar of incense and the seven-branched candlestick.

Beyond this room, and separated from it by a rich curtain, was the chamber called the Holy of Holies. In Solomon's Temple this sanctuary held the Ark of the Covenant, containing the two Tables of the Law, Aaron's rod which had blossomed, and a pot of manna. After the destruction of the First Temple the Ark of the Covenant was lost, and in the Second Temple only a black stone marked its place within the Holy of Holies. Into this sacred spot none but the High Priest entered, and he but once a year on the Day of Atonement, when, after filling it with the smoke of incense, he went in with the blood of victims to pray God to forgive the sins of the people.

No place was so dear to a true Israelite as this Temple of the Lord. David cried out: "How lovely are Thy tabernacles, O Lord of Hosts, my soul longeth and fainteth for the Courts of the Lord." To pray within these sacred Courts was their greatest happiness, and every Jewish boy looked forward with eagerness to his twelfth birthday, because thenceforth he would be bound to go up three times a year at the great feasts to worship there. When, after days of weary march, pilgrims climbed Mount Olivet, and from its summit caught sight of Mount Moriah and the golden roof of the Holy Place glittering in the sunshine, they forgot all the fatigues of the journey and broke out into loud songs of joy and praise.

Herod's Temple, it is true, lacked that which had made Solomon's so glorious. The Ark of the Covenant was gone, and the bright cloud above it which showed the Presence of God in the Holy of Holies. But had not Aggeus comforted his people by telling them that this Second Temple would be more hallowed than the First, because the Lord of the Temple would Himself visit and sanctify it? "Great shall be the glory of this last house more than of the first. The Desired of all

In the Temple

nations shall come, and I will fill this house with glory, saith the Lord of Hosts."

These words of the prophet must have been in the thoughts of Joseph and Mary when, with the Infant Jesus, they presented themselves at the foot of the steps which led to the highest of the Temple Courts. A priest came down to receive their offering. They gave him the shekels, and then Mary laid her Child in his arms to be offered to God. This was no mere ceremony. The Divine Infant begged to suffer in our stead the punishment our sins deserved, and His offering was accepted. He was indeed given back to Mary, but as a little lamb to be kept for sacrifice later.

Having done all things according to the Law, Mary and Joseph were turning to leave the Temple when a venerable old man came forward, took the Holy Child into his arms, and, smiling upon Him, gazed long and earnestly upon the little face, whilst tears of joy trickled down his cheeks. Mary watched and wondered. Here, then, was another that knew her secret, and had come forward to worship the Hidden God. Such a smile of welcome, such a loving embrace! The old man might have known the Child and been expecting Him. And so in truth he had. For this was the aged Simeon who had been promised that he should not die until he had seen the Christ of the Lord. God always gives more than He promises. Simeon was to see the Child, and here he is, not seeing only, but holding and fondling Him, and knowing what is to befall Him.

The Presentation in the Temple

"Now Thou dost dismiss Thy servant, O Lord, according to Thy word in peace."
(Luke 2:29)

In the Temple

But God expects us to trust Him; He often keeps us waiting for a long time. Day after day Simeon had come into the Temple praying and hoping; day after day he had gone away disappointed and a little weary of waiting. This day, just at the right time, the Holy Spirit put it into his mind to go there, just at the right moment made him lift his eyes and fix them on that Child in the young mother's arms. There was nothing about the Holy Family to attract notice—a poor couple presenting their first-born, bystanders would have said. But the aged priest saw by faith what others could not see, and in a transport of joy blessed God and said:

"Now Thou dost dismiss Thy servant, O Lord, according to Thy word in peace. Because my eyes have seen Thy salvation, which Thou hast prepared before the face of all peoples: a light to the revelation of the Gentiles, and the glory of Thy people Israel."

Then, turning to Mary, he went on in tones of sorrowful compassion: "Behold this Child is set for the fall and for the resurrection of many in Israel, and for a sign which shall be contradicted. And thy own soul a sword shall pierce, that out of many hearts thoughts may be revealed."

Joy and sorrow come together all through Mary's life. She has just had the happiness of presenting to God an offering worthy of Him. She has seen her Child welcomed as the Messiah. And now, suddenly and unexpectedly, all is changed. The day that began so brightly is dark with coming woe. He whom she loves more than her life is to be contradicted, and so cruelly used, that her soul will be pierced with sorrow. But because this terrible future is God's Will for her Son and for herself, she bows her head and says once more: "Behold the handmaid of the Lord, be it done unto me according to His Will."

There is still another meeting to-day. Whether Anna, the aged prophetess, knew of the promise to Simeon and kept near him, hoping to have a share in his joy, we are not told, but we know that "she departed not from the Temple, by fasting and prayers serving night and day." And thus it happened that when he went forward and took the Child Jesus into his arms, she followed and joined the group, and not only adored in silence, but spoke of the Child to all around who were expecting the Redeemer. The only persons that we know of who preached and praised Him in that glorious Temple of His were this aged woman, at the beginning of His life, and the fearless children with their Hosannas six days before the end.

X.
The Star in the East

One day a party of strangers on richly trapped camels passed through the streets of Jerusalem causing great excitement. Their riders, noble looking men, wore the high head-dress and mantle thrown back over the shoulders, which marked them as Persians.

They told a strange story. Months ago, whilst studying the midnight heavens, as was their wont, a star of extraordinary brightness had suddenly shone forth. They felt that it was sent to announce some great event. They knew that the whole world was expecting a Deliverer, and that the holy books of the Jews said a star should arise out of Jacob. This must be the star of the great King, sent to call them to His feet. They must go at once with the costliest gifts they could provide and offer Him their homage. Their people had mocked them; their families had tried to keep them back; but they were resolved to seek and find the Messiah at any cost. And so they had set out, three of them, towards Jerusalem, where they supposed He would be found.

"Where, then," they asked, "is He that is born King of the Jews? For we have seen His star in the East and are come to adore Him?"

Those who heard all this shook their heads and muttered as they turned away that it was a pity these travellers did not know what kind of a ruler Herod was, and that no man who valued his life would dream of speaking in Jerusalem of another king.

The news of their arrival and of their errand soon reached the palace, and Herod in great alarm summoned all the chief priests and the scribes to enquire of them where Christ should be born. They answered as with one voice: "In Bethlehem of Juda, for so it is written by the prophet: And thou, Bethlehem, the land of Juda, art not the least among the princes of Juda, for out of thee shall come forth the captain that shall rule My people Israel."

The strangers now receive a courteous invitation to visit the king, with the assurance that he will do all in his power to aid them in their search. Simple and unsuspecting, they present themselves before him as he lies, splendidly robed, on his magnificent couch. He makes careful inquiries as to the star: "What was it like? When and where had they first seen it? How long had they been on their journey?" They are delighted to find him so interested and tell him the whole story. He shows himself very gracious and says he is pleased to be able to give them the information they require. Bethlehem, six miles south of Jerusalem, is to be the birthplace of the Messiah. It is a little place, they cannot fail to find Him there:

"Go," he says, "and diligently inquire after the Child, and when you have found Him, bring me word again that I also may come and adore Him."

The Magi thank him and set off without delay. No one cares to go with them; the priests and scribes who have told them where to find Christ do not trouble to seek Him themselves. "Herod was troubled and all Jerusalem with him." Thus did His own people receive the good news the strangers brought.

Surprised, but not disheartened, the Magi pursue their way, when, suddenly, the star they had seen in the East appears again and goes before them until it comes and stands over the place where the Child is. And, seeing the star, they rejoice with exceeding great joy. And entering into the house they find the Child with Mary His Mother, and, falling down, they adore Him.

They expected to see the King of kings in a splendid palace surrounded by courtiers. Instead of this they find in a poor cottage a child without attendants or comforts of any kind. Only a youthful mother and a humble tradesman keep watch beside Him. Can this be really a king? Can this be the great Deliverer the world is awaiting? Yes, such is their faith they believe Him to be both. They spread a carpet at His feet in Eastern fashion, humbly kneel down before Him, and, opening their treasures offer Him gifts—gold, frankincense and myrrh. In the East no king is ever approached without gifts. The Magi have brought the most precious their country produces, and very suitable gifts they are, for gold is a fit tribute to a king, incense is offered to God, and myrrh, the herb used for preserving bodies from corruption, shows that our Lord, though truly God, is man as one of us.

The Holy Kings

"We have seen His star in the east, and are come to adore Him."
(Matt. 2:2)

The Star in the East

We are specially told that they found the Child "with Mary His Mother." It was by Mary that our Blessed Lord came to us: in the Holy Bible the Son and the Mother appear side by side, and in the Catholic Church they are never separated. His Mother was the dearest treasure our Lord had in this world, and, poor as He was, He had this treasure to the end. How glad we ought to be that when He came to this cold and sinful world, where there was no room for Him, He had her arms to fold Him, and her immaculate heart on which to rest His head!

He did not speak as He lay in her lap. Was He then like any other child? "Whence art Thou?" we can imagine the Magi asking as they knelt before Him. Mary answered for Him. She told them that He who had sent His star to fetch them was a real, little human child, but He was also the God of Heaven and earth, and they must worship Him. He had two natures, the human nature which they could see, the Divine Nature which they could not see, but He had only one Person, which was the Person of God the Son. They listened humbly, and bowed down, and kissed the little feet, and adored Him. And Mary gave them His little hand to kiss and blessed them with it.

At last they had to go. They were so happy, so glad that they had come. They would go back now to their own land and tell their people all they had seen and heard. And as long as they lived they would remember their visit to Bethlehem, and keep in their hearts the memory of the Mother and the Son. They had arranged to return by way of Jerusalem, but, being told by God not to go back to Herod, they went to their own country another way.

Meanwhile the king was waiting and wondering. Why did not the Magi come back? Could they have found him out and have tricked him who thought himself so clever in tricking others? How foolish he had been not to have them followed and watched by some of his own people. Finding at last that he had been outwitted by these simple-looking men, he was furious, and, sending his soldiers, killed all the male children that were in Bethlehem and in all the country round from two years old and under. In vain did the poor mothers try to hide or to defend their little ones. At their play, in their cradles, in the very arms of their mothers, these innocents were seized and slain, while shrieks and piteous cries were heard on every side.

And where was He whose life the cruel king was seeking?

The night after the departure of the Magi, as Joseph slept, an Angel of the Lord appeared to him:

"Arise," he said, "and take the Child and His Mother, and fly into Egypt, and be there until I shall tell thee. For it will come to pass that Herod will seek the Child to destroy Him."

Without asking a single question, Joseph arose, went to Mary and told her of the order. Like him, asking no questions, she rose quickly, put together some provisions, took her little Babe and wrapped Him up in the few garments she had, whilst Joseph collected his

The Flight into Egypt

"Arise, and take the child and his mother, and fly into Egypt: and be there until I shall tell thee."
(Matt. 2:13)

tools and went out to saddle the ass. Then he helped Mary to mount, laid the Holy Child in her arms, closed the door of the cottage and went out into the night.

Days and weeks they journeyed on, first through wild and hilly country, then across the trackless desert. There was no shelter for them when the rays of the sun beat fiercely down by day and the chilly dews fell at night. Day after day that dreary waste of sand stretched out before them. Springs of water were rare, and they suffered terribly from thirst. As they plodded on under the white light of the moon, or lay down to rest, they heard the bark of the jackal and the roar of the distant lion. The burning breath of the sirocco, with its whirling sand, might overtake them, robbers might swoop down upon them. But they were not afraid, for they knew that the little Child they had with them—was God.

At last the yellow wilderness is broken up by patches of refreshing green; further on they come upon fertile fields and the dwellings of men, and Joseph begins to look about for a place where they can settle down. But the idolaters view with suspicion these Jewish strangers; no one knows them, and they are homeless wanderers till Joseph is able to hire a little house. Then it is hard to get work, and though he and Mary stint themselves for the sake of the Child, they are so poor that many a time when He asks for bread they have none to give Him.

It seems to have been soon after the slaughter of the Innocents that Herod died and went to Judgment.

The Star in the East

What an awful account he had to give! To keep a throne of which death must soon deprive him, he had murdered his nearest and dearest, the priests of the Temple, and at last a whole troop of little children, among whom he hoped was the Saviour of the world.

There was nothing now to keep the Holy Family in exile, and the Angel who had ordered the Flight into Egypt appeared in sleep to Joseph saying:

"Arise, and take the Child and His Mother and go into the land of Israel, for they are dead that sought the life of the Child."

And he arose and took the Child and His Mother and came into the land of Israel. But hearing that Archelaus reigned in Judea in the room of Herod his father, he was afraid to go thither. He therefore determined to return to Nazareth in Galilee and settle there.

XI.
Jesus of Nazareth

If their home at Nazareth was dear to Mary and Joseph before they left for Bethlehem, what was it now when the sound of little feet was heard upon its floor, and a childish voice called for "Father" or for "Mother!" Joseph's trade, that kept him away all the morning and afternoon, seemed harder than ever, but he consoled himself by thinking that his loss was Mary's gain.

Yes, she had the Child all to herself during those early years. He sat at her feet as she spun, or stood by as she did the kneading, or the baking, or the washing of the little house. When she dropped anything, He was quick to pick it up. He noticed what she wanted before she knew herself, and ran to fetch it; and as soon as He was able He helped in the household work. Neighbours would stand at their doors to watch the young mother and her beautiful Boy as they went together to the fountain. They were all in all to each other, it was plain, and His manner towards her, so reverent and so tender, was delightful to see.

How happy were Mary and Joseph, when, sitting down to their simple meal, they had the little Jesus between them; when, morning and evening, they knelt beside Him, knowing that He whose prayer went up with theirs was Himself the God to whom they prayed. See them—how reverent they are, how still, how attentive. Was there ever a scene on earth more beautiful than morning and night prayers at Nazareth!

In the synagogue they heard the Prophecies read which told of the coming Messiah . . . "Despised and the most abject of men, a man of sorrows . . . I have not turned away my face from them that spat upon me." What did Mary feel as she watched the calm, grave face of her Boy and thought of the dishonour that was to come!

On Sabbath evenings they walked together through the flowery fields or up the grassy slopes of Nazareth, drinking in every word, as the Child spoke to them of the God who had made all these things for our use and enjoyment, who so loved the world as to give His only Son to save it.

As Jesus grew older, He swept the house, washed the dishes, ground the corn, and at last went with Joseph to the workshop to learn such rough carpentry as His Foster-father could teach Him. No work was too lowly or too commonplace for Him who had made all things out of nothing. Mary and Joseph were never tired of watching Him and admiring the care with which all was done and finished; not once or twice, or when the work was interesting or new to Him, but day after day, year after year when it was dull and tiresome. They never forgot who He was; never got used to the thought

His Boyhood at Nazareth

"And the child grew, and waxed strong, full of wisdom; and the grace of God was in Him."
(Luke 2:40)

that He who came at their call, and went errands, and brought home the modest pay for Joseph's work, was the Lord of Angels and of men. "Whence art Thou?" their hearts would cry, as they saw the readiness with which He obeyed their slightest wish, the cheerfulness and grace with which He served them.

It must have been from Mary's lips that St. Luke gathered all we know of those long years at Nazareth which we call the Hidden Life. Twice in the same chapter he speaks of her habit of pondering the words and actions of her Divine Son, and all that befell Him. And he tells us what about Him was most marvellous to that pondering heart of hers: "He was subject to them." *He—to them!*

Indeed, He was the Hidden God of Nazareth. His cousins, James and Joseph, and Simon, and Jude, little thought that He who played with them, or with sweet words settled their childish disputes, was the Desired of all nations, the long-promised Messiah whom the whole world was expecting. And their elders, who, as we are told, would say in their troubles: "Let us go and have a talk with the Son of Mary," did not know that He was able to dry their tears and refresh the heavy-laden—because He was God.

We wonder, perhaps, why He gave so much time—twenty years and more—to this Hidden Life, or why He remained hidden at all. He was to be on earth only three and thirty years. There was so much to teach and to do, and He could have begun at once. But do we not all know that the best teaching is by example?

Whether the lesson is needlework, or swimming, or painting, or drill, what we want is, not merely to be taught by words, but to be shown by our teacher what we have to do.

We may be sure our Blessed Lord did not want to lose time, for no one knew as He did how much had to be done. He had us all to teach—men, women, and children—and to teach in the best way, by example. Therefore He would begin at once, as soon as He came into the world. And He would begin with the children. They are His first class. He calls them all round Him, the children of America, and Europe, and Africa, and Asia, and says to them:

"Look at Me in My home. It might have been a rich home, provided with all kinds of comforts and conveniences. But because most of My followers would be poor and unable to have these things, and all of them would be inclined to care far too much for the pleasant things of this life, I chose to be poor. We had nothing unnecessary at Nazareth, nothing pretty or curious—a table, a few stools and mats, a meal-tub, a chest for clothes. My Foster-father had to rise early to go to his work. My Mother mended and washed for us and cooked our homely meals; we had no servant. For all of us it was hard labour, early and late.

"Will not those who are poor among you be comforted by seeing Me poor? Will not those who are better off deny themselves something for My sake, and give to those who are poor like Me? And will not all children try to give up their own way, to obey cheerfully, to reverence father and mother as well as love them when they see how for long years I did all these things in My little home at Nazareth?"

XII.

In the Temple Again

A boy's twelfth birthday was a great event in a Jewish family. Up to this age he was called "little," afterwards he was called "grown up" and became a "Son of the Law." He must put away now the things of a child and behave and be treated as a man. The same strict subjection to his parents as before was not expected of him. He was consulted as to the trade or profession he wished to follow. In the synagogue he wore the phylacteries, narrow bands of parchment inscribed with sacred texts. And he was bound to go up to the Temple at the three great yearly festivals.

The first of these was the Passover. It commemorated the preservation of the first-born of the Jews on the night when all the first-born of the Egyptians were killed. It lasted seven days. The first-fruits of the barley harvest were offered to God on this Feast. Seven weeks, or fifty days later, came the Feast of Pentecost, commemorating the giving of the Law to the Israelites on Mount Sinai. On this Feast the first-fruits of the wheat harvest were offered.

Lastly, in the autumn, when the fruits of the vineyards and the cornfields had been fully gathered,

In the Temple Again

came the Feast of Tabernacles in memory of that time in the desert when the people lived in tents. This was a festival of thanksgiving for the blessings of the year. Every Jew who had come of age was bound to be present in Jerusalem at each of these Feasts. So great were the numbers congregated together at these times that they often exceeded two millions.

When Jesus, therefore, was twelve years old, He accompanied His parents to Jerusalem for the Feast of the Passover, joining the caravan which was going up from Galilee.

For greater safety against robbers many thousands travelled together, the men and the women in separate companies, the children with either father or mother. As they neared Jerusalem and fell in with other caravans, the concourse of pilgrims grew more and more dense, and in the neighbourhood of the Holy City husbands and wives reunited and finished the journey together.

See Mary and Joseph walking with Jesus between them. There is bustle and noise all around, but they are not distracted; their eyes are ever turned towards Him; their ears catch each sound of His voice. We are told of Him at this age that He advanced in wisdom and grace before God and men; that is, He showed more and more of the wisdom and grace which were perfect in Him from the first. If ordinary neighbours perceived this, how much more Mary and Joseph. Each day He was more beautiful and more winning, more lovable and more loving. The Temple to which they were journeying held nothing so holy as this Child of theirs, this little Pilgrim of twelve, and when from the summit of Mount Olivet the dazzling roof of the Holy Place appeared to view, and a shout of joy broke from every heart, they turned to the Boy between them and worshipped Him with profoundest adoration.

Yet they were glad to go to the Temple, and, during the seven days the Feast lasted, the blessed Three were seen continually at the various services.

The Paschal lamb had to be without blemish; to be slain in the evening and carefully prepared for the supper, for not a bone must be broken. It was eaten with unleavened bread and wild lettuce. The youngest present had to ask his father the meaning of these sacred rites, and the father was to tell him it was to remind God's people how on the night their fathers were delivered from the slavery of Egypt, a lamb was slain and its blood sprinkled on the doorpost of their houses that the destroying Angel who was to pass in the night and slay the firstborn throughout the land, might spare the dwellings marked by that sign. God had commanded that every year they were to keep the anniversary of that night by eating the Paschal lamb till He should come whom the lambs of the Passover had represented.

So when the Holy Family meets for the supper, Jesus asks the meaning of the ceremonies, and St. Joseph tells the story whilst Jesus and Mary listen. See Mary looking with tenderness and pain on the Boy by her side. His eyes are fixed, now on the lamb before Him, now on the unleavened bread; His thoughts seem far away.

In the Temple Again

When the Feast is over, the caravan from Galilee returns home. Joseph travels with the men, Mary with the women as before, both generously rejoicing in the happiness of the other. Jesus had gone, of course, with His Mother, Joseph thinks. He is with His father, Mary says to herself again and again through the long desolate day; what joy it will be to see Him when evening comes.

At last a halt is called. The vast multitude stops its march and prepares to encamp for the night. Such a scene of confusion as it is. Such unlading of asses, and setting up of tents, and preparation for supper; husbands coming in search of their wives, children running about, delighting in the hubbub and the prospect of camping out. Joseph and Mary meet. Each is alone. Their troubled look says plainer than words: "Where is Jesus?" Neither has seen Him since they started. They make inquiries but can hear nothing of Him.

They go here and there, threading their way among the various parties settling down for the night. No one has time to listen to them, rough or careless words are the only replies they receive. Darkness falls and with it a stillness. Perhaps now He will come to them. They sit by the roadside and wait and pray. The hours go by. They cannot disturb the sleeping camp, and surely He would have come to them before now had He been anywhere there. He must have remained behind in Jerusalem. Joseph looks at Mary, tired out with her day's march and weary search, but she smiles through her tears and tries to cheer him. "Yes, surely,

Jesus will be in the Temple," she says, "let us go to Him." And they set out.

She is quite spent by the time they reach Jerusalem. But there can be no rest for her till Jesus is found. They go to the Temple; they search the Courts and the colonnades; they question the talkers; they look among the worshippers. No, He is not here. They go out and wander up and down the still thronged streets of the Holy City, feeling for each other at every new disappointment, trying to keep up each other's hope.

Three days they search; the market, the bazaars or shops, the synagogues—all are visited, the Temple again and again. Joseph wonders how Mary keeps up. The anguish of her heart can be seen on her face, but there is never a complaint, never anything in the tone of her voice to tell of aught but patient suffering and resignation to God's Will.

On the third day, as they are passing a group of rabbis or doctors, met, as was their wont, in one of the porticos of the Temple to discuss difficult questions of the Law, Mary is startled by the sound of a Voice coming from the midst of that attentive throng. There is no other voice like that. She lays her hand on Joseph's arm and they stand and listen. Now they can see within the circle.

There He sits, the carpenter's Son, the centre of that learned gathering. Every eye is fixed on Him in wonder and admiration. He has put questions to which none can reply; simple questions they seemed and in keeping with His years, and asked with the reverence

In the Temple Again

with which a child should address his elders, yet He waits in vain for an answer. Old men are there whose lives have been spent in the study and explanation of the Law. But they have found their Master to-day and are forced to keep silence before Him.

"Who is this Child? Does anyone know anything of Him?" they ask each other.

Mary and Joseph wait. They must not interrupt Him. He has a work to do here. They wait patiently and delightedly as He answers His own questions and explains hard passages of the Scripture and clears away difficulties from the minds of these men. He shows them that the time of the Messiah as foretold by the prophets is come and that they must be ready for Him. There is no disputing what He says, for He speaks with authority and such wisdom that all are astonished. Silent and thoughtful, one after another leaves the group.

Now the Child Teacher is alone, and Mary and Joseph come up to Him.

"Son, why hast Thou done so to us? Behold Thy father and I have sought Thee sorrowing."

At last her full heart finds vent. There has been no word of complaint to Joseph, but to Him who knows her pain and her submission to His Will in all things, to Him who cannot misunderstand, she may say in loving complaint: "Why hast Thou done so to us?" He looks up into her tear-stained face and says tenderly:

"How is it that you sought Me; did you not know that I must be about My Father's business?"

Christ in the Temple

"They found Him in the temple, sitting in the midst of the doctors, hearing them, and asking them questions."
(Luke 2:46)

In the Temple Again

Mary understood Him and His words and ways better than any other has ever done. But He was God, and what He did and said was not always plain even to her. We are told she did not understand Him here.

It was to give her an opportunity of practising many virtues that He did not tell her He was staying behind in Jerusalem. And He had another reason. He wanted her to know by experience the misery and the pain of separation from Him, that she might be able to feel for those who lose Him by sin, and to pray for them that they may find Him again.

He wished also to give an example to those many followers of His who would have to go through the agony of leaving father and mother in order to do their Father's business by working for the salvation of souls. He would comfort them by bearing this trial first Himself. For His was the tenderest of hearts, and it cost Him very much to grieve those who were dearer to Him than all the world beside, and who were so worthy of His love.

God's way is to try His servants for a little while and then to reward them. He filled with overflowing joy the hearts of Mary and Joseph as, with the Holy Child between them, they set out on their way home. How sadly they had trod that road three days before! But what a difference the presence of Jesus makes now! They held Him fast, one by each hand. They had Him all to themselves, for the caravan was far ahead. And He was making up to them in all manner of sweet ways for the pain they had had.

When they got home they wondered if He would be any different; if the time was come for Him to be less subject to them; if He was going to continue the work of teaching He had begun in the Temple. No, He was just the same as before; the twelfth birthday had made no change. There was the same ready obedience, the same eagerness to find out their wishes, to spare them trouble, to make the little home happy for them.

XIII.
The Hidden Life

Next time the doctors of the Temple met they wondered if that marvellous Child would come again and teach them. They went over together all He had said, and when they got puzzled afresh they wished they had asked Him who He was and where He lived. He was very young to be a prophet, but surely none of the prophets had spoken as He had done; those who called themselves masters in Israel were no more than children beside Him. He knew the hidden meanings of the Scripture, and, as some of them had found out, He could read their most secret thoughts. They made inquiries and talked about Him for a time, and then, as they could learn nothing, the memory of Him faded from their memory, and most of them forgot Him.

And what is He doing who made such a stir among these learned men? Standing by Joseph's side in the workshop to see how yokes and ploughs are made; how the hammer and the saw and the chisel are used; guiding the tools with weak, unsteady hand; learning to be a carpenter. Later on He works under Joseph's direction, and during the hot hours of the morning and afternoon the two may be seen day after day at their heavy toil. Then our Lord sweeps up the shavings, tidies the shop, and takes the finished work to the little homes around. He waits to see if it gives satisfaction, and holds out His hand for the pay.

Then comes the meeting at the evening meal that makes up for the hard work of the day. The joys and sorrows of these blessed Three are the same, and their hearts are so united that nothing ever happens to disturb their peace. Troubles there are every now and then, and hardships always, for they are poor people. But Jesus makes up to Mary and Joseph for all beside.

No mother ever had such joy as Mary, because none ever had a son so perfect and so loving. But she had sorrows too that were hers alone. Some of us find it hard to keep a secret. God's greatest secret was trusted to Mary, and at times she found it hard to keep. Let us see why.

We know how reverently the Church treats the Blessed Sacrament. Her priests alone may touch it. Their hands must be clean; the corporal on which It rests spotless. A veil must hang before the tabernacle door where It is reserved, a lamp must burn day and night before it. Flowers are to be set around the little throne where It is exposed for Benediction, sweet incense must rise up before It, and hymns be sung in Its praise. And when It is waved above their heads, the faithful bow down in adoration. All we can do must be done to honour the Hidden God who makes Himself so little for love of us.

The Hidden Life

Now Mary knew as no one else has ever known who He was that went out to work each morning and came home tired at night, who took orders from the villagers, and helped to earn the daily bread. We get used to the miracle of the Blessed Sacrament, as our genuflections before the tabernacle show. But the Real Presence at Nazareth was always as wonderful to Mary as It had been at the first. Her love and her worship, so far from growing less, grew more intense as time went on. And when she spoke to her Son with the authority of a mother, she never forgot that she was His creature and little handmaid. She knew that whilst He slept on His hard mat at night, or worked in the shop by day, legions of Angels were prostrate in adoration before Him.

It was the keenest pain to her to see Him treated with any want of reverence. When neighbours came into her little home in Egypt, and, meaning to be kind, took up her Babe and dandled and played with Him as if He had been an ordinary child, still more when the townsfolk of Nazareth spoke to Him roughly, found fault with His work, ordered Him here and there, it was hard to look on and say nothing. But she had God's secret to keep, and until the hour had come for her Son to show Himself to the world she must be content to adore in silence and try to make up to Him by her loving reverence for the neglect of those who knew Him not.

Time went on, went quickly in the Holy House, for they were all so happy. Our Lord was quite grown up now, and did all the hard work at the shop. For Joseph's strength was failing. Still he liked to go to the little timber yard, for Jesus was there, and He could sit and watch Him even if he could not help. And there he did sit hour after hour, his eyes fixed on his Foster-Son, watching and wondering why he should have been chosen to be His guardian, why people were allowed to call that Holy One "the Son of Joseph."

At last he could no longer get to his place in the yard. Then, a little later, the end came. There was no illness; the old man simply seemed to fade away. Our Lord prepared him for death, making with him the acts of Faith, Hope, and Charity which get us ready to die. Joseph had always willed just what God willed. It was this habit that made his face so peaceful that his neighbours used to wonder if he had any troubles. Yet sometimes the Will of God was hard. It was hard now.

When other saints die they are glad because they are going to God whom they love, going to be with Jesus and Mary for ever. But Joseph had lived with Jesus and Mary almost all his life. He had toiled for them, provided their daily bread, gone and come with them wherever they went. To look upon the face of Jesus, to be trusted and loved by Mary—this had made the happiness of his life.

And now he must leave them and go down to Limbo, the dark, dreary place of waiting. Our Lord knew it was hard. But He comforted him by telling

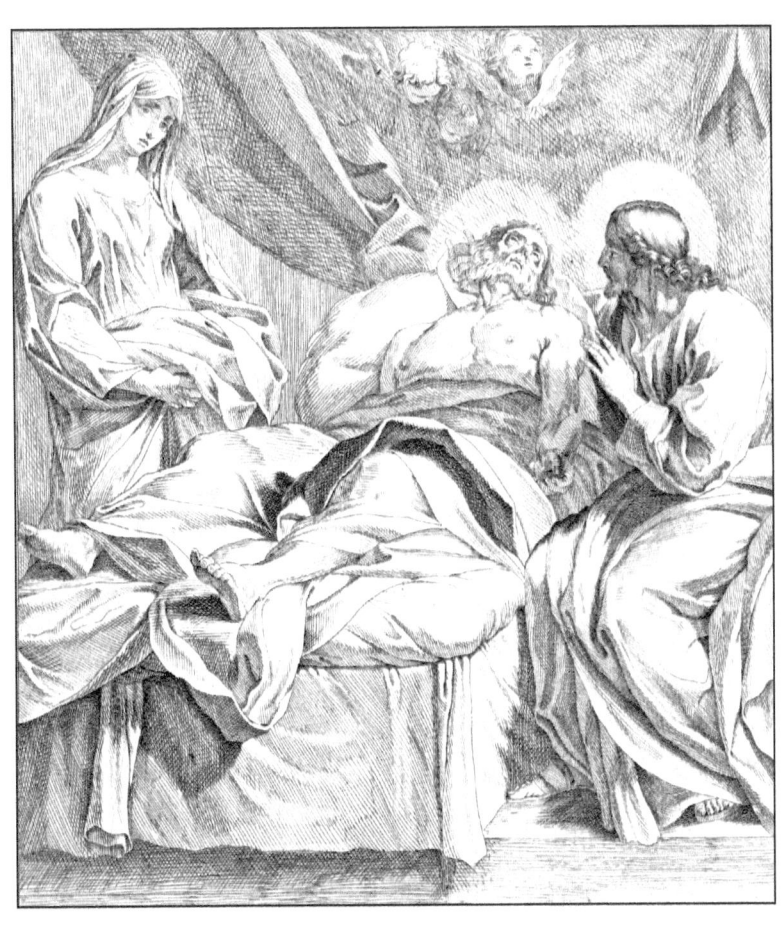

The Happy Death of St. Joseph

*Jesus, Mary, and Joseph, assist me in my last agony.
Jesus, Mary, and Joseph, may I breathe forth my soul
with you in peace.*

him that the separation would not be for long, and gave him sweet messages to take to the waiting souls. Only three years more and the world would be redeemed, and as soon as the price was paid on Calvary He would come to them and turn Limbo into Paradise.

The end of Joseph's wonderful life was come. His head lay on the breast of Jesus, his hand was clasped in the hands of Mary—and so he died. How they had loved him and how they missed him now! By the parting at that holy deathbed, and by the vacant place in the little home, Jesus and Mary learned to weep with those that weep, and to feel for hearts torn and bleeding by the breaking of the ties that God Himself has made.

It is because of the happiness of St. Joseph's death, with Jesus and Mary by to help and comfort, that we beg this blessed Saint to be with us with Jesus and Mary when we come to die, and get us the faith, hope, and charity, the contrition, and resignation to God's Will which we shall need in that most dreadful hour:

Jesus, Mary, and Joseph, assist me in my last agony.

Jesus, Mary, and Joseph, may I breathe forth my soul with you in peace.

Our Lord now became the carpenter at Nazareth. Morning and afternoon the sound of the hammer was heard in His shop. Passers by looked in now and then—looked carelessly, their attention attracted by the noise. No one stopped to watch reverently, no one so much as dreamed that this—was God!

The Hidden Life

He was expected to make and mend all the simple village furniture, to be grateful for orders, and to do His work cheaply and well. He must be at every one's beck and call, work after hours, leave what He was about, to do something wanted at once; this table must be altered, that plough was too dear. He listens patiently; He undoes His work and does it again. He tries to please His humble customers; He treats them with respect and obeys them cheerfully.

And this day after day, all through the Hidden Life!

There need not have been all those years of heavy toil. Our Lord might have had a comfortable and a beautiful home. He might have taught in the synagogue, or written books, or trained disciples. Or, if He chose to work with His hands, His tasks might have been easier and more interesting. Had He thought of Himself things would have been different. But we are told that "He pleased not Himself." He knew that most of His followers would spend their lives in hard, distasteful labour—nothing to look forward to when they get up in the morning, always the same dreary round of little duties. The thought of Nazareth and of the Son of God earning His bread by the sweat of His brow would comfort and cheer these heavy-burdened ones. This is why He spent almost His whole life in a cottage and a workshop. And there was another reason.

What a prince touches, or does, or likes, receives a value which it had not before. When the Son of God came into the world, He found labour despised and shunned. So He consecrated it by the touch of His divine hands, and now it has become honourable and dear to those who love Him. We should esteem it as all the saints have done. How much better is a life of labour than one of ease and luxury! Let us thank God if we have to work hard with our heads or our hands. This will save us from the dangers that idleness brings; and if like our Lord we do our work for the love of God, it will be very pleasing in His sight and deserve a great reward.

When evening came our Lord and His Blessed Mother took their simple meal and said their night prayers together. He would speak to her of the time fast approaching when He must leave her to go out into the world and save the souls of men. She would see Him now and then during the time of His preaching, but His Father's business would fill His days, and prayer His nights. She must be content to follow Him with the holy women who would minister to Him, and mix in the crowd and see and hear Him from afar.

In His tender, loving talks during those last days at Nazareth, He would tell her many things about that Kingdom of His, the Church, which He was going to found—many secrets which, because of her holiness, she was fit to hear. When our Lord came to mix with men, we find Him sighing again and again at their want of faith, at the dullness of their understanding, at the slowness of their hearts. What a joy it must have been to Him to have such a one as Mary to teach, and how freely He must have spoken to her during those years of the Hidden Life when she was His one companion.

The Hidden Life

At last the day of parting came, and as they stood together at the door she bade Him farewell. He was leaving the little home in which God had had such perfect service, and going out into a world in which God was little known and loved. He left behind the one heart that understood His own, the Mother to whom He had trusted His joys, His sorrows, His plans for the souls of men. As time went on He would find many followers and a few devoted friends, but none like those who had made Nazareth a little Heaven upon earth.

Mary's heart was breaking when she saw Him go. No one has ever known Jesus as she knew Him, and therefore no one can have any idea of the love with which she cherished and clung to Him. She alone among mothers was allowed, nay, was bound to worship her Son. For thirty years He had been the Life of her life. To part with Him was worse than death. Yet she would not have kept Him a day from the work to which He was going. She was the first and most faithful of His disciples, and she had learned from Him the worth of souls. She knew how dearly He loved them, how He was longing to give His blood to save them from sin and hell, and she was willing and eager to see them saved even at this tremendous price. He was going to torments and to death; the sword of sorrow must pierce her soul; but she bowed her head and said: "Behold the handmaid of the Lord, be it done according to His Will."

SEEKING OUR HEARTS

"Behold, I stand at the gate, and knock."
(Apocalypse 3:20)

THE PUBLIC LIFE

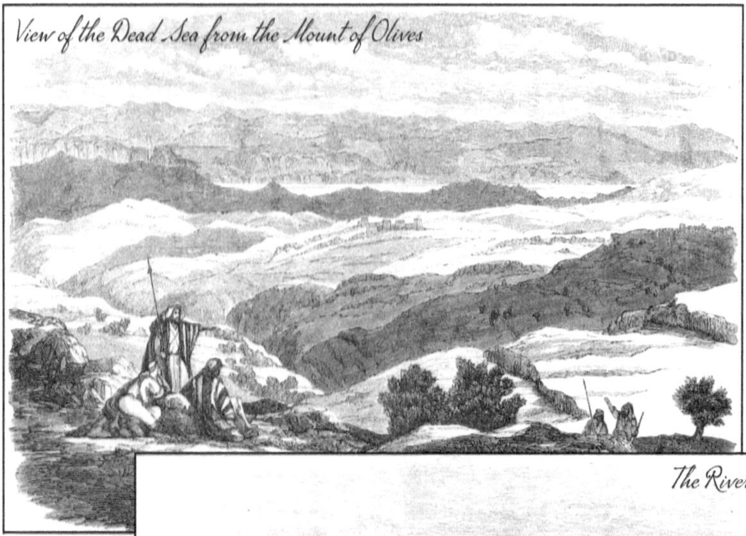

View of the Dead Sea from the Mount of Olives

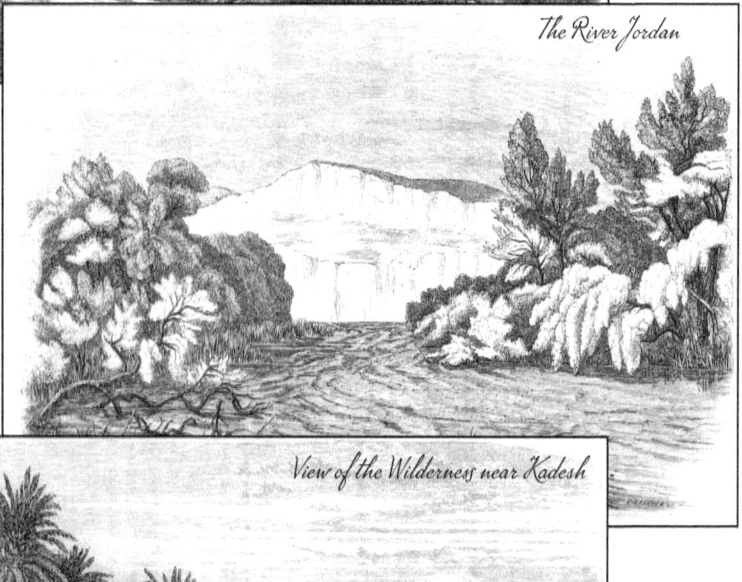

The River Jordan

View of the Wilderness near Kadesh

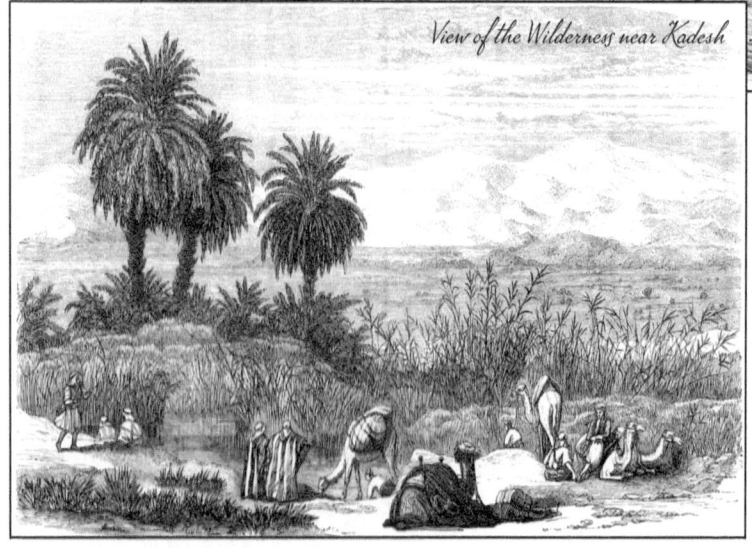

XIV.
Palestine and its People

"Too long hast Thou been silent, O Lord Jesus, and very much too long; begin now at last to speak," says St. Bernard in one of his sermons.

We can scarcely imagine a greater contrast than the thirty years of our Lord's Life now past, and the three that are to come. Hitherto He has been hidden away as the carpenter of an obscure village, unknown except to His humble relations, and very imperfectly known even to them. Now, with a band of devoted disciples, He is to come and go along the highways of the land, to be a familiar Figure in the Temple at the time of the great yearly Feasts, a Teacher in the synagogues up and down the country, the Guest of Pharisees of distinction. He will be followed from city to city, and across the wilderness and up the mountain slopes by multitudes of every age and class and calling. He will be found amidst friends and enemies, at festive gatherings, at the bedside of the sick and lonely poor.

To know Him better we will try to get some idea of the land to which He is coming as Teacher of its people.

If we take a map of the world we shall find that the little country of Palestine lies just in the heart of the Eastern hemisphere. It forms part of Asia, it adjoins Africa, and the same sea that bathes its shore washes all those of southern Europe; as if to show by its very situation that the Land from which salvation flowed to all lands should be the centre to which the men of every age and race and clime should turn with love and thankfulness.

It seems to belong to all lands in another way—by sharing what is special to each. Nowhere out of Palestine are to be found natural features so opposite, and the animal and vegetable life of such different parts of the globe.

In a country about the size of Switzerland are snow-capped mountains, parched deserts, beautiful lakes; plains scarlet with poppies, and desolate stony wastes; groves of feathery palms, and oaks, chestnuts, pines, and firs; vines, melons, pomegranates, the sugar cane; and apples, nuts, and fields of waving grain.

The lion, rhinoceros, wild bull, and bison, are no longer found, but there are camels and bears, wolves and hyenas, jackals and apes, with the horses, asses, sheep, and goats, hares and foxes of our own land.

Palestine has our birds, too, all the warblers of our woods and hedges, the blackbird, thrush, and cuckoo, with sparrows, rooks, and jackdaws. The robin spends his winter there; all about Bethlehem the goldfinch is common, wild ducks abound in the Jordan valley, whilst soaring above most rocky ravines are the vulture and the eagle. Might we not think that the various creatures familiar to us in different parts of the world are gathered together in the Holy Land to be blessed for every land?

To bring home to ourselves the Life of our Blessed Lord on this earth of ours, it helps us to know the kind of country and scenery that lay around Him, the animals and birds and flowers He would see; to be able to picture to ourselves the little white houses with their low roofs and blinking windows that would come within sight when He neared a village; the sort of people with whom He would have to mix, their manners and customs and dress. We must not, then, think it dull and uninteresting to learn something of the state of the country when He came. Trouble is well bestowed if it helps us to know Him better, to feel as well as to know what His life on earth must have been, and what He went through, not uncomplainingly only, but willingly and brightly for the love of us. A word, then, about the government of the country.

When Abraham, the father of the Jewish people, was led thither out of Mesopotamia, he found there the fierce and wicked race of Canaan, from whom it takes the first name by which we know it. God promised it to Abraham and his children, who called it the Land of Promise. They did not, however, get possession of it till more than five hundred years after Abraham. Then Jewish kings reigned there for five hundred years, till the Jews were taken into captivity by the Assyrians, and again for another hundred years before they came under Roman rule. It was because two royal brothers quarrelled about the crown that the Romans were called in. They soon settled the dispute by making the country a Roman province, obliging the Jews to pay a yearly tribute to Rome, and setting over them as king a foreigner, Herod the Great, in whose reign our Lord was born.

The Jews hated everything that reminded them of their subjection to Rome, the sight of the Roman eagles set up in public places, of Roman soldiers stationed here and there to keep them in order, of the Roman coins with which they had to pay the tribute; they even hated and despised their fellow-countrymen, the publicans, who collected the taxes for the Romans. They were always ready for revolt, always prepared to follow any of the imposters who at this time of universal expectation pretended to be the long-looked-for Deliverer of the people. It was as a deliverer from the Roman yoke, a king who would shower upon them honours and riches, and make them the first nation of the earth, rather than as One coming to free them from sin and teach them the way to Heaven, that they regarded and ardently desired the Messiah. We have to bear this in mind in order to understand how the whole people could turn against Him and deliver Him up to the Romans and to death.

He came at a time when things were at their worst, not only in the great pagan world that lay outside His own Land, but in that favoured Land itself. The priests, even the High Priests, were men of evil life and a scandal to the nation. It was they who became the bitterest enemies of our Blessed Lord and stirred up the masses against Him.

The people, instead of being united in fervent preparation for the coming Redeemer, were divided into sects and parties, bitterly opposed to one another. There were the Pharisees who made pretence of being better than the rest of men. "Whited sepulchres," our Lord called them: fair without, loathsome within. There were the wealthy, luxurious Sadducees who denied the existence of spirits and the resurrection of the dead, men determined to enjoy this world as they did not believe in another, wanting no Messiah who would disturb a state of things with which they were quite satisfied. And there were the Herodians, who flattered those in power in order to gain their own ends and have a comfortable, easy life.

The Pharisees appear so often in the Gospel story that we must try to have a clear idea of them. Their name describes them well, for it means "the Separated," the holy ones set apart from the multitude. They looked down upon the poor and the ignorant who had not studied the Law of Moses, and called them "accursed." They prided themselves on their knowledge of the Law and their exact observance of all it required as to fasting, purification, the paying of tithes and particularly as to the keeping of the Sabbath. According to them it was unlawful to make a knot, to kill a stinging insect, even to clap one's hands on the

Sabbath day. They were most strict about the washing of hands, and cups, and dishes. But the holiness of the soul they did not trouble themselves about. The greatest saint was not he who most loved God and his neighbour, but he whose phylactery was the broadest and tassels longest, and face the gloomiest on fasting days. These men had great influence with the people, who looked up to them with awe, called them "Rabbi;" that is "Master," and showed their veneration by touching respectfully the tassels of their mantles.

Our Lord showed Himself condescending but firm with the Pharisees. He meekly bore their rudeness and even their blasphemy. He went to their houses, though He knew He was invited only that they might watch and inform against Him. But, when at the end of His ministry He saw that they remained obstinate, hindered His work, and turned the simple folk against Him, He spoke to them with terrible severity, and boldly reproved them for their pride and deceit. He called them hypocrites who might indeed deceive men with their show of goodness, but could not escape the All-seeing eye of God. His fearless exposure of their wickedness enraged them, and the people's admiration for Him filled them with envy and hatred. For they wanted to be the leaders of the nation, and could not bear to be put into the shade by this carpenter of Galilee. The divine beauty of our Lord's character and teaching and works they did not wish to see. To them He was only a rival who must be got rid of. And because they feared as well as hated

The Pharisees

"Woe to you scribes and Pharisees, hypocrites!"
(Mt 23:29)

Him they leagued with their enemies the Sadducees to bring about His destruction.

Such were the masters to whom the people looked for guidance and example. It was amongst such as these that our Lord found Himself when He left the wilderness and began His work of teaching.

Palestine was at this time divided into six districts. West of the Jordan were Galilee in the north, Samaria in the centre, Judea in the south. East of the river were Ituria, Trachonitis and Perea.

Herod the Great had ruled as a vassal king under the Romans over all Palestine. On his death his kingdom was divided among his three sons, Archelaus, Herod Antipas, and Herod Philip, who governed their territories with the title of *tetrarchs*. Archelaus ruled over Judea and Samaria, but after ten years of a cruel reign he was deposed and banished and his tetrarchate was made into a Roman province under a *procurator* or governor. Herod Antipas governed Galilee and Perea with the title of king, though he was only a tetrarch. He was still reigning at the time our Lord began His public ministry. Pontius Pilate was procurator of Judea and Samaria. Tiberias Cæsar was Emperor of Rome.

The scenes of our Blessed Lord's Life lay occasionally in Samaria, oftener in the towns and highways of Judea, oftenest in Galilee, among the towns and villages dotted along the western shore of its beautiful lake, and up the grassy slopes to the east.

XV.
The Banks of Jordan

Leaving Nazareth behind Him, our Lord made His way to the banks of the Jordan, and following the river southward through Galilee, Samaria and Judea, arrived at a ford near Jericho. On His road He had fallen in with troops of people of all classes going in the same direction, and here assembled at the ford was a vast multitude covering both banks. On one point all eyes were fixed. Standing on the river bank was a man of rough and uncouth appearance. His face, from constant exposure to sun and wind, was of the colour of brown parchment; his eye was bright and piercing; his frame lean with fasting, and freely over his shoulders fell his long hair, for his locks had never been shorn. He wore a garment of coarse camel's hair gathered in at the waist by a leathern girdle.

Who was this extraordinary man? People said he was the son of the priest Zachary, who, thirty years ago, whilst offering incense in the Temple had seen an Angel and been struck dumb by the vision. His name was John. He had spent his life from childhood in the desert, where his food was locusts and wild honey. And now he had suddenly appeared on the borders of his desert and was telling the crowds who went out to see him that they must repent of their sins and prepare for the Messiah, for the Kingdom of Heaven was at hand.

"The Kingdom, the Messiah's Kingdom at hand!" A cry of rapture rang through the land. He was near, then, who should free them from bondage and raise the fallen fortunes of Israel; who should march at their head against the heathen Gentiles, bring the whole earth under His rule, and begin a thousand years' reign of prosperity and glory for the people of God! Men, women and children from Jerusalem and all the country about the Jordan, nay, from distant towns and villages, flocked in thousands to the wilderness—Pharisees and Sadducees, priests, publicans, soldiers, forgetting in the common joy and expectancy their mutual jealousy and hate.

But John's speech to them was not of coming pomp and pleasure, but of penance. He flattered none; he told all to confess their sins and be baptized. In stern and fearless words he rebuked the proud, the self-indulgent, the unrepenting sinner. Seeing among the crowd some Pharisees and Sadducees, he cried out:

"Ye offspring of vipers, who hath shewed you to flee from the wrath to come?"

But he spoke gently to the humble and the poor.

Standing one day on a hillock, his voice thundered over the wilderness:

"Now the axe is laid to the root of the trees. Every

The Banks of Jordan

tree, therefore, that bringeth not forth good fruit, shall be cut down and cast into the fire."

The people terrified cried out: "What, then, shall we do?"

And he said: "He that hath two coats, let him give to him that hath none, and he that hath meat let him do in like manner."

And the publicans who came to be baptized said to him: "Master, what shall we do?"

And he said to them: "Do nothing more than that which is appointed you." For as collectors of taxes they were accustomed to cheat.

And the soldiers also asked him saying: "And what shall we do?"

And he said to them: "Do violence to no man, neither accuse any falsely, and be content with your pay."

He did not tell men to lead a hard life like his own, but to keep the Commandments of God and be faithful to the duties of their state of life. In this way they would be getting ready for the Messiah.

The rugged appearance and stern speech of the young preacher, so far from scaring the people away, drew them to him. His words that the Messiah was about to appear caused the greatest excitement throughout the country; thousands were baptized by him in the Jordan confessing their sins, and disciples began to gather round him. And as people were thinking that perhaps John might be the Christ, he said to them:

"I indeed baptize you with water, but there shall come One mightier than I, the latchet of whose shoes

I am not worthy to loose. He shall baptize you with the Holy Ghost and with fire."

The Coming of Christ—this was always the subject of his instructions. It was this that made his dark eye kindle and his countenance glow. Men who knew how stern his speech could be marvelled at the burning love that from his heart overflowed upon his lips when he spoke of Him whose messenger and forerunner he was.

Day by day his words of prophecy grew clearer, and the expectation of his hearers more intense. The Messiah was close at hand. John had said it, and all men held John to be a prophet. He was at hand; when and where would He show Himself?

One day John was preaching as usual and as usual the stillness of the vast audience showed that his words were reaching every heart. Suddenly he broke off and fixed his gaze with a look of reverent wonder on something or someone at a distance. All eyes followed his. From the midst of the throng a Man was quietly advancing towards the little height on which the Baptist stood. His garments were poor, yet there was an indescribable majesty about Him joined to an innocence, simplicity and gentleness capable of winning every heart. He was a stranger, unknown to all but one. John saw Him, knew Him, and his heart leapt forth to welcome Him.

Painters have loved to show us the little Baptist standing with the Child Jesus at Mary's knee. The two were cousins, but we are not told that they had ever seen each other before this meeting by the Jordan. How, then, did John know our Blessed Lord? He himself tells us: "I saw the Spirit coming down as a dove from Heaven upon Him."

The Precursor thought his work was now done; the Master had come, it was the place of the servant to retire. What, then, was his amazement and awe when our Lord, mingling with the sinners who were coming down to the water, and waiting His turn, stood at length before Him and humbly asked for baptism.

"I ought to be baptized by Thee," he said trembling, "and comest Thou to me?"

"Suffer it to be so now," replied Jesus in a low tone, "for so it becometh us to fulfill all justice."

Then John with reverent hand poured the water on that sacred head, and that which was one day to make us children of God and heirs of Heaven was consecrated by the Baptism of Christ. As He came out of the water there was a glorious sight: the heavens opened, and in the midst of dazzling light the form of a Dove with outstretched wings was seen to overshadow Him, whilst a Voice like soft thunder was heard:

"Thou art My Beloved Son, in Thee I am well pleased."

This is the first time the Holy Trinity, One God in Three Persons, showed Itself to men—the Father in the Voice from Heaven, the Son in the Sacred Human Nature, the Holy Ghost in the form of a Dove.

The Hidden Life was over, our Lord's Public Life had begun, and it began with an act of deep humility. But He that humbleth himself shall be exalted. So it

The Baptism of Our Lord

"Thou art my beloved Son; in thee I am well pleased."
(Mark 1:11)

has ever been; so it was by the Jordan now. Christ, the All-Holy, had humbled Himself, appearing among sinners as a sinner. And His Father had glorified Him by declaring before that vast multitude that He was no sinner but His own well Beloved Son.

We might have thought that at last His time for preaching had come. He was thirty years of age; the people prepared by John were in eager expectation. They had heard Him proclaimed from Heaven to be the Son of God. How they would flock to Him and welcome Him if He were to come among them and teach them now!

But God's ways are not like ours. Our Lord was indeed going to teach; not, however, the people of His own land, but His followers in every land and throughout all time, to teach us all one of the most important lessons we have to learn in this world. And He was going to a battlefield to meet a cruel and powerful adversary. What was this lesson? Where was this battlefield? Let us follow Him and see.

XVI.
In the Desert

When the people on the river banks looked around for the wonderful Stranger they could find Him nowhere. He had quietly left the place where He had been glorified, and, climbing the steep side of a mountain, had entered a lonely country full of barren rocks and gloomy caves, a region rugged and dreary beyond description. There He spent forty days and forty nights, neither eating nor drinking. The wild creatures of the wilderness were His only companions. The tortoise came out of its rocky hole, the lizard darted across His path as He walked. When evening fell He heard far off on the mountain side the jackal's mournful cry. Lions and leopards passed Him on their way to a stream, or came up and fixed their great, wondering eyes on Him as He knelt in prayer. He was their Lord and Master, and He was sinless—they did not harm Him.

After He had fasted forty days and forty nights the devil, who had been watching and suspecting, came to Him. He wanted to find out who this extraordinary man was. He knew that the time was at hand for His Coming who was to redeem the world and save us

In the Desert

from sin and hell. Was this holy One the Redeemer, or only another of the prophets? If he was no more than man, He could be tempted and fall into sin like other men.

There are three desires which, unless resolutely checked, lead people into sin—the desire of pleasure, such as the enjoyment of the body in eating and drinking; the desire of notice and admiration; the desire of riches, and of the comforts, power and importance that riches bring.

We must bear in mind, however, that these three p's—pleasure, plenty and praise—are things not bad in themselves, nor is the moderate desire of them wrong. What is bad is the immoderate desire, the reckless use of them simply because they are nice. The devil knows that we are inclined to rush after enjoyment for enjoyment's sake, so he uses these things as baits to catch and ruin us. Men, women, children, all are tempted, some by one bait, some by another, but no one escapes, the Saints least of all. They do not go to Heaven alone, but take many with them, hence the enemy of souls hates and fears them more than others. With what hate, then, did he look upon this Holy One who might be not a Saint only but the Saint of Saints and the Redeemer of men.

The forty days were over, and Jesus, who had been six weeks without food, was sitting worn and weak on a rock in the midst of the desolate country. Scattered around were great stones something in the shape of loaves. And the tempter coming said to Him:

"If Thou be the Son of God, command that these stones be made bread."

By these cunning words he meant to find out what he wanted so much to know, for God alone could change a stone into bread. But we wonder, perhaps, where the temptation was. Our Lord was very hungry and He was asked to change a stone, not into anything dainty but into bread. It was temptation because He was urged to satisfy His hunger before the time appointed by His Father, and to do this by a miracle. He had come into the world to suffer, not to use His divine power to escape suffering. His miracles were to be for others, not for Himself. And He had something far more important to do at that time than to provide for His bodily need. And so the answer came promptly:

"It is written; Man liveth not by bread alone but by every word of God."

He would suffer as long as His Father willed, and wait patiently till His Father should send relief. The devil had found out nothing and his temptation had been treated with contempt. But he had two more in reserve.

He took our Lord into his loathsome grasp and bore Him away to the holy city, Jerusalem. There he set Him on one of the lofty pinnacles that overlooked the Temple Courts and said to Him:

"If Thou be the Son of God cast Thyself down, for it is written: that He hath given His Angels charge over thee, and in their hands shall they bear thee up lest perhaps thou dash thy foot against a stone."

THE TEMPTATION

"If thou be the Son of God, command that these stones be made bread."
(Matt. 4:3)

As if he would say: "At the sight of Angels flocking round Thee to guard Thy sacred feet, the worshippers in the Courts below will fall prostrate before Thee and adore Thee as the Son of God." See how determined he is to get our Lord's secret from Him, how cunningly his tricks are devised, and how he can turn even holy words to his own purposes. Jesus answered calmly:

"It is written again: Thou shalt not tempt the Lord thy God."

Did He mean that He Himself was the Lord God? The crafty spirit could not tell; he was foiled again. But there was a third trial, he might succeed yet. The man, if he was only man, was very weary, very suffering, he might yield just to purchase peace.

Again the devil took Him up into a very high mountain and showed Him all the kingdoms of the world and the glory of them and said to Him:

"All these will I give Thee if falling down Thou wilt adore me."

"Begone, Satan! for it is written: The Lord thy God shalt thou adore and Him only shalt thou serve."

Like a thunderclap from a cloudless sky came those tremendous words. Jesus was weary even to exhaustion. But when His Father's honour was assailed He spoke in words of power which terrified the coward that thought to take advantage of His weakness.

"Begone!" The Evil One quailed before Him and fled. And behold Angels came and ministered to Him. They had been hovering near all through this marvellous scene, wondering and worshipping. And now in joyful throngs they offered Him their service, who, though so spent and suffering, they knew to be very God of very God. They brought Him refreshment in His hunger and thirst, and by their bright, beautiful forms gladdened His sight.

You will ask, perhaps, how our Lord could see from one mountain all the kingdoms of the world? Or how it was that Satan, who is so clever and watchful, did not know from all that had gone before who He was?

Many people are asking nowadays how certain things we read in Holy Scriptures are possible, how they can be explained. These are two distinct questions, not two forms of the same. How things that we cannot understand are possible, should be no difficulty to us in these days of marvellous discoveries and inventions. A hundred years ago, wireless telegraphy, the X-rays, the cutting off of a man's leg without hurting him, would have been pronounced impossibilities had anyone predicted them, and any genius who should have made them facts would in the Middle Ages have run the danger of being treated as a wizard for his pains.

Wise folks are becoming very wary of declaring anything impossible. It is a thought to make us humble that we are perhaps only beginning in this twentieth century to find out the possibilities of this wonderful kingdom of Nature which is *beneath us*. It ought to make us ready to believe that in the spiritual world which is *above us*, there are multitudes of things which we cannot understand. We know from the testimony of our senses that the gramophone and chloroform are facts. But very few of us could give a satisfactory explanation of these marvels; knowledge and terms would alike fail us were we to try. Nay, for the same reasons we should hardly understand the explanation of an expert, even were he to do his best to be simple and clear by the use of our own familiar words.

What wonder, then, that we cannot comprehend those spiritual things which we can neither see, nor hear, nor touch, nor reach by any of our bodily senses! Even God Himself cannot make these things perfectly clear to us now; we are too ignorant, and the words of our poor human speech are too weak to express the wonders that Angels understand perfectly, and that we shall understand some day. When God speaks to us in the Holy Scriptures He has to use our imperfect words to express His divine thought. He is like a father who, in answer to his children's questions, tries to put some grand astronomical fact into their childish language. We are all children now, and even the most learned must be content to say when it comes to the mysteries of faith: "I know it is so, because God has said it. I do not know *how* it is, because of my ignorance. God cannot at present explain it to me. But I shall know some day, and meantime I can wait."

But there are plenty of things which, with a little thought, we can understand quite well in Holy Scripture, and God means us to learn from the Life of our Blessed Lord all we can. This wonderful fact of His conflict with the devil was for our sakes, to teach us how to meet temptation. Our enemy is stronger than we are, but he has been completely conquered by our Leader, and this gives us an immense advantage over him. For a foe that has been beaten again and again comes on to the field in a very different spirit from one who has never known defeat. We have to fight the same enemy who fled in terror at our Lord's word "Begone!" And our Lord stands beside us always. He encourages us to use His own word: "Begone, Satan!" and promises us victory if we only ask Him for it and do our best. He has taught us by His own example that temptations are not sins; that we are not to be surprised or frightened when temptation comes; and even if it comes again and again and in different shapes we are to meet it calmly and patiently, trusting in His strength whose soldiers we are.

XVII.
The First Disciples

We must go back to our Lord whom we left in the desert surrounded by Angels.

Coming down the mountain side He made His way again to the bank of the Jordan where John was still preaching and baptising. The crowds were greater than ever and more enthusiastic. John, they said, was either Christ or Elias who was to announce His Coming. At last the great Council of the nation, called the Sanhedrin, determined to find out the truth. They therefore sent messengers to the Baptist to ask him:

"Who art thou?"

"I am not the Christ," he said.

"What, then; art thou Elias?"

"I am not," he replied.

"Art thou the Prophet?"

He answered: "No."

"Who art thou, that we may give an answer to them that sent us?"

"I am the voice of one crying in the wilderness: Make straight the way of the Lord, as the prophet Isaias said."

John the Baptist

"A voice of one crying in the desert,
Prepare ye the way of the Lord, make straight his paths."
(Matt. 3:3)

And they asked him: "Why then dost thou baptize if thou be not Christ nor Elias nor the Prophet?"

John answered them saying: "I baptize in water, but there hath stood One in the midst of you whom you know not. The same is He that shall come after Me, who is preferred before Me, the latchet of whose shoe I am not worthy to loose."

If we want to see a perfect servant of God, we have only to look at St. John. For months the stream of people, rich and poor, learned and simple, had been coming and going; his name was in every mouth, everyone wanted to see him, hear him, show him reverence. But he cared nothing for all this homage. His one thought was his Master, to turn the minds of the people from himself and fix them upon Him, to hand over his own disciples to Him at the first opportunity. This came at last.

One day he saw Jesus coming towards him. Turning to those who stood about, he said:

"Behold the Lamb of God, behold Him who taketh away the sin of the world, this is the Son of God."

The next day he was standing with two of his disciples when Jesus passed by:

"Behold the Lamb of God," he said again, as he pointed Him out to them.

Everyone is attracted by a lamb. St. John wanted to draw the hearts of his disciples to Jesus, so he called Him by this name. Yet not "Lamb" only, but "Lamb of God," for they must know who He was, and worship as well as love Him.

The First Disciples

"Behold the Lamb of God!" The priest says these words to us just before Holy Communion, that we may not be frightened of Him who comes to us, and on the other hand that he may not thoughtlessly forget how great and holy He is. In every Mass, at the end of every litany, the Church calls upon our Lord by this beautiful name of His, "the Lamb of God." He has many names, and among them some are His favourites— the Holy Name, "JESUS," (that is, Saviour), "Jesus of Nazareth," "Son of David," "the Lamb." It is by this last name that St. John the Evangelist calls Him when he sees Him in His glory. He tells us that he saw "a great multitude whom no man could number, of all nations and tribes and peoples and tongues, standing before the Throne of God and in sight of the Lamb," to show us what a happiness it is to be where we can see face to face and to our heart's content our dear and gentle Lord. Among these blessed ones he saw some specially favoured "who follow the Lamb whithersoever He goeth."

It was these words: "Behold the Lamb of God," that won the hearts of the disciples. They looked earnestly, and drawn they knew not how, followed Him. He turned and, seeing them following, said graciously:

"What seek you?"

"Rabbi, where dwellest Thou?" they answered timidly, not knowing what else to say.

"Come and see," He replied.

They followed Him joyfully now, and He took them to a little hut or shelter He had on the river bank.

It was about four in the afternoon, "and they stayed with Him that day," says one of them who has left us the account. This one was John the Evangelist, called later "the Disciple whom Jesus loved." The other was Andrew, a fisherman who lived on the shore of the Lake of Genesareth.

It seems that they stayed with our Lord not only the rest of that day but the following night. What they said to Him and He to them we are not told, but when day was come and they took their leave, our Lord had gained His first two disciples, the oldest and the youngest of the Twelve Apostles. From what they had seen and heard they were quite sure that this was He who was come, and they went off at once to tell their brothers. Andrew found his first:

"We have found the Messiah!" he exclaimed joyfully. And he brought him to Jesus.

St. John seems to have been present at the interview, for he tells us very carefully what happened. Jesus, looking upon the newcomer, said:

"Thou art Simon, the son of Jona, thou shalt be called Cephas" (which is interpreted as Peter).

Well might our Lord look earnestly upon that weather-beaten, eager face, all aglow with expectation. Here was His first Vicar upon earth, the Rock on which He was to build His Church. He looked, and thought of all He was to be to Peter and Peter to Him, of the long line of successors this Galilean fisherman was to have, of all they would gather into their net and land safely on the eternal Shore.

The First Disciples

Those who heard these words of our Lord must have been startled. A Jewish name was not given lightly as ours often are, for the sake of the sound, or because one of the family has borne it before. It was intended to show the character or the calling of the person who bore it. To change a name was to show a change of position or of office. It was an important act, and allowed only to the rulers among the Jews.

Now here was One who, on seeing this fisherman for the first time, not only told him his name and his father's, but changed his name from Simon, which means "Son of a dove," to Peter, which means "a Rock." Andrew and John looked at one another in astonishment. What such a change meant they could not tell, but they did not forget it. New disciples as they came in were told about it, and Peter at once came to be looked upon as the first and chief among them. The Evangelists, who have written the Gospel story, all name him first in their lists of the Apostles. He was not the oldest, not the first called, but he was "the Rock."

Simon, Andrew and John had, like so many others, left their homes in Galilee to come down to Judea that they might hear the preaching of John the Baptist. The fourth disciple, Philip of Bethsaida, was another Galilean fisherman. He came from the village of Simon and Andrew on the shore of the Lake.

The day after His words to Peter, our Lord was returning with His little company to Galilee when "He found Philip," says St. John. To the disciples this meeting, first with one, then with another of them, might seem to be chance. But there is no chance with God. Each of this chosen band was sought out by the Master, and at the right moment found.

Looking on Philip He said to him:

"Follow Me."

Two words, but enough. Philip followed, and was so happy in the company of his new Master that he could not rest till he had made Him known to a friend of his named Nathaniel. Nathaniel was sitting alone under a fig tree when Philip broke in upon his solitude exclaiming joyfully:

"We have found Him of whom Moses in the Law and the prophets did speak, Jesus of Nazareth."

"Of Nazareth." His little speech could scarcely have had a more unfortunate ending, the effect of the good news was spoilt completely.

"Can anything good come from Nazareth?" Nathaniel replied coldly.

"Come and see," was the answer. It took some persuasion, but at length the two were on their way to our Lord. When they had come up to Him He said in the hearing of Nathaniel:

"Behold an Israelite indeed in whom there is no guile."

Nathaniel in amazement replied: "Whence knowest Thou me?"

Jesus looking upon him said: "Before that Philip called thee, when thou wast under the fig-tree, I saw thee."

The First Disciples

The fig-tree was a long way off, and what had happened there we do not know. Perhaps Nathaniel had been praying to see the Messiah before he died, and be numbered amongst His followers. Any way there had been some act or thought which God alone could know. Who was this Stranger that in that secret place had seen him and read his heart? Nathaniel was a man without guile, that is without cunning or deceit. He only wanted to know what was right, and seeing what a mistake he had made he owned it at once.:

"Rabbi," he exclaimed, "Thou art the Son of God, Thou art the King of Israel."

Jesus answered: "Because I said unto Thee: I saw thee under the fig-tree thou believest? Greater things than these shalt thou see."

Many believed Nathaniel to be the same as St. Bartholomew the Apostle. "Bar" means "Son," "Bar-Tolmai" means "Son of Tolmai." The full name may have been Nathaniel Bar-Tolmai, just as we have Simon Bar-Jona. One reason for this belief is that in the lists of the Twelve Apostles Philip and Bartholomew are always put together.

XVIII.
Galilee

> Clear silver water in a cup of gold,
> Under the sunlit steeps of Gadara,
> It shines—His Lake—the Sea of Chinnereth-
> The waves He loved, the waves that kissed His feet
> So many blessed days. Oh, happy waves!
> Oh, little silver, happy Sea, far-famed,
> Under the sunlit steeps of Gadara![1]

And now they were in Galilee, our Lord and His five disciples—six, if we count Nathaniel.

Let us try to see the place where the greater part of the Public Life was spent: the home of those who, after Peter, were to be the foundation stones of the Church. It must be dear to us for their sake, and much more for the sake of Him who is our Master as well as theirs.

The Sea of Galilee, or of Tiberias, or the Lake of Gennesareth, is a pear-shaped sheet of water, fourteen miles long and six broad in its widest part. In our Lord's time it was a scene of wonderful beauty. Its deep blue waters were crossed and recrossed by boats of many shapes and sizes. There were heavily laden

---

1   *The Light of the World.* Sir Edwin Arnold.

barges bearing the costly merchandise of the East to the custom-house on the shore; there were pleasure skiffs darting here and there with gay parties bound for one or other of the handsome Roman villas by the Lakeside; and there were fishing smacks in hundreds, some with nets lowered for a draught, others bringing home the fruits of the night's haul. The white beach showed boats being unladen, children looking on as the silvery load was landed and sorted, men and boys mending their nets on the strand or stretching them out to dry.

Dotted all about were the cottages of the fishermen, and, coming down almost to the water's edge, glowed rich, waving cornfields and flowers of every hue. In the Jordan valley, where, sheltered from the winds, the vegetation was tropical, the sugarcane flourished, and palm trees with their feathery foliage. Higher up grew figs, almonds and olives. Higher still, walnut, oaks, apple trees, each of these needing its own kind of soil and temperature, yet all at home here. Here, too, were the richest and busiest cities of Galilee—Tiberias, Magdala, Bethsaida, Capharnaum, Chorazin. Behind them soared the solemn mountains framing the beautiful picture.

Very different was the country to the east of the Lake. The mountains rise steeply from the shore, and it was difficult to land except in a few places. Owing to the winds that rush between them from the colder heights beyond, the Lake was subject to sudden and dangerous storms. All around lay a wild and desolate region, desert or grassy plain, or rocky highland, with none of the life and stir and busy population of the district to the west.

Dear Sea of Galilee! We love it for His sake who crossed it in Peter's boat, and spoke to its angry waves, and walked upon them to come to the help of His disciples. Here He sat with them on the shingly beach; here He taught and healed and comforted all who came to Him. Up yonder are the bleak mountains to the east which He so often climbed with weary feet, there to spend the night alone in prayer.

How glad Mary must have been to welcome her Divine Son back to Galilee! She was waiting for Him at Cana, a little town five miles north-east of Nazareth, for there was to be a marriage there and they were both invited. It seems likely that the bridegroom and the bride were her relations and that she had something to do with the arrangements for the feast.

Jewish weddings took place in the evening, and it was often dark when the bridal procession, the grandest part of the ceremony, started. Attired in a white and gold-embroidered robe, veiled from head to foot, and with a crown of myrtle on her head, the bride awaited at the door of her father's house the coming of the bridegroom. Waiting and watching with her were ten virgins, her companions carrying lamps. At last a cry was heard: "Behold the bridegroom cometh!" He came with ten youths, his friends, and taking his bride by the hand led her forth. The whole family then formed in procession, and by the light of the torches, with the music of flute and tambourine, and with joyous shouts and song, the bridal pair were escorted to their home, where a great feast was prepared.

These two at Cana were of humble rank and poor. And our Lord had brought His disciples with Him. Perhaps this was the reason why the wine ran short. Mary's quick eye saw the mishap at once, and her motherly heart felt for the confusion of the young couple. Accustomed to take every trouble to her Son, and to be granted all she asked, she went to Him and whispered:

"They have no wine."

"Woman," He answered, "what is it to Me and to thee? My hour is not yet come."

To our ears these words sound strange, but to Eastern ears they would not. "Woman" was a title of reverence, and "what is it to Me and to thee?" meant: "It is no concern of ours that the wine has failed; the time for Me to work miracles has not yet come."

There are some who think that our Lord was displeased with His Blessed Mother for telling Him of the need. They do not consider what Jesus and Mary were to each other; how for thirty years they had lived together under the same roof, she using her authority over Him as His Mother, though always with the profoundest reverence, He showing her the honour and giving her the obedience of a Son. Did she not know Him better than any other has ever done, and know what pleased and what displeased Him? And who understand best the meaning of

The Wedding at Cana

*"Jesus saith to them: Fill the waterpots with water.
And they filled them up to the brim."*
(John 2:7)

words? Is it not those who saw the speaker, heard the tones, noticed the actions? Nothing that Jesus said or did was lost on Mary. Did she think He was displeased? On the contrary, as if He had told her beforehand what she was to do, she turned to the waiters and said:

"Whatsoever He shall say to you, do ye."

Now there were set there six water-pots of stone, according to the manner of the purifying of the Jews. They were very particular to wash their hands before and after eating, and wherever a meal was provided there was always plenty of water for washing. The water-pots contained two or three measures, or about seven and a half gallons apiece. Jesus said to the waiters:

"Fill the water-pots with water."

And they filled them to the brim. Then He said:

"Draw out now and carry to the chief steward of the feast."

This was usually a friend of the bridegroom's, appointed to preside and give directions to the servants. He had to taste the wine before it was served to the guests. The waiters said nothing to the steward, but watched him as he raised the cup to his lips. When he had tasted he put the cup down, and, surprised that poor people could afford to have such wine, and that they should have kept it to the end of the feast, he called the bridegroom and said playfully: "Every man at first setteth forth good wine, and when men have well drunk, then that which is worse; but thou hast kept the good wine till now."

But the faces of the servants showed that something extraordinary had taken place. They were questioned and told their tale again and again, and what had happened under that humble roof was soon spread far and wide.

About a hundred and twenty gallons of water had been changed into the purest wine. Why? Because Mary had asked? No, she had asked nothing. And the time for working signs and miracles had not yet come. Our Lord expressly said so. Why then did He work this wonderful miracle? Because He wanted us to know that whatever His Mother desires He will grant, and that for her dear sake He is ready to hasten His hours of mercy to us. He knew the wine had failed. He meant to give more, but He waited for her to speak that the gift might be hers as well as His.

He wanted to teach us also by His Blessed Mother's example not to be discouraged if He seems to be displeased with us, and to show us that our little troubles are no concern of His. It is only seeming. Everything that touches us interests Him and His holy Mother. They think for us before we think for ourselves. They feel for us, not in big troubles only, but in the least little annoyances and inconveniences. And they are always ready to help.

Our Lord went to this feast, then, on purpose to show honour to His Mother. He went also to bless that marriage union which He was soon to raise to the dignity of a Sacrament, and to bless all innocent joy and merrymaking. He was pleased to see the brightness all round Him at Cana, and He likes to see us, too, happy and gay.

There was still another reason for the miracle. St. John, who was present and gives us the account, says: "This beginning of miracles did Jesus in Cana of Galilee, and He manifested His glory, and His disciples believed in Him." Day by day the disciples were growing in the knowledge of their Divine Master. From His words to Peter and to Nathaniel they had seen that He could read the future and the secrets of hearts. This splendid miracle at Cana showed that He had power over Nature. Their reverence as well as their love was deepening continually. St. John speaks particularly of the way in which this miracle increased their faith—as well it might. The other Evangelists tell us later of another and still greater miracle than this of Cana, a more stupendous change, and one that was to be wrought not once only, but thousands of times daily, all the world over, wherever Holy Mass is said by a Catholic priest.

The thought of Cana helped the disciples when our Lord first spoke to them at Capharnaum of the Mystery of the Holy Eucharist, and when at the Last Supper "He changed the bread and wine into His most sacred Body and Blood. And it helps us too who live so long after Him, but believe in Him as firmly as did His first disciples, and cry out to Him with Nathaniel:

"Rabbi, Thou art the Son of God!"

XIX.
The Court of the Gentiles

Immediately after the miracle at Cana, our Lord went with His Mother, His brethren, and His disciples to Capharnaum, a prosperous commercial town on the north-west coast of the Sea of Galilee.

These brethren of Jesus, so called by Jewish custom, were His near relations, the children of Mary, wife of Cleophas or Alphaeus, and sister or cousin of the Blessed Virgin. They were James, Simon, Jude and Joseph. James and Jude (also called Thaddeus), and perhaps Simon, became Apostles.

They remained at Capharnaum not many days, for the Passover was at hand, and the caravan from Galilee was starting for Jerusalem. Our Lord joined it, and on His arrival in the Holy City went to the Temple.

It must always have been painful to Him to go there at this time and see what went on within those sacred walls. The lowest and largest quadrangle, the Court of the Gentiles, was like the rest of the Temple, a place for prayer, but at the time of the Passover it looked like a market. The beautiful cloister and colonnades that ran along the inner side of the Court were filled with oxen, sheep and lambs innumerable. The tables of the

The Court of the Gentiles

money changers, piles upon piles of caged doves, stalls stocked with oil and incense, and whatever was needed for the various sacrifices, blocked up the space in every direction. As Roman subjects the Jews used Roman coins, but when they had to buy anything needed for the service of God, these had to be changed for sacred money. The wrangling that went on over this exchange, the lowing of the cattle, the bleating of the sheep, the shouting as the animals were driven here and there, all the uproar of a huge market in which the purchasers numbered many thousands, was a daily profanation of this sacred Court, the only place open to the Gentiles when they came to the Temple for prayer.

Time after time our Lord had seen this desecration of His Father's House when He came up to worship. He came now, not as a worshipper only but as an Avenger of His Father's glory.

For a moment He looked around. Then, picking up from the pavement some bits of cord lying about, He twisted them into a scourge, and with uplifted arm came suddenly upon the traders and their merchandise, and drove them all out of the Temple, the sheep also and the oxen, and the money of the changers He poured out, and the tables He overthrew. And to them that sold doves He said:

"Take these things hence and make not the House of My Father a house of traffic."

Imagine the scene—the flight of the dealers and the changers; the terror of the beasts which broke loose and rushed right and left; the panic and cries of the

Traffic in the Temple

"My house is the house of prayer; but you have made it a den of thieves."
(Luke 19:46)

crowd; on every side silver shekels rolling and lying, no one daring to pick them up, as men, women and children fled before Him. No need for Him to use the scourge. It was the Divine indignation of His eye that drove them forward. His disciples remembered that it was written: "The zeal of Thy House hath eaten Me up." Yet, even in His zeal He was kind. Whilst scourge in hand He drove the beasts, He stayed His hand before the caged doves. The timid, gentle things He would not frighten. He only said to those who sold them: "Take these things hence."

At length He stopped and again looked round. The vast enclosure was deserted, but what a scene it presented! tables, stalls, benches, overturned and, lying all about, the silver coins that will be picked up quickly when the crowd recovers itself and returns. Already a party of Jews are advancing to call the Nazarene to account for causing this disturbance. They keep close together, and the spokesman, trying to show a bold front, asks:

"What sign dost Thou show unto us, seeing Thou dost these things?"

"Destroy this Temple, and in three days I will build it up," Jesus replies.

They are indignant and say: "Six and forty years was this Temple in building, and wilt Thou raise it up in three days?"

But He spoke of the Temple of His body.

The people of the East express themselves constantly in figurative language. They explain things difficult to understand by likening them to things which are well known, which can be seen or heard or felt. And they are quick to perceive the hidden meaning intended. By David's words: "The Lord is my rock," they understand that God is strong and will support and shelter us. From those other words: "The Lord is my Shepherd," they see that He is tender to us and takes care of us. A temple is built for the service of God and contains what is holy. The sacred body of our Lord was a beautiful shrine for the Divinity which dwelt within. Thus, when our Lord spoke of a Temple that was to be destroyed and raised up in three days, it was not difficult for them to know that He was speaking of His body. That they did understand this, we know from the fact that when they had destroyed this Temple by putting Him to death, they went to Pilate and asked for soldiers to guard the sepulchre where He was buried until the third day, because He had said He would rise again. Of His disciples too we are told that "when He was risen again from the dead they remembered that He had said this, and they believed the word that Jesus had said." It was our Lord's custom to teach by means of figures and parables, because He knew that we all like a story, and that lessons in this form are more easily and pleasantly learned.

    The purifying of the Temple Court was not the only proof of His Divine Power which our Blessed Lord gave at this Passover, "for many believed in Him seeing the signs which He did."

The Court of the Gentiles

A sign is something we see which makes known to us something we do not see. A high temperature is a sign of fever; smoke, of a fire. We might have thought that the wonderful deed of power in clearing the Temple would have been taken by the Jews as a sign that our Lord was some holy one of God, perhaps the Holy One whom all men were expecting. John the Baptist had told them that He was in the midst of them, and had pointed out our Blessed Lord as the Lamb of God. A Voice from Heaven at His Baptism had declared Him to be the Son of God. We should have thought that when a Man appeared showing "signs" there would have been rejoicing from one end of the land to the other, and that all men would be saying:

"Here, perhaps, is the Messiah!"

Some did believe in Him "seeing the signs which He did." But others, as we have seen, came round Him asking in a carping spirit: "What sign dost Thou show unto us?" They were always asking for signs and always shutting their eyes to those which God gave them. At this first Passover began the series of splendid miracles which for three years were to make Palestine a Land of wonders, miracles wrought with generous hand to supply every need, to cure every disease and every infirmity. And the reward of Him who thus went about doing good would be to see His enemies multiplied and to hear them saying with evergrowing blindness and obstinacy: "By what authority dost Thou do these things? and who hath given Thee this authority?"

The cleansing of the Temple was an act of authority which the Jewish leaders never forgave. From this time we find priests, Pharisees, Sadducees and Herodians, who were usually so opposed to each other, united by a common hatred of Christ. They laid snares for Him to catch Him in His speech, they were always trying to set the people against Him, they said His wonderful works were done by the power of the devil, they charged Him continually with breaking the Sabbath and blaspheming against God.

Yet not all were so perverse. Some among them were simple and upright souls, ready to see what God was showing them. One of these was a Pharisee named Nicodemus, a rich man and a ruler of the Jews, that is the president of a synagogue. This man came to Jesus by night and said to Him:

"Rabbi, we know Thou art come a Teacher from God, for no man can do these signs which Thou dost unless God be with him."

He came by night, for, although he half believed in our Lord and wanted to be taught by Him, he was afraid of what men might say. It would never do to have it noised abroad that a member of the Sanhedrin, "a master in Israel," was going for instructions to this new Teacher, the Son of a carpenter. Nicodemus did not want to be the talk of the city, and so he went by night. We can see him making his way through the deserted streets, and guided by the lamp burning in the guest-chamber on the roof, reaching it by the outside stair. Our Lord did not reproach him or think it waste

Nicodemus

"For God so loved the world, as to give his only begotten Son; that whosoever believeth in him, may not perish, but may have life everlasting."
(John 3:16)

of time to instruct so timid a disciple. But He received him kindly and was patient with him, and answered all his difficulties. It was to Nicodemus He taught the necessity of Baptism for salvation in the words we have in our Catechism: "Unless a man be born again of water and the Holy Ghost, he cannot enter into the kingdom of God."[1]

It was to him He first spoke of His coming death on the Cross: "As Moses lifted up the serpent in the desert, so must the Son of Man be lifted up." And it was to this earnest but timorous soul that He spoke of the incomprehensible love of God to us in giving us His Son: "For God so loved the world as to give His Only-Begotten Son that whosoever believeth in Him may not perish, but may have Life Everlasting."

The graces of that night so enlightened Nicodemus that he became our Lord's faithful disciple. But it was still in secret. We do not find him mingling in the crowd. Once only, overcoming his timidity, he defended his Master before the Sanhedrin. And that good Master had patience with him as He had patience with us all. He thinks, not so much of what we are, as of what we desire to be, of what we shall be some day. And so He waits for us.

A day came when, hanging on the cross of shame, lay the lifeless body of Jesus of Nazareth. His own people had delivered Him up to death. He had been betrayed by one apostle, denied by another, forsaken by all. His Mother stood beside the dead body of her

---

[1] John 3:5.

Son. She had no friend to take Him down from the cross, to give Him a grave, to help her to bury Him. She looked around. Two men of noble bearing were coming towards her, two who had been disciples of Jesus, but secretly for fear of the Jews. The Jews were triumphant now. They had tortured Him to death, they had called down His blood upon themselves and upon their children, they hated His Name and all that were His. The two men drew near. They brought myrrh and aloes and linen cloths. And, whilst His Apostles were hiding and His enemies were rejoicing, they reverently took down the sacred body from the cross and bound it in linen cloths with spices, and laid it in a new sepulchre in a garden. And one of them was Nicodemus.

XX.
At Jacob's Well

When the Passover was over, our Lord went up and down the country of Judea preaching and baptizing by the hands of His disciples. Some take this baptism to have been, like that of the Precursor, merely a sign of repentance and of a desire to be cleansed from sin. Others believe it to have been the Sacrament instituted by Jesus Christ. The sweetness and attractiveness of our Blessed Lord drew to Him all hearts that evil passions had not spoiled, and it seemed as if His Ministry were beginning happily, when opposition arose from an unexpected quarter.

St. John the Baptist still continued to preach and baptize, but his work was nearly done, and every day some of his followers left him to become our Lord's disciples, to the great displeasure of those who remained with him. These said to him one day—and we can almost hear the peevish tones of their complaint:

"Rabbi, He that was with thee beyond the Jordan, to whom thou gavest testimony, behold He baptizeth, and all men come to Him."

Did they not know their master better than this? Did they think he would be jealous of Him who was to come, when his one thought and desire was to prepare hearts for Him? He had called our Lord "the Lamb of God." He gave Him now another beautiful name, and tried to show the troubled disciples that souls were right to go after Him to whom all souls belong as the bride belongs to the bridegroom. "He that hath the bride," he said, "is the Bridegroom, but the friend of the Bridegroom," meaning himself, "is not jealous, but rejoiceth with joy because of the Bridegroom's voice. He must increase, but I must decrease."

Yes, the end of that noble, unselfish life was nearly come. Soon after this St. John fearlessly rebuked Herod Antipas for wanting to marry Herodias, the wife of his brother Philip. Herod, stirred up by the wicked Herodias, was provoked, and taking John, cast him into a strong and gloomy prison.

"And when Jesus had heard that John was delivered up, He retired into Galilee. And He was of necessity to pass through Samaria."

Have you ever noticed—dove-tailed into a piece of wood—a small bit of wood of another kind? The difference of colour and of grain strikes the eye at once, and shows the intruder to be no part of the natural growth, but a chip thrust in later from without.

Something like this was the province of Samaria between Galilee and Judea. Its inhabitants were a mixed race, partly Jews, partly Gentiles. When Salmanaser, king of Assyria, took the Ten Tribes into captivity, he sent some of his own subjects from Assyria to repeople the land of Samaria. They were idolaters, and continued their heathen practices till, terrified by a plague of lions sent by God, they begged for one of the captive priests to teach them how to worship the God of the country.

The priest was sent, but they would not give up their idols altogether, and worshipped them as well as the true God. For this reason the Jews of the Two Tribes, on their return from captivity, would have nothing to do with their idolatrous neighbours. In vain did the Samaritans beg to be allowed to help in rebuilding the Temple: their aid was harshly refused. This was the beginning of the hatred between the two nations, displayed in the haughty contempt of the Jews and in continual annoyance on the part of the Samaritans. A Jew would draw his garments closely round him lest a Samaritan passing by should brush against them and defile him. He would consider himself grossly insulted to be called a Samaritan. Hence the contemptuous words to our Lord: "Thou art a Samaritan and hast a devil."

The Samaritans on their side lost no opportunity of insulting and troubling the Jews. They would not go up to the Temple of Jerusalem, and set up a rival temple of their own on Mount Gerazim. When the Jews lit beacon fires upon the hills to guide the caravans from Galilee to the Holy City at the time of the yearly Feasts, the Samaritans lit false beacons to mislead them. They ill-treated travellers going up to Jerusalem, and often refused them a passage through their country, so that

At Jacob's Well

pilgrims had to go down the eastern bank of the Jordan and cross the river twice.

Yet our Lord was not angry with these poor people, nor did He despise them as idolaters and outcasts. He is the Good Shepherd and all are His sheep, loved and cared for one by one. He guards those that are in the fold, and follows the wanderers when they stray. He was following a wanderer now as He toiled over the hilly country of Judea and entered one of Samaria's beautiful valleys. His Divinity did not save Him from fatigue and pain, for He was truly man, like us in all things excepting sin. And so He was footsore, weary and thirsty when about noon He neared the little town of Sichem.

There was a well by the roadside, a very old one, that had been dug by Jacob and given by him to his son Joseph. It was much prized by the people of the country, both for its own sake, because water is precious in the East, and for the sake of the patriarchs to whom it had belonged. A welcome sight to the traveller in this sultry land was that well of Jacob with its sheltering archway and stone margin on which he might sit and rest.

When our Lord, with His little party of five, reached the well, He was too faint and spent with His journey to go further. Seeing this, the disciples begged Him to sit and rest whilst they went on to the town to buy food.

Presently a woman of Samaria came to draw water. She had filled her pitcher and was going to poise it on her head, when Jesus said to her:

The Samaritan Woman

"Whosoever drinketh of this water, shall thirst again; but he that shall drink of the water that I will give him, shall not thirst for ever"
(John 4:13)

"Give Me to drink."

Surprised at such a request, for a glance had shown her the Stranger seated there was a Jew, she replied:

"How dost Thou, who art a Jew, ask of me to drink who am a Samaritan woman?"

Jesus answered: "If thou didst know the gift of God and who He is that saith to thee: Give Me to drink, thou perhaps wouldst have asked of Him and He would have given thee living water."

What was this gift of God? That of which He had spoken to Nicodemus when He said: "God so loved the world as to give His only-Begotten Son." Had she known that the Son of God was there before her, that she had all to herself Him whom the world was expecting, how eager she would have been to do Him this little service, and in exchange for a drink from her pitcher ask for that living water of grace which would cleanse her sinful soul, refresh its thirst, and preserve it for eternal Life! But she did not know the Gift of God, nor did she understand what the Stranger said. Still the words "living water" sounded delightful in her ear, and in a puzzled, wistful way she said:

"Sir, give me this water that I may not thirst nor come hither to draw."

It is God's way to move us to ask for a grace which He means to grant. The poor woman had asked as well as she knew how. Now, then, He would give. The first thing He gives is sorrow for sin. To bring her to this He let her see that He knew all her past life. Overwhelmed with astonishment she exclaimed:

"Sir, I perceive that Thou art a Prophet." Then, thinking this a good opportunity of putting such a question, she asked if God was not as much pleased with their worship on Mount Gerazim as with that of the Temple in Jerusalem. She did not understand our Lord's answer and said:

"I know that the Messiah cometh who will tell us all things."

She wanted to be taught, she longed for her Redeemer. Jesus could hide Himself no longer.

"I am He who am speaking with thee," He said.

This is the first time He had declared plainly who He was.

During the three years of His Public Life His "signs," that is His wonderful miracles, showed plainly that He was God. Only a few times did He say distinctly that He was the long-expected Messiah, the Son of God. And the first time was to this poor Samaritan woman.

How we should like to know her answer! But at that moment the disciples came up, and she, eager now for all her friends and all the townsfolk to come and know our Lord, hastened into Sichem saying to all she met:

"Come and see a Man who has told me all things whatsoever I have done. Is not He the Christ?"

Her earnestness impressed those who heard her. She had evidently seen and heard something wonderful. And was there not a rumour that Christ had appeared in Galilee and Judea and was doing marvels? But could He have come to them—Samaritans? Oh, if He had,

At Jacob's Well

how welcome they would make Him! Yielding to the woman's entreaty, the simple people flocked out in crowds to Jacob's well, asking her questions all the way.

In the meantime the disciples gathered round their Master and pressed Him affectionately to take the food they had brought, saying:

"Rabbi, eat."

But He said to them: "I have meat to eat which you know not."

They looked at one another astonished and said: "Hath any man brought Him to eat?"

Jesus said to them: "My meat is to do the Will of Him that sent Me."

He meant that as men long for the food of the body to satisfy their hunger and thirst, so did He long to see His Father's Will done, and the souls of men redeemed and saved. Pointing to the cornfields, which in Palestine are silvery not golden at harvest time, as with us, He said:

"Do you not say there are yet four months and then the harvest cometh? Behold I say to you, lift up your eyes and see the countries, for they are white already to harvest."

He was thinking of the Samaritans now hastening to Him, and was rejoicing in the thought of the faith already springing up in their hearts, that faith which at the preaching of His Apostles was to ripen and bring forth all manner of beautiful virtues.

Many of the Samaritans believed in Him on the word of the woman—"He told me all things whatsoever

I have done." And when they had themselves seen and heard Him, they were so charmed that they desired Him to tarry with them, says St. John. And He abode there two days. And many more believed in Him, because of His own word. And they said to the woman: "We now believe, not for thy saying, for we ourselves have heard Him and know that this is indeed the Saviour of the world."

What wonder that later on when the Jews obstinately refused to acknowledge Him as the Messiah, our Blessed Lord should have thought of those happy days at Sichem, and that when He wanted to teach a lesson of gratitude or of kindness to strangers, He spoke of the Samaritans!

As He watched the woman hastening with her joyful message to her fellow-citizens, He must have thought of a day to come, the brightest earth has ever seen, when another woman would hasten from an empty Sepulchre to tell His friends: "I have seen the Lord!"

And both these chosen messengers of His had been sinners!

XXI.
A Sabbath at Nazareth

Our Lord was now on His way to Galilee. His fame was spreading far and wide, and His fellow townsmen of Nazareth and other Galileans, many of whom had gone up to Jerusalem with Him year after year at the time of the great Feasts, were curious to see again and consider more attentively this Man of whom they had thought so little in the past. He came among them as before, simple and gentle, but with that charm of manner, that power of attracting hearts which has had nothing like it before or since.

What we would give to have a true picture of Him as men saw Him when He went to and fro among the people of His day! If only we knew what it was that made the crowds flock after Him, forgetting food, sleep, business, weariness, anything and everything so they might be with Jesus of Nazareth, so they might look upon His Face, and hear the tones of His Voice, and drink in His beauty as the thirsty ground drinks in the summer rain!

But we have no such picture. In one of the Roman catacombs is a very old painting of Him. There we see an oval face, the beard not long and ending in a double point, the eye dark and penetrating, the expression of the countenance grave and sad, yet full of sweetness, the long hair parted on the forehead and flowing over the shoulders. He wore a long tunic gathered in at the waist with a leathern belt, over this a kind of mantle or cloak, a veil bound round the head to protect the forehead and neck from the sun, and sandals on His feet. His garments seem to have been white and of the same kind and shape that may be seen in the East today.

So we may picture Him to ourselves. But the charm that hung about Him, this we cannot picture, this we must have felt to understand. There was something about Him that made men feel He was above them; His presence and manner awed as well as attracted them. They knew that He read the secrets of hearts. Yet the love that beamed in His glance, the sweetness of His smile, the grace of His every movement, won love no less than admiration and reverence. What man noticed in Him chiefly was the gentleness, the simplicity, the guilelessness of the lamb. This is what drew all hearts to Him.

The Galileans had heard of the "signs" in Judea and they had not forgotten the miracle at Cana. There was the greatest excitement and enthusiasm then when the news got abroad that the great Wonderworker was coming.

A certain ruler living at Capharnaum had a son who was dangerously ill of a fever. Hearing that Jesus was

THE RULER AT CAPHARNAUM

"Unless you see signs and wonders, you believe not."
(John 4:48)

at Cana, he hastened to Him and begged Him to come down and heal the boy, for he was at the point of death.

Jesus said to him: "Unless you see signs and wonders you believe not."

"Lord, come down before that my son die," was the answer.

Every moment was precious. What if the Master should be too late! The ruler's faith, we see, was far from perfect, for he thought our Lord must be on the spot to cure.

Jesus said to him: "Go thy way, thy son liveth."

The man believed the word which Jesus said to him and went his way. And as he was going down his servants met him, and they brought word that his son lived. He asked, therefore, the hour wherein he grew better. And they said to him: "Yesterday at the seventh hour the fever left him." The father therefore knew that it was at the same hour that Jesus said to him: "Thy son liveth," and himself believed and his whole house.

The people of Nazareth, as was natural, were impatiently awaiting our Lord's coming amongst them. They were getting proud of Him. They liked to hear Him called "Jesus of Nazareth." They hoped He would preach in their synagogue as He had been preaching in the other synagogues of Galilee. At last He came, and they looked forward eagerly to the next Sabbath. Let us try to see the synagogue on that day.

A long hall, divided by a balustrade into two parts, the men on one side, the women on the other. Facing

A Sabbath at Nazareth

them in a kind of sanctuary, a wooden ark or chest covered with a veil and enclosing the rolls of parchment on which the Law of Moses was written. Before this ark a lamp that burns day and night. Pharisees coming in with heads erect, marching to the top seats, all respectfully saluting and making way for them. Husbands and wives separating at the door and taking their places, children going with father or mother.

They have come for prayer and instruction, not for sacrifice, which may be offered only in the Temple of Jerusalem. They have come also to see Jesus of Nazareth and to hear Him, for any Rabbi or distinguished stranger may be asked to read and explain the passage from the Prophets appointed for the day. They hope, too, to see some miracle, and are full of eager curiosity.

He comes in, puts on the scarf of white wool with blue stripes and fringes worn by every Jew on entering the synagogue for worship, goes to His place, not up there with the honoured, but with the poor, and kneels down to pray. All heads are turned towards Him, all faces glow with admiration as they watch Him.

The service begins with the usual prayers, and then the minister takes a scroll from the ark and looks around to see if anyone will offer to read and explain. See the delight on every face as Jesus rises and holds out His hand for the scroll. He mounts the raised platform in the centre of the building from which the Rabbis speak to the people, unrolls the book and reads:

"The spirit of the Lord is upon Me, wherefore He hath anointed Me to preach the Gospel to the poor, to heal the contrite of heart, to preach deliverance to the captive, and sight to the blind, to preach the acceptable day of the Lord and the day of reward." He folds the book, returns it to the minister and sits down. The eyes of all in the synagogue are fixed upon Him, not a sound is to be heard.

He tells the people that these words refer to Him and to the work He is come to do. He is sent to preach good tidings to them, to heal their sick souls, to free them from their sins. His grave and beautiful face beams with loving interest as He looks round upon them. They are those among whom He has lived nearly all His Life. Hitherto He has had to be silent, but now He may speak and help. He teaches them in words so full of grace and power that His hearers are filled with wonder. And yet—you remember the kind of people these Nazarenes are—they seem to take it amiss that their village carpenter, who has been at their beck and call all His life, who has never studied, and understands nothing but His tools, should now be their teacher, and even make Himself out to be the Messiah.

"Is not this the son of Joseph?" they whisper to one another. "He has said nothing about the glorious Kingdom of the Messiah, nor of what He is going to do for us. And there have been no signs in Nazareth as in the places round about. Surely the place where He was brought up and His fellow-citizens should be more to Him than a young couple at Cana and a sick lad at Capharnaum?" Notice the Pharisees scowling their disapproval, the restlessness beginning to show itself all round. Hear the discontented words.

Now, have they any right to behave like this? Is it reverent so to treat One whose words and works show plainly that He comes from God, if indeed He is not Himself God? "No man can do these signs unless God be with Him," said Nicodemus. So should these Nazarenes be saying.

Look at our Blessed Lord, calm amid the growing excitement. He hears the whispering, He sees into every heart. Now He is speaking:

"Doubtless you will say to Me: Physician, heal Thyself, as great things as we have heard done in Capharnaum, do also here in Thy own country. But I say to you no prophet is accepted in his own country. There were many widows and lepers in Israel in the days of Elias and Eliseus, yet not to them but to Naaman the Syrian and to a widow of Sarepta were the Prophets sent."

This is too much. What! does He mean to say that strangers and Gentiles are to be preferred to them, the children of Abraham! In a frenzy of rage they rush upon Him, drag Him out of the synagogue up the steep street and on to the brow of the hill whereon their city is built, that they may cast Him down headlong. He is on the edge of the rock, they are going to hurl Him down, and—passing through the midst of them He goes His way.

This, then, is the end of that Sabbath day's welcome. The men of Nazareth, like those of Jerusalem later, reject Him and drag Him up a hill to make away with Him.

Between these two murderous scenes how much ill usage and ingratitude He will have to bear from those whom He wants to help! There will be no resistance, no complaint—but oh! what pain in that affectionate sensitive Heart of His!

XXII.
His Own City

Up to this time our Lord's disciples have not been always with Him. Now they are to be called by Him in a solemn manner to be His constant companions.

On leaving Nazareth, He went to Capharnaum, which you will remember was on the shore of the Sea of Galilee. Walking one day along the beach, He saw Peter and Andrew casting a net into the sea. And He said to them:

"Come after Me and I will make you to be fishers of men."

And immediately leaving their nets they followed Him. And going a little farther He saw James, the son of Zebedee, and John, his brother, in a ship with Zebedee their father mending their nets, and He called them. And they immediately, leaving their nets and their father, followed Him. All they had—father, mother, the fishing by which they earned their living, all their little possessions—they left for His sake, not willingly only but joyfully. They did not care where He took them, or what He did with them, or how much they might suffer in His company. To be with Him, to belong to Him, this was enough.

You notice that we have now a sixth disciple, James, the brother of John, and like him a fisherman. Most of those who were to be after our Lord the founders of the Church were fishermen, about the last class of men we should have thought suitable for such a work. Go down to any seaside place and watch the fishermen putting out to sea or tugging in their nets. Do they look fit to be the teachers of the world? They know the ways of fish, and something about the weather, and how to manage their craft—and that is about all. The fishermen of Galilee were much the same as those you have seen: rough, simple, ignorant. And out of them our Lord made the Princes of His Church. He would not have it said that the world was converted by the learning of the teachers He sent to preach the Gospel, but He would force men to own that if such preachers could convince the wise and the great of the truth of the religion which they taught, it must be because God was with them, and therefore this religion must be divine.

Our Lord was so much at Capharnaum and so many of His miracles were worked there, that it came to be called "His own city." It was a busy place. Roman soldiers with their centurion passed to and fro, for it was a garrison town. Pharisees and Doctors of the Law, courtiers of Herod, custom-house officers and fishermen thronged its streets; and in its market place and bazaars the traders of many nations were found.

His Own City

Let us follow our Blessed Lord through one of His days in Capharnaum: a Sabbath day, of which three out of the four Evangelists have left us an account.

At the hour of prayer He was in the synagogue, a handsome structure built for the Jews by the Roman centurion of the place, who, though a Gentile, was kind to the conquered people, and reverenced their God. Our Lord, according to His custom, was speaking to the congregation, when, suddenly, a shriek was heard, so piercing, so unearthly, that it was hard to believe it was the cry of a human being. Yet this it was, though not of a human being only.

Before the coming of Jesus Christ, evil spirits had much more power than they have had since. They used this power to torment cruelly those who were "possessed" by them, throwing them into the fire and into the water, and making them say and do things which of themselves they would never have done. One of these poor creatures had got into the synagogue, and in the midst of our Lord's discourse cried out saying:

"What have we to do with Thee, Jesus of Nazareth! Art Thou come to destroy us? I know Thee who Thou art, the Holy One of God."

Dismal and fearful cry! The evil spirits knew that Jesus had not come for them. They had nothing to do with Him. They hated Him and all that were His. How glad and grateful we must be that He has come for us, that we have everything to do with Him, that we belong to Him and He to us, that He has saved us from sin and hell.

Jesus rebuked the Evil One saying: "Hold thy peace and go out of him."

And the devil, when he had thrown him in the midst, tearing him and crying out with a loud voice, went out of him.

What a fearful scene! At the cry of the possessed man the people had sprung to their feet in terror. Then, curiosity overcoming fear, they came and stood round him as he lay on the ground, freed at last from his enemy, and looking up with tears of gratitude into the face of his Deliverer. But when he rose and went quietly away admiration broke forth in words of wonder and praise:

"Who is this that with power commands even the wicked spirits and they obey Him?"

Soon all Capharnaum knew what had happened in the synagogue, and on and on from town to town the news flew till all Judea had heard.

Encouraged, no doubt, by what they had seen, the disciples tell the Master that Simon's wife's mother is lying sick of a great fever, and they ask Him to go to her. He goes at once with James and John, making His way with difficulty through the crowds who are discussing the event of the morning.

Standing over the sick woman, He commands the fever and it leaves her. And He lifts her up, taking her by the hand. The Evangelists notice that when our Lord and His disciples sat down afterwards to their humble meal, it was the invalid of an hour ago that served them. St. Luke, who was a doctor, notes particularly that it was "a great fever," and that "immediately rising she ministered to them." Our Lord's cures left no weakness after them.

The tidings of the cure at Simon's house soon spread and increased the enthusiasm caused by the event in the synagogue. If Jesus of Nazareth could cure the possessed and the fever-stricken, why should not all the sick in Capharnaum be healed? The excitement was intense. The diseased and afflicted of every kind, even those blind, deaf or dumb from birth, must all be brought to Him; there was hope for all.

As soon as the sun was down and the Sabbath over, a sad procession was on its way to Peter's house. But was it sad? Oh, no: the lame were hastening along on their crutches, the quiet faces of the blind beamed with hope, even the deaf and dumb had somehow come to understand what was in store for them. Of course there was trouble in getting the possessed to go forward, and there was risk in bringing out the dying. But what were risk and trouble provided every one of them could get to Him in the end!

"And all the city was gathered together at the door," says St. Mark; the sick in their beds filling the street, the other afflicted ones massed together, pressing against the door; whilst choking up all the narrow thoroughfares an immense throng moved slowly forward, "all the city" coming to see what would happen. Could those who saw that sight ever forget it, ever forget the faces of that multitude when the door opened and Jesus of Nazareth stood on the threshold?

HEALING THE AFFLICTED

"And when the sun was down, all they that had any sick with divers diseases, brought them to him. But he laying his hands on every one of them, healed them."
(Luke 4:40)

His Own City

He came out, and, going up and down among the rows of sick and dying, laid His hands tenderly on all and healed them by that touch. We are expressly told that not one was sent away disappointed. "He, laying His hands on every one of them, healed them. And devils went out of many crying and saying: Thou art the Son of God."

Think of the streets of Capharnaum that evening: the cured being surrounded, questioned, congratulated on all sides; the wonder, the thanksgiving, the delirium of joy everywhere. Was there any going to bed that night?

And where was He who had made them all so happy? Tired in body and sad at heart, He lay down for a little rest when at last all had gone home satisfied. But, rising very early in the morning, He went out into a desert place and there He prayed. The crowds, however, came in search of Him. And Simon followed after Him and said to Him:

"All men seek for Thee."

And He said: "Let us go into the neighbouring towns and cities that I may preach there also, for therefore am I sent."

Well might He be tired in body after such a day, but why was He sad at heart? Because He was God as well as man, and therefore suffered as no mere man could do. He saw into every heart, He knew what was to come. He knew that His own city after all these miracles would refuse to believe in Him and would have to be punished. One day, when His time of preaching was drawing to a close, He began to upbraid the cities wherein were done the most of His miracles, for that they had not done penance:

"Woe to thee, Corozain! Woe to thee, Bethsaida! And thou, Capharnaum, thou shalt go down even unto hell. For if in Sodom had been wrought the miracles that have been wrought in thee, perhaps it had remained unto this day. But I say unto thee that it shall be more tolerable for the land of Sodom in the Day of Judgment than for thee."

XXIII.
"We have seen Wonderful Things today."

One day the multitudes pressed so eagerly upon Him as He was walking by the Sea of Galilee, that our Lord got into a boat, which was Simon Peter's, and told him to push off a little from the land. Then, sitting down in the boat, He taught the people who came crowding down right to the water's edge. When He had finished speaking He said to Simon:

"Launch out into the deep and let down your nets for a draught."

Now, Simon and his partners had been out all night casting their nets first on one side then on the other, and all to no purpose. "What was the use," a fisherman might have said, "of trying any more at present?" But Simon had seen enough by this time to make him obey without a word.

"Master," he said, "we have laboured all night and have taken nothing, but at Thy word I will let down the net."

And when they had done this they enclosed a very great multitude of fishes and their net broke.

The Miraculous Draught of Fishes

"And Jesus saith to Simon:
Fear not: from henceforth thou shalt catch men."
(Luke 5:10)

And they beckoned to their partners that were in the other ship that they should come and help them. And they came and filled both the ships so that they were almost sinking. Lower and lower sank the boats till the water was almost level with the edge. It was scarcely safe to move. Peter was overpowered with the greatness of the miracle. How near God was! How unfit was he to be in His Presence! Trembling, he cast himself at the feet of Christ, crying out:

"Depart from me, for I am a sinful man, O Lord!"

For he was wholly astonished and all that were with him at the draught of fishes which they had taken. And so were also James and John, who were Simon's partners.

And Jesus said to Simon: "Fear not, from henceforth thou shalt catch men."

And, having brought their ships to land, leaving all things they followed Him. Simon must have followed, wondering what those words could mean: "Henceforth thou shalt catch men."

As our Lord was walking one day through a certain city, whose name we are not told, a miserable object that had managed to escape notice darted from out a hiding place and flung itself on His path. It was a man, but in so frightful and loathsome a state as to appear scarcely human. Coarse white hair half covering what remained of a face, eyes glassy and staring, eyelids and lips gone, cheeks eaten away by disease, neck and hands covered with white scales—

he is described by St. Luke the physician in three words: "a man full of leprosy."

He had no business in the city, for lepers were forbidden to approach their fellow-men. They carried about with them the corruption of the grave, their presence polluted the air; they were counted as already dead, whose place was among the tombs, not in the homes of the living. Their nearest and dearest fled from them, they were driven out into the wilderness with the beasts. Without shelter, or food, or medicine, or covering for their misery, they wandered about, objects of fear and horror to all. If any came near them, they were bound to cry out their dismal warning—"Unclean! Unclean!" From a distance they begged of passers by a morsel of bread, an old rag to cover their sores. Men shouted after them, threw stones at them and reviled them, not because they were wicked but because they were so sorely afflicted, because they were lepers.

This poor leper knew that by coming into the city he was breaking the Law. But he had heard that Jesus of Nazareth healed every disease and every infirmity, perhaps He would have pity on Him. There he lay, his mouth in the dust of our Lord's feet, hiding his disfigured face. But as he fell down there a cry had gone up:

"Lord, if Thou wilt Thou canst make me clean."

And Jesus having compassion on him stretched forth His hand and touched him and said:

"I will; be thou made clean."

A word would have been enough, but He touched

him. He did not shrink from those loathsome sores. He beheld them with divine compassion, and—perhaps because the leper is the image of the sinner—He touched them with infinite gentleness. And instantly the leper was cleansed. There was no time for the indignant crowd to revile him, to catch up stones and cast at him, for before the sound of his prayer had died away he was a leper no more. "Lord, if Thou wilt Thou canst make me clean." "I will; be thou made clean." The words came back like the echo of his own.

Oh, words and touch of Christ! All he had lost they restored. He felt the life blood coursing freely through his veins. The pain, the unsightliness, the misery of mind and body—all with those hideous scales had fallen from him. He was a free man once more, free to stand up erect among his fellow-men, to go back to the old home and to all he loved.

Our Lord looked down kindly on the radiant face lifted to His and said:

"See thou tell no one, but go, show thyself to the priest."

Willingly would he present himself to the priest to have his cure attested. But keep silence when his heart was bursting with joy and praise, how could he? Surely, he thought, this command did not bind him, and going away he began to blaze abroad what Jesus of Nazareth had done for him.

A vast crowd gathered one morning round a house in Capharnaum. Within the Master sat teaching. There was no room; no, not even at the door, for the cure of the leper had made a great sensation throughout the country, and "Pharisees and doctors of the Law from every town of Galilee, and Judea, and Jerusalem," were there. It was not with any hope of gaining admittance that the patient crowd waited, but to catch a glimpse of the great Teacher, perhaps to hear the tones of His voice as He came out.

Presently four men appeared carrying on his mattress bed a man sick of the palsy. Round and round the throng they went, and at last succeeded in making their way through and reaching the door. But no persuasion could win them entrance, and they were told angrily to go away and not make a disturbance. They seemed to yield, but after a while were seen hauling their helpless burden up the narrow outside staircase that led to the roof. Then they began to lift up the tiles of the roof, not without much noise and grave displeasure of the audience within. At last a hole large enough to admit the bed was made, and the sick man was let down into the midst before Jesus.

And when Jesus had seen their faith, He said to the sick of the palsy:

"Be of good heart, son, thy sins are forgiven thee."

Our Lord saw the state of the soul as distinctly as that of the body, and because He knew the much greater value of the soul, He thought of its health first. The poor man held up his trembling hands and looked wistfully at the great Physician, thinking only

The Palsied Man

"Which is easier, to say to the sick of the palsy: Thy sins are forgiven thee; or to say: Arise, take up thy bed, and walk?"
(Mark 2:9)

of the healing of the body, or afraid, perhaps, that his sins would render him unworthy of cure. In reward of his faith our Lord gave him true sorrow for his sins, without which there can be no forgiveness, and then He forgave them.

Now notice carefully what happened, for this scene, like another at Capharnaum later, is one of the most important in our Lord's Life. Remember who sat there: quite an unusual gathering, Pharisees and doctors of the Law from every town of Galilee and Judea. These men began to think in their hearts:

"Why doth this Man speak thus? He blasphemeth. Who can forgive sins but God only?"

And Jesus seeing their thoughts said to them: "Why think you evil in your hearts? Which is easier to say: Thy sins are forgiven thee, or to say: Arise and walk? But that you may know that the Son of Man hath power on earth to forgive sins"—He said to the sick of the palsy:

"I say to thee, arise, take up thy bed and go into thy house."

And immediately, rising before them, he took up his bed on which he lay and went his way in the sight of all, glorifying God. And all were astonished and glorified God saying:

"We have seen wonderful things today."

Notice in how many ways our Lord here shows Himself to be God. He sees the faith of the poor paralytic and his friends; He sees the evil thoughts of the Pharisees; He sees the sin on the soul; He forgives it, and works a miracle on the body to prove His power over the soul.

St. Matthew says "they glorified God who gave such power to men." That is, they glorified God, not only for the cure of this poor man, but because the miracle had proved in the sight of such a multitude that it was possible to give to men the power of forgiving sin.

If people laugh at us for going to confession, and say they tell their sins to God and not to man—"*who can forgive sins but God alone?*" Let us think of this scene at Capharnaum and of another in Jerusalem on Easter Day, when our Blessed Lord, appearing to the Apostles, passed on to them His own power, saying: "Whose sins you shall forgive they are forgiven." And let us, with the simple grateful people of Capharnaum, glorify God who has given such power to men.

Followed as usual by the crowd, our Blessed Lord took the road from Capharnaum to the Sea of Galilee. Vessels were coming up to the little quay and discharging their cargoes, which were then carried up to the toll-booth of Matthew the publican, whose duty it was to tax them. He was sitting in the midst of bales of goods and piles of money, when, suddenly, amidst the noise and confusion of men coming and going, a Voice from without was heard:

"Follow Me."

Matthew turned round, met the glance of Jesus of Nazareth, who was passing by, rose up immediately, and went out. He had probably seen our Lord before this and heard Him preach. But to be noticed by Him, to be called to be His disciple—this was an honour he had never dreamed of. Not another thought for the business he was leaving, for the money just taken, for what people would say. The great Prophet and Wonderworker had called him—*him, a publican!* His heart leaped with joyful surprise: It seemed too good to be true.

Publicans were looked upon as traitors to their country and to their God, because they collected the taxes for the Romans, and as enormous sinners because of the injustice of which many among them were guilty. Every Jew, even the poorest, shunned and despised them. The righteous Pharisees drew away their garments lest those of a publican should touch and defile them. It must have astonished the disciples themselves to find a publican admitted into their little band. As for Matthew, he was obliged to find an outlet for his joy by giving a feast at which many publicans and sinners sat down with Jesus and His disciples. How delightful it is to think of our Blessed Lord making Himself at home in such company!

But some Pharisees came in at the open door to look on, as was usual in the East, and to find fault and disturb the happy gathering, which was not usual.

"Why doth your Master eat and drink with publicans and sinners?" they asked the disciples.

Jesus hearing it said to them: "They that are well need not the physician, but they that are sick. I came not to call the just but sinners."

Perhaps these just ones went away ashamed. Anyway we hear of no further objections at that time.

XXIV.
The Twelve

And now the second Passover of our Lord's Public Life had come. The country from one end to the other was ringing with the sound of His Name. In the crowded cities, in lonely hamlets, in the synagogues, the bazaars, the streets, and in the Temple itself, Jesus of Nazareth and His marvellous works were the talk of high and low. Herod Antipas in Galilee, Pontius Pilate in Judea, came to hear of Him, and in their own households He had found adherents. Joanna, the wife of Herod's steward, Claudia Procula, the Governor's wife, and many others of rank and influence, either followed Him openly with the crowd, or believed in secret. The news of fresh cures sped like wildfire through the land, and kept up an enthusiasm which grew daily. For the miracles of which we are told in the holy Gospels are samples only of the immense numbers wrought. Day after day, in all sorts of places, and at all hours He was amongst the sick and suffering. He "went about doing good." This was the business of His Life.

It was blazed abroad how on one Sabbath He had healed a man whom all Jerusalem knew, the paralytic

At the Pool of Bethsaida

"Him when Jesus had seen lying, and knew that he had been now a long time, he saith to him: Wilt thou be made whole?"

(John 5:6)

at the Probatica pond, who for nearly forty years had lain there looking wistfully at the water that would have cured him could he have found a friend to help him into it when it was troubled. Jesus of Nazareth had seen him, and, unasked, had cured him, bidding him take up his bed and go into his house. The people did shout when he swung his bed over his shoulder and walked away. But he had not gone far when some Pharisees came and stopped him, telling him He was breaking the Sabbath by carrying his bed.

On another Sabbath He was teaching in a full synagogue. There was a man before Him whose hand was withered. Everyone was crowding up to the top seats where the Pharisees were and to the raised desk at which Jesus sat. Of course the man would be healed, and of course the Pharisees would be scandalized and shake their heads, and the people wanted to see and enjoy it all.

And so it happened. The Scribes and Pharisees watched Him to see if He would heal on the Sabbath. And Jesus looked steadily at them, and there was no fear on His face. Then He looked at the man and said to him:

"Arise, and stand forth in the midst."

And rising, he stood forth. Then Jesus said to them:

"I ask you if it be lawful to do good on the Sabbath day?"

But they held their peace. And He said:

"What man among you whose sheep hath fallen into a pit on the Sabbath day will not take hold on it and lift it up? How much better is a man than a sheep. Therefore it is lawful to do a good deed on the Sabbath." And He looked round about on them with anger, and His countenance was terrible to see. And He said to the man:

"Stretch forth thy hand."

And he stretched it forth sound and strong like the other.

It was always the same thing, said the crowd. If the Pharisees would not believe in Him, they might at least let Him alone. But no, they must follow Him everywhere with their "Why?" and "It is not lawful."

He was walking through the cornfields on another Sabbath, and His disciples who were hungry began to pluck the ears of corn, rubbing them in their hands. At once the Pharisees were down upon them:

"Why do you that," they said "which is not lawful on the Sabbath day?"

The Pharisees and the priests never joined in the people's shouts of praise. Not they; it would have been beneath them. Instead of being glad when the sick and the demoniacs came from Him cured and happy, they rebuked them sharply and told them it was wrong to have anything to do with Jesus of Nazareth, because it was only with the help of the prince of devils that He cast out devils and wrought these cures.

After this fashion the people talked about Him and about their rulers, whose jealousy and hatred were plain to all.

Our Lord began the second year of His Ministry by an act of the greatest importance, an act which concerns the eternal welfare of every one of us. He founded the Apostolic College, and thus laid the foundation of His Church which was to carry on to the end of time His work for the souls of men.

The world was dark and the way to Heaven difficult to find before He came. How dark it would be again when He was gone! So those thought who loved Him and followed Him. Well might they cry out: "Stay with us, O Lord!" He was everything to them. They had no need to seek for the truth, but only to believe Him and do as He bade them. If their enemies were cunning and strong, He was at hand, always ready to help. If trouble came they could cling to Him, and He would take care of them. But what would become of His followers when He had gone away?

Our Lord, too, asked Himself this question. To understand His own answer to it we must bear in mind His tender love, not for those only who flocked to Him during His Life on earth, but for every soul redeemed with His Precious Blood; that is, for every one of us. However unimportant in the eyes of men, however sinful we may be, we have each of us a place in the Heart of Christ; each one may say with St. Paul: "He loved me and delivered Himself for me."

Because He loves us He had to find a way by which the Gospel or good tidings He has brought to the world might reach us, by which we who have never seen His face or heard the sound of His voice may know what we must do to save our souls. Like those who crowded about Him in the villages of Judea and the towns of Galilee, we should want to be taught and comforted, we should have sins to be forgiven. And because we are most of us poor and simple and have to work hard for our daily bread, we should need a plain and simple way to Heaven. We have no time, even were we clever enough, to think out hard questions.

Our dear Lord knew all about us, and this is what He did. From among those who believed in Him and listened with docility to His teaching, He chose twelve whom He called Apostles, or messengers "sent," because they were commissioned by Him to carry on His work among men and teach what they had themselves been taught. These Twelve He kept constantly with Him. He instructed them very carefully in all they would have to know. He answered their difficulties. He told them secrets not made known to the crowd. What He taught to others in parables He explained to them apart.

Our Blessed Lord made a very solemn preparation for this choice of His Apostles. The evening before, says St. Luke, "He went out into a mountain to pray, and He passed the whole night in the prayer of God," not because He needed prayer, but for our example, who need it very much when we have any important work to do or decision to take.

"And when day was come He called unto Him His disciples, whom He would Himself. And He made that twelve should be with Him that He might send

THE APOSTOLIC CHURCH

"And going, preach, saying: The kingdom of heaven is at hand. Heal the sick, raise the dead, cleanse the lepers, cast out devils."
(Mt. 10:7-8)

them to preach." He gave them His own power to heal the sick, to cast out devils, to raise the dead, to forgive sins. When He was leaving the earth He bade them go into the whole world and preach the Gospel to every creature. He promised to send down upon them His Holy Spirit, who should abide with them for ever and lead them into all truth, and to be with them Himself even to the end of the world.

Because they were to teach His truth, and with His authority, men were to listen to them as to Him. "He that heareth you heareth Me," He said, "and he that despiseth you despiseth Me." By "you" our Lord must have meant, not the Apostles only but their successors. For these twelve men were to die, but their work was not to stop with their death. They were to pass it on to their successors, and with these as with the first Twelve Christ promised to remain till the end of time.

Those who heard the Apostles and believed what they taught were to form a society or Church whose members would be, some in Heaven, some in Purgatory and some on earth. Those who have reached Heaven are the Church Triumphant, those in Purgatory are the Church Suffering, those on earth are the Church Militant or Fighting. The Church Militant consists of two classes, the teachers and the taught. For Christ did not say to all His followers but only to the Twelve and their successors: "He that heareth you heareth Me." The Apostles, then, and their successors, the Bishops, are the Church Teaching, the laity are the Church Taught.

The first Christians knew their place as learners. They did not argue with the Apostles, or pick and choose among the doctrines taught them. So earnestly did their teachers impress upon them the necessity of holding fast what they had been taught, that St. Paul said to his converts: "If an angel from Heaven preach a gospel to you besides that we have preached let him be anathema;"[1] that is, accursed.

Why such tremendous words? Because St. Paul knew that what he and his fellow-Apostles taught was not their own doctrine, but the teaching of their Divine Master, which was to be passed on unchanged till He should come again.

Our Lord prayed that His followers might be one, all believing the same truths, all uniting in the same worship, all using the same means of salvation which He had provided for them, all obeying the ruler He had set over them. To keep them one, He put them all into Peter's charge, as we shall see later, and by His prayer for Peter and promises to Peter He secured him and his successors against the possibility of leading the Church astray.

We must learn something about these Twelve whom Christ our Lord chose out of all men to carry on His work, to preach the Gospel and to plant the Church.

Peter. In the four lists drawn up by the Evangelists, St. Peter is always named the first. St. Matthew says: "The names of the twelve Apostles are these—the first Simon, who is called Peter, and Andrew his brother;

---

[1] Gal. 1

James, the son of Zebedee, and John his brother; Philip and Bartholomew; Thomas and Matthew the publican; James, the son of Alpheus and Thaddeus; Simon the Canaanean, and Judas Iscariot, who also betrayed Him."

"The first Simon." Our Lord had made him first, and they all acknowledged him as such. When a question was asked they let Peter answer for them. They noticed that their Master taught from Peter's boat, that He treated him differently from the rest, expected more of him, reproved and warned him specially, promised him favours that were for himself alone, and gave him charge of the rest. Peter's was an ardent, impetuous nature. His heart was full of deep, devoted love of his Master. But he trusted too much in himself. In the hour of trial his courage failed him, and he thrice denied Him for whom he had left all things and thought he was ready to lay down his life. But if he fell grievously he rose quickly and grandly. His was the kind of repentance our Lord loves. He wept bitterly, and all his life, his cheeks were furrowed with his tears. But there was no gloom, no mistrust, no damping of the courage which had made him do and dare great things.

Peter's faith in our Lord's Divinity made him shudder with horror when he heard of the mocking and the scourging and the spitting that were to come. "Far be it from Thee, O Lord," he cried, "this shall not be to Thee." And at the Last Supper he would not suffer our Lord to wash his feet: "Thou shalt never wash my feet," he said. But when Jesus threatened to have nothing more to do with him, he went to the other extreme and offered his hands and his head. When the hour came for Peter to lay down his life for Christ in the persecution of Nero, he showed his humility by begging to be crucified with his head downwards, deeming himself unworthy to suffer in the same posture as his Lord.

Andrew, his brother, the "Bringer to Christ," has the glory of being the first called of the Apostles, and of having brought Peter to Jesus. He seems to have been the oldest of the Twelve, and when we hear of him he is generally presenting someone to our Lord.

James and John, the sons of Zebedee and Salome, were called by our Lord "*Boanerges*," or the "Sons of Thunder." They had much to learn before they became like their Master, meek and humble of heart. All who would not welcome Him they would have liked to see destroyed by fire from Heaven. And they were ambitious, too, asking to sit on His right hand and on His left in the Kingdom they thought He was going to set up on earth. Think of rough, ignorant fishermen applying for the chief places at Court, to be royal ministers in the new Kingdom!

Yet with all their faults, their love for their Master was deep and generous, and they were His special favourites. He took them, with Peter, to places where the other Apostles were not admitted. They were at the Transfiguration, at the Agony in the Garden, and at the raising to life of Jairus' little daughter. And He gave them something better than the first places they wanted. James was the first among the Apostles to give his life for his Master, and John was first in his Master's love, and suffered for Him more than martyrdom at the foot of the Cross. He was the youngest of the Apostles, and calls himself "the disciple whom Jesus loved," because of the special affection our Lord showed him.

Thomas was a practical man. He had no idea of a service of Christ that costs nothing. It was all very well to go out preaching and to return to their Master saying joyfully they had been working miracles and casting out devils in His Name; but if they were really His followers they must be ready to follow Him always and everywhere, not only when the multitude cried out in admiration, "We never saw the like," but when the Samaritans refused Him a passage through their country and when the rulers persecuted Him. And so when the other Apostles tried to dissuade their Master from going into Judea where danger threatened, Thomas said boldly: "Let us also go that we may die with Him."

His courage, like Peter's, failed him at the last, but his idea of what our Lord had a right to expect of His disciples never changed. It accounts in part for his obstinate refusal to believe in the Resurrection. All the others, Peter included, told him they had seen their risen Lord. He would not believe. He knew better. What! that Christ should raise Himself to life when He had been dead three days, and come back to them with the old love when they had all failed Him in His hour of need—it was impossible. Our Lord had to show Himself to Thomas before he would believe that

His rising again and coming to comfort His poor, weak disciples was not too good to be true.

Matthew. After his call to the Apostleship we hear no more of Matthew in the Gospels. He wrote the first and longest of the Gospels, in which his chief object is to show how our Lord fulfilled all that was foretold of Him by the Prophets, and that He is therefore the long-promised Messiah and Son of God.

Philip, Bartholomew, Simon and Jude. Of the friends Philip and Bartholomew, or Nathaniel, we have seen something. Of Simon, the Canaanite, and Jude we know little beyond their names. Jude wrote an Epistle in which he earnestly exhorts the first faithful to stand fast in the faith first delivered to the Saints and taught by the Apostles.

James, the son of Alphaeus, called "the Less," to distinguish him from St. James the Great, the son of Zebedee, was brother to St. Jude and cousin of our Blessed Lord. We hear little of him in the Gospels. He was the first Bishop of Jerusalem, and for his holiness was revered even by the Jews.

Judas Iscariot comes last in all the lists. Some of the Evangelists add to his name "who also betrayed Him," terrible words that pass down for the detestation of all ages the crime of the miserable disciple who thus repaid the love and preference of His Master. Out of all men our Lord had chosen Judas to be one of His best loved and trusted companions. He had a most real and tender love for him. He chose him because He loved him. He gave him special graces, and with the rest, the gift of preaching, of healing the sick, of casting out devils. He gave him warning after warning. But all in vain. A fault which he might easily have conquered in the beginning grew and grew till he became its slave. He did not ask the help he needed, and when strong temptation came he fell, never to rise again.

This was the little company gathered round our Blessed Lord—poor, uneducated men, more used to employing their hands than their minds, looking like the rest of the nation for a golden age of temporal prosperity, for the people of God to come with the Messiah. They lived with their Divine Master as His intimate friends. They took their simple meals with Him, they prayed and slept at His side. After Mary and Joseph, none knew Him like the Twelve.

Because they were to help Him in the great work of saving souls which brought Him down from Heaven, and because He saw beneath their rough exterior grand qualities to be developed, He loved them dearly and trained them carefully and patiently. In character they were very different, but in their love of Him, and in the readiness with which they left all they had for His sake, they were alike. When they were chosen by Him they were dull and ignorant, unable to take in the sublime thoughts of their Divine Teacher. But little by little His instructions, His example, His gentle influence began to tell, and when the Holy Ghost came down upon them at Pentecost they were fit for the great work that lay before them—to preach the Gospel and to plant the Church.

XXV.
The Sermon on the Mount

One day a vast multitude follows our Blessed Lord up a mountain side. They come trooping after Him, men, women and children; their homes, their business, all the cares of this life by common consent left behind; no one to blame them, for all are under the same spell, all attracted by that Form in white moving before them and rising higher and higher up the grassy slope. Now He has stopped and turned round facing them. He waits long and patiently as they come toiling up, guiding them with His hand to go here and there where they may hear Him best.

It is His first great Sermon that He is going to preach, this Sermon on the Mount, and it is not only for the numbers beyond all reckoning gathered together here, but for all that shall come into this world and have to be taught what they must do to save their souls. Therefore He would speak so solemnly and from such a lofty place. He sits down, and the Twelve come and stand around Him, or sit on the ground at His feet. The people press round as close as they can, and when all are seated and quiet He begins to speak.

The Sermon on the Mount

*"And seeing the multitudes, he went up into a mountain...
And opening his mouth, he taught them"*
(Mt. 5:1-2)

A preacher chooses a text, some sentence which in a few words sums up all he has to say. What will the text of this great Preacher be? What is the thought uppermost in His mind and heart? This—to teach us what we must do to be happy. He knows that we are made for happiness, and that we long to be happy. But He knows, too, that very many try to find happiness in things that will not satisfy them; in the riches, pleasures, and honours of this world which can never content our hearts, because we are made for something much greater and better—for God Himself. And so He tells us, in the beginning of His Sermon on the Mount, who are really blessed or happy:

"Blessed are the poor in spirit, for theirs is the kingdom of Heaven.

"Blessed are the meek, for they shall possess the land.

"Blessed are they that mourn, for they shall be comforted.

"Blessed are they that hunger and thirst after justice, for they shall have their fill.

"Blessed are the merciful, for they shall obtain mercy.

"Blessed are the clean of heart, for they shall see God.

"Blessed are the peacemakers, for they shall be called the children of God.

"Blessed are they that suffer persecution for justice' sake, for theirs is the kingdom of Heaven."

Blessed the sufferers for whom Heaven is waiting! This is the text of the Sermon on the Mount.

The poor in spirit are those who, having little of the good things of this life, are content with what God has given them, bear patiently the want of many things they would like to have, and do not envy those who are better off. Those, too, who having a sufficiency or an abundance of the pleasant things of this world, do not let their hearts get too fond of them, are ready to give them up if God should take them away, and are generous in sharing them with those in need. To poor, such as these, our Lord promises all the riches of Heaven by and by.

The meek are those who have gained a mastery over anger and revengeful thoughts. They possess as conquerors three lands—the land of their own soul, which they control as lords and masters; the Land of Heaven, where nothing will trouble them any more; and, strange to say, that very land in which they seemed to be overcome. For in the little difficulties and differences of daily life, it is those that yield who are really victors. How many conquests has meekness made! "I can convince the Calvinists," said a learned man, "but to convert them I must send them to Francis de Sales," that gentle saint who, by the constant study of the Lamb of God, had so conquered a passionate nature as to become a perfect likeness of Jesus, "meek and humble of heart."

The mourners are those who all their lives long have a quiet, loving sorrow for their sins—not as though they were unforgiven, but just because they are forgiven, because they have offended Him who forgives so readily and so often. Those, too, are blessed mourners who remember when sorrow comes that He who loves them only permits it for their good, and that in a very little while He will wipe away all tears from their eyes, and they shall be comforted, "nor mourning, nor crying, nor sorrow shall be any more."

Who hunger and thirst after justice. The soul, like the body, has its hunger and thirst. Our Lord says those are blessed who take care to feed it with those things which keep it alive in the grace of God, with prayer, and instruction, and the Sacraments. Blessed are those who hunger after this spiritual food, who are always trying to get more and more of God's grace, who go hungry to prayer, hungry to Confession and Communion. Almighty God says: "Open thy mouth and I will fill it." And our Blessed Lady sings in her canticle: "He hath fed the hungry with good things." It was because all the saints hungered like this that so much was given them.

The merciful. There is nothing our Lord tells us so often and so plainly as this—that to obtain mercy from God we must ourselves be merciful. If we wish Him to judge us kindly and to forgive our many faults, we must be forgiving and kind. "Be merciful," He says, "as your Heavenly Father is merciful." He tells us that at the Last Day He will say "Come" to those who have been merciful to others for His sake, and "Depart from Me" to those who have been unmerciful to the poor and needy, and therefore to Him. For what we do to His least brethren He counts as done to Himself. If, then, we want to hear His sweet invitation on that dreadful Day, we know how to secure it—"Blessed are the merciful, for they shall obtain mercy."

The clean of heart. The reward and the joy of the next life is to see God. There are many joys in Heaven —freedom from pain and care, the delights of the glorified body, the society of the Angels and Saints, reunion with those we loved on earth. But all these are as nothing compared with the Vision of God. It is this that makes Heaven what it is. Without this all the rest would not satisfy us. But to see the All Holy God, we must be holy. In Heaven all are clothed with white robes, and the nearer the approach to the Great White Throne, the more dazzlingly white is the raiment. We must be getting ready to join that spotless throng. How? By taking as much pains to keep our soul free from stain as we do to prevent soiling our dress when we go along a miry road; by shunning with care all mortal sin and deliberate venial sin; by being careful in our examination of conscience, and often cleansing our soul in the Sacrament of Penance, and by frequent acts of contrition. If we do this we shall be among the clean of heart, and one day we shall see God.

The peacemakers. "Some there are who are neither at peace with themselves nor suffer others to be at peace. And some there are who keep themselves in peace and study to restore peace to others."[1] Gladness goes with

---
1 *Imitation of Christ,* ii. 3.

these peacemakers; they turn aside little words and jokes that would give pain, and come among us like our Blessed Lord whose favourite word of greeting was: "Peace be to you." They are so like their Father who is in Heaven that they deserve to be called in a special way His children.

The persecuted. If our Lord had not told us these are blessed, should we ever have guessed it? To be persecuted seems such a terrible thing, and so indeed it is unless we can bring ourselves to think more of Him for whose sake we suffer than of the suffering itself. Perhaps we may have known the quiet happiness of being by the side of one we loved who was in pain. The thought that our presence and our sympathy soothed that dear one was greater joy than any pleasure to be found elsewhere. Something like this is the gladness those have even now who for our Lord's sake are hated and persecuted. They know that the thought of their companionship was a consolation to Him when He was on earth, and they know, too, that if they are like Him in His suffering they will be like Him one day in His glory. Are they not blessed then?

And now let us stop awhile to look at our dear Master and His hearers. The Twelve are listening with reverent and fixed attention, their eyes riveted on His blessed face. They are so proud of Him, so proud to be His, so anxious that all should come to know and love Him. The people gaze at Him in amazement and delight. It is all so new, so comforting, so different from the teaching of the rabbis, the scribes and doctors of the Law. They have been taught to hate their enemies, to seek revenge, to think that poverty and suffering are the signs of God's anger, that an abundance of corn and wine and cattle are the rewards for which a good man must hope.

Their beatitudes would have been: "Blessed are the rich and the successful, those that laugh and are held in honour by men." How unlike these to the blessed ones of Jesus of Nazareth! His way to happiness was a hard way, but they knew as they looked up into His face that it was the right way, that He could not deceive them. And they felt that He could not only teach but help them. Had they known the story of His Life as we do they would have seen that He had first practised all He taught. He was so poor that He had not where to lay His head. He was meek and humble of heart, the Man of sorrows, the great Peacemaker, the Holy One who was to be persecuted even unto death.

After the Sermon our Lord comes down from the Mount, conversing familiarly with His disciples, His simple congregation flocking after Him, trying to get near Him, all so refreshed by His company and His words. Hear them talking of Him among themselves, saying: "We never heard the like."

Oh, if we had seen our Blessed Lord as these happy people saw Him, if we had followed Him about with the crowd, had sat at His feet as He taught, and watched Him as He laid His hands on the eyes of the blind and the sores of the poor lepers—how we should have loved Him! He knew that we should want to hear all about Him, and it was to satisfy us that He would have the story of His Life written in the holy Gospels. We must try as we read His Life to bring the scenes before us, to make them real to ourselves, as if it were all going on before our very eyes, as if it had all been done for us, as indeed it was, that we may come to know Him better and love Him more.

XXVI.
"Who went about doing Good"

The Roman centurion of Capharnaum was in sore trouble. A servant very dear to him lay at the point of death, every effort to save him had proved unavailing, and now his master, as tender by the sickbed as he was brave in battle, watched beside him and waited for the end. Suddenly it was told in the house that Jesus of Nazareth was entering the city. The centurion had heard of His deeds of mercy, and hope sprang up in his heart. Thinking himself unworthy as a Gentile to approach the great Prophet, he sent to Him the ancients of the Jews. And when they had come to Jesus they besought Him earnestly, saying:

"He is worthy that Thou shouldst do this for him, for he loveth our nation and he hath built us a synagogue."

And Jesus went with them. And when He was near the house the centurion met Him, and, falling on his knees before Him, said:

"Lord, trouble not Thyself, for I am not worthy that Thou shouldst enter under my roof, but say the word and my servant shall be healed. For I also am a man subject to authority having under me soldiers; and I say

The Faith of the Centurion

*"Lord, I am not worthy that thou shouldst enter under my roof:
but only say the word, and my servant shall be healed."*
(Mt. 8:8)

to this one: Go, and he goeth, and to another: Come, and he cometh, and to my servant: Do this, and he doth it."

As though he had said: "If the word of one who is himself a subject meets with prompt obedience, how much more will the word of Him who is Almighty be obeyed." And Jesus hearing, marvelled, and, turning to them that followed Him, said:

"Amen, I say to you, I have not found so great faith in Israel."

The faith and frankness of this Roman soldier delighted Him:

" Go," He said, "and as thou hast believed, so be it done to thee."

And the servant was healed at the same hour.

We should like to know what became of one whose faith won the admiration of the Son of God. This at least we know: that the Church sets him before us as a model. In the solemn moment when we are receiving Jesus Christ into our hearts, she puts upon our lips as our most fitting preparation the *Domine, non sum dignus* of the centurion.

One evening our Lord, attended by the Twelve and by the vast crowd that always followed Him now, began to climb the hill on which stood the little city of Naim. As He neared the gate a sad procession streamed out—first, women weeping and wailing and beating their breasts; then, flute players with their mournful music; then, a bier on which lay the body of a young man wound round and round with linen cloths. A great throng of people followed, not only because the Jews held it to be a religious duty to accompany the dead to the grave, but also because this was "the only son of his mother, and she was a widow." Our Lord saw her among the hired mourners, and His heart was filled with pity. Making His way through the crowd, He came to her and said:

"Weep not."

She looked up bewildered, and her red eyes met the divine compassion of His. Then He led her to the bier and touched it. The bearers stood still and laid their burden on the ground. There was a thrill of expectation all around. The procession broke up, the crowds mingled, and a breathless multitude closed round Him. For a moment He stood there looking down on the boyish face. Then in a tone of authority that none who heard it could ever forget, He said:

"Young man, I say to thee, arise!"

Instantly the eyes opened, the marble cheek flushed, and he that was dead sat up and began to speak. His mother fell on her knees, and, with tears of joy streaming down her face, stretched out her arms to her boy. A great awe fell upon the people, and for some moments there was silence. "There came a great fear on them all," says St. Luke, "and they glorified God." This was always the effect of our Lord's wonderful works on the simple folk that followed Him—fear because God was so near, thanksgiving and praise because God was so pitying and so good.

The Young Man at Naim

"Young man, I say to thee, arise."
(Luke 7:14)

We notice that it is chiefly the poor who form the audience of our Blessed Lord when He preaches. They are attracted to Him. He is one of themselves, they feel at home with Him.

But one day there appears in their midst a listener whose attire and bearing show nothing of the simplicity and bashfulness of the poor. Her dress is of the richest, her veil thrown back displays the costly gems that hang from her ears and gleam on her forehead and in her hair. What can she, with her perfumes and long braided tresses and embroidered sandals, be doing here? Has she come, like a Pharisee, to scoff at the Master? Her humble neighbours eye her with curiosity and no little indignation. For this is Mary Magdalen, whom all the city knows, and who all the city would say is here strangely out of place. Yet here she stands, her gaze riveted on the Speaker yonder.

An hour ago she was passing this way, and, attracted by the crowd, drew near, to see Him who had just raised to life the widow's son. And now she stands, swaying with the throng, heeding nothing but Him, impatient only when some movement in front hides Him from her sight.

His sermon ended, He goes away, and the crowd breaks up. Yet, still, she stands there, gazing after Him. She had darted forward as if to follow Him, but looking down upon her dress came back with a sigh. She watches now till He is out of sight, then, drawing her veil over her face, hastens home.

Doing Good 219

Some hours later Simon, the Pharisee, is dining with a party of friends in a room that opens into a courtyard. Handsome lamps, couches with rich cushions for the head and arms, tables laden with choice wines, figs, grapes, pomegranates—all show a wealthy home. Near the tables, which form three sides of a square, are placed the low couches on which the guests recline, their feet stretching back from the tables.

Among those present is Jesus of Nazareth, whose Name since the miracle of Naim is in every mouth. Simon has invited Him, but has not thought it necessary to show Him any further courtesy. He is only a carpenter and will not expect it. So no water was offered Him for His feet when He came in. There was no kiss of welcome from His host, and He took His place, not on the couches reserved for "the worthiest," but with the less distinguished guests.

The meal is nearly over when one of the rabbis present points with a contemptuous expression of surprise to the couch on which Jesus reclines. A woman is kneeling there at His feet. Her dress is coarse, her long hair streams loosely over her shoulders and face, and on the floor beside her stands an alabaster box of precious ointment. Her tears are falling fast upon His feet, and as they fall she wipes them away with her hair. Again and again she stoops and kisses His feet. And then she takes the box and breaks it over them, and the fragrance of the perfume fills the house.

Simon is indignant. How dares Mary Magdalen enter his house! And how is it Jesus of Nazareth does

The Penitent Woman

"Many sins are forgiven her, because she hath loved much"
(Luke 7:47)

Doing Good

not drive her away? If He were a prophet He would surely know that she is a sinner.

From His lowly place Jesus looks at Simon and says:

"Simon, I have somewhat to say to thee."

And he says: "Master, say it."

"A certain creditor had two debtors, the one owed five hundred pence and the other fifty. And as they had not wherewith to pay, he forgave them both. Which, therefore, of the two loveth him most?"

Simon answers in a surly tone: "I suppose he to whom he forgave most."

And Jesus says to him: "Thou hast judged rightly."

Then, turning to the woman, He says to Simon: "Seest thou this woman? I entered into thy house, thou gavest Me no water for My feet, but she with tears hath washed My feet, and with her hair hath wiped them. Thou gavest Me no kiss, but she since she came in hath not ceased to kiss My feet. My head with oil thou didst not anoint, but she with ointment hath anointed My feet. Wherefore I say to thee many sins are forgiven her because she hath loved much. But to whom less is forgiven, he loveth less." And He says to her:

"Thy sins are forgiven thee."

At once all the company begin to think: "Who is this that forgiveth sins also?" Jesus takes no notice of them, but says to the woman:

"Thy faith hath made thee safe, go in peace."

Not one word had Magdalen spoken, either of sorrow for her sins or in self-defence. She let her Lord speak for her, she trusted herself to Him. Not by words but by her tears, and kiss, and costly gift she showed Him her contrition. And she knew from His own words that not one of her loving acts had escaped Him. He had accepted all. And now she goes away, her heart full of peace and joy, teaching us all by her example not to be afraid of our merciful Lord when we have sinned, but to go to Him like her with our sorrow and our love, and like her we shall be forgiven.

Magdalen never forgot that much had been forgiven her. To try to repay her Lord with loving service—this was her one aim now. With other holy women who had become His disciples, Joanna, wife of Herod's steward, Mary of Salome, Mary of Cleophas, and many others, she followed Him about and provided for His wants. For we must remember that from the time He left Nazareth He had no home, and with His twelve Apostles depended on the charity of those who believed in Him and loved Him. "The foxes have holes and the birds of the air nests," He said, "but the Son of Man hath not where to lay His head." These holy women were devoted to Him, faithful and brave when even Apostles wavered, but bravest and most faithful of all was Mary Magdalen.

Where His Blessed Mother lived during the three years of the Public Life we are not told; some think she remained at Nazareth, others that she settled with her relatives at Capharnaum. Twice we find her mentioned in the Gospel. Jesus was speaking one day to the multitude when a man in the crowd said to Him:

"Behold Thy Mother and Thy brethren stand without seeking to speak to Thee."

Our Lord would not interrupt His teaching, and again taught the lesson given long years ago in the Temple, that before any call of affection, however holy, however tender, must come His Father's business. Answering him that told Him, He said:

"Who is My Mother and who are My brethren?" And stretching forth His hand towards His disciples He said:

"Behold My Mother and My brethren. For whosoever shall do the Will of My Father that is in Heaven, the same is My brother and sister and Mother."

Again, when a woman in the crowd, filled with admiration for the Son, had broken out into words of blessing on the Mother, Jesus said:

"Yea, rather, blessed are they that hear the word of God and keep it."

He did not mean that as Mother of God Mary is not blessed among women, but that she is more blessed for hearing His words and doing His will, for that habit of pondering in her heart of which St. Luke tells us twice in the same chapter.

"Hail, full of grace!" said Gabriel first. And then—"Blessed art thou among women."

Teaching the Multitudes

"Behold the birds of the air, for they neither sow, nor do they reap, nor gather into barns: and your heavenly Father feedeth them."
(Mt 6:26)

XXVII.
"Never spake like this Man"

Preaching was the chief occupation of our Blessed Lord during His Public Life. He was always teaching, now on the seashore, now from a boat on the lake, on country roads, in houses, in the synagogues. And everywhere He was surrounded by huge crowds of men and women, boys and girls, fathers holding their children high to see and hear, mothers with their little brown babies in their arms, old folk bent and tottering, scarce able to keep their footing amidst the thousands that stood about Him, crowding and crushing "so that they trod upon one another," says St. Luke.

St. Mark tells us that "they ran flocking to Him from all the cities. And Jesus going out saw a great multitude, and He had compassion on them because they were as sheep not having a shepherd, and He began to teach them many things." The teaching and the Teacher were so delightful that the hearers never tired; fathers of families who had the daily bread to earn, mothers with their household cares upon them, little restless children, stood or sat about Him, silent, spellbound. There was a majesty and a grace in His look, and words, and gestures that held them captive.

He taught as a Master, with an authority none could gainsay, and when He prefaced His words with that solemn: "Amen, amen, I say unto you," there was not a wandering eye nor an inattentive ear in the crowd.

All could understand Him. He did not preach dry sermons like the Scribes and Pharisees, who made the Law harder by explaining it. He taught by parables, stories with a hidden meaning that the people were to find out. By the things they saw around them every day He explained truths which they could not see.

"Be not solicitous," that is, over anxious, "what you shall eat or what you shall put on," He said to them one day. "Consider the ravens, for they sow not, neither do they reap, neither have they storehouse nor barn, and God feedeth them. How much more valuable are you than they." And pointing to the lilies bespangling the fields all round, He went on: "Consider the lilies how they grow; they labour not, neither do they spin. But I say to you, not even Solomon in all his glory was clothed like one of these."

The sparrows, innumerable in Palestine, were hopping about in His path.

"Are not five sparrows," He said, "sold for two farthings? and not one of them is forgotten before God. Fear not, you are of more value than many sparrows." Then, looking round on the fathers who with their little ones were standing by, He said:

"What father is there here who when his child asks for bread will give him a stone, or for a fish will give him a serpent? If you then, being evil, know how to give good gifts to your children, how much more will your Father from Heaven give good things to them that ask Him."

When He spoke of a net filled with all kinds of fish and of the sorting on the seashore, the rough men of the Lake gave an approving nod, and understood that while the world lasts, good and bad men will be together, and that at the end of the world there will be a great separation, the good will be taken to Heaven and the bad cast away.

He said that a woman who has lost a little coin lights a candle and sweeps the house and seeks diligently till she finds it. The wives and mothers looked at one another and smiled, and understood what He wanted to show them—the value of the soul, stamped with the image of the King of kings, who has taken such pains to find it when it was lost.

The farmers and the labourers liked the parables which told of men being hired to work all day and being paid when evening comes; and about the seed that was sown on different kinds of soil, and was wasted in one place whilst in another it sprang up and yielded good fruit; about the fig-tree, too, which its master had taken every care to cultivate and which never made him any return, so that at last he ordered it to be cut down and destroyed. And all, even the little children, understood the parable of the cruel rich man who when his life of feasting and pleasure was over was punished in terrible torments, whilst Lazarus, the patient beggar at his gate,

The Parables of Jesus

"All these things Jesus spoke in parables to the multitudes: and without parables he did not speak to them."

(Mt 13:34)

who had been refused even the crumbs that fell from his table, was comforted.

Jewish children, like all others, loved to play at being grown up, and to have weddings and funerals. Our Lord had Himself played at these things with His little companions at Nazareth. When He spoke about their games in His preaching, the children in the crowd were delighted to see He knew all about them and could make parables of them.

One day He told the people a parable to show them how foolish it is to think only of this life which is going so fast, and not to be getting ready for that life which is to last for ever.

There was a certain rich man who had so much corn that his barns were full to overflowing. "What shall I do?" he said to himself, "for I have no more room to store my corn. This will I do. I will pull down my barns and build greater, and I will gather therein all that I have. And I will say to my soul: Soul, thou hast much goods laid up for many years; take thy rest, eat, drink, make good cheer." But God said to him: "Thou fool, this night do they require thy soul of thee, and whose shall those things be which thou hast provided?"

The little ones in the crowd were listening attentively, and could see quite well why this man was called a fool. For who but a fool would speak to his soul like that, or think that barns full of corn could satisfy the soul that is made for God and for Heaven! What use were the man's riches to him when he came to die, and "what would it profit a man," as our Lord asked, "if he were to gain the whole world and lose his own soul?"

Those words, "lose his soul," are very terrible. Sometimes our Blessed Lord spoke to the people about terrifying things, as a father or mother will frighten a child of the fire lest it should go too near and fall in. He told even His dear disciples to fear that fire which is never put out, which will burn body and soul for ever. He spoke in terrible words of that "place of torments" to make us all fear sin, which alone can take us there. He said that as we part with eye, or hand, or foot to preserve our life, so must we give up anything, however useful or pleasant, rather than let it lead us into sin. And, as He spoke, the crowd could see by His face and by the tone of His voice that He knew all about that dreadful place and wanted to save them from going there.

He told them they must be like servants in charge of a house who have to be watching, ready to open to their lord whenever he knocks, either at midnight, or at cockcrowing, or in the morning. They knew what He meant. The house which belongs to the lord is our soul. And we are in charge. He calls us to Him by death when we least expect it. We must keep our soul always in the state of grace and ready for Him. This is to be found watching. The people delighted in finding out our Lord's meaning as He went on, and sometimes their admiration broke out in joyous exclamations:

"This is the Prophet indeed! This is the Christ!"

"Never spake like this Man"

Because their hearts were simple and upright they understood the Divine Teacher better by far than the Scribes and Pharisees who were eaten up by pride and envy. Some of these were generally found among His hearers, not to learn of Him—they would have scorned to do that—but "to lie in wait for Him," says St. Luke, "seeking to catch something from His mouth that they might accuse Him."

One day they sent officers to seize Him. Provided with cords to bind Him and lead Him away prisoner, these men joined the listening crowd. But when they beheld the majesty of His countenance and heard His wondrous words, they stood as if transfixed, not daring so much as to think of laying a finger on Him. Until He ceased to speak they stood there with the crowd, still, reverent, charmed. Then they returned to give an account of themselves.

"Why have you not brought Him?" said their angry masters.

"Never man spake like this Man," was the answer.

XXVIII.
"Talitha Cumi"

When we try to picture to ourselves our Blessed Lord in the midst of the poor of Palestine, we must bear in mind that a crowd of poor, such as we are accustomed to, is respectable compared with an Eastern crowd. Dirty, ragged, and afflicted beyond anything we can imagine, were those among whom His days were spent. They "thronged Him, pressing upon Him to touch Him as many as were diseased. They stayed Him that He should not depart from them." They poured into the house where He was, "so that He could not so much as eat bread," says St. Mark. Think what this means.

Everything in our Lord was most delicate and refined. He was more sensitive than any of us to what is unsightly and unpleasant. Yet He never complained, or seemed to notice what must have distressed Him sorely. He bore with these poor people. He let them press upon Him and touch Him. How often He was weary of standing and speaking, of going here and there as He was wanted, of satisfying the endless needs of such a multitude! For they could never have enough of

Him. Used to seeing themselves objects of contempt and disgust to the Pharisees, they beheld with wonder and delight the gentleness and tender compassion of their new Rabbi, and in His company forgot everything else, even consideration for Him.

It was not often that He sought to escape from the people. But one evening as they showed no signs of returning home for the night, He said in a low voice to His disciples: "Let us go over to the other side of the Lake."

They were only too glad to obey, for He was quite spent, and this was the only way to get Him a little rest. So a few of them hurried Him down to the beach, and when the others who had stopped behind to dismiss the crowd joined them, they all got into the boat and pushed off. He seated Himself in the stern, resting His head on a rough pillow there, the steersman's cushion, and very soon was asleep. The disciples watched Him in silence or talked quietly among themselves about the parables which, in the intervals of that long day's preaching, He had explained to them apart. They did not like to come out with their difficulties before the people, but when alone with their Master they put their questions to Him, and He was so careful to explain all, that He used to ask them: "Have you understood all these things?"

He was asleep, and, as the boat glided smoothly over the still, moon-lit waters, they sat around Him, speaking little, content to gaze upon that calm, beautiful face, so

Christ Calms the Waves

"And rising up, he rebuked the wind, and said to the sea: Peace, be still. And the wind ceased: and there was made a great calm."
(Mark 4:39)

tired and yet so restful. They were half way across the Lake, some dozing, some talking round the pilot, when a shriek of the night wind made them all start.

In a few minutes a furious tempest was upon them. Down between the mountains swept the hurricane, lashing the water into wild, crested billows. Helpless on the heaving sea, the boat rose and fell, now sinking into the hollow, now mounting a monstrous wave, now plunging again into the depths. The water poured in, it was filling fast—and still He slept. For a while the disciples dared not wake Him, but fear overcoming at length every other feeling they crowded round Him crying:

"Lord, save us, we perish!"

He woke, and looked calmly into those terrified faces.

"Why are you fearful," He said, "O ye of little faith!"

And rising up He rebuked the wind, and said to the sea:

"Peace, be still!"

And the wind ceased, and there was made a great calm. And they feared exceedingly. They did not fall at their Master's feet pouring out their thanks in eager words. But they crouched before Him, whispering in trembling tones to one another:

"Who is this, that He commands the wind and the sea and they obey Him?"

To these men of the Lake the first feeling brought by this sudden stilling of the storm was one of overpowering fear. Who was it they had amongst them, that treated them as familiar friends, that ate, and drank, and slept in their midst? Who was it?—God, the Lord of the wind and sea. Jesus their Master, their Friend, was very God—and they feared exceedingly.

Smoothly over the placid waters the boat made the rest of its way. It was early morning when they ran it into a little bay on the eastern shore of the Lake, the land of Gadara, or Gergesa. The disciples were stepping on shore, scarcely recovered from the terrors of the night, when a new fear seized them.

Bounding down from one of the caves hollowed in the cliff came a wild creature, more like a beast than a man. His eyes glared in a frightful manner. He had long since torn to shreds the clothing that hung about him. He lived in the gloomy caverns in the rocks that were used as graves, and "he was exceeding fierce, so that no man could pass that way." No man could tame him; iron chains he snapped like flax. Day and night he roamed about the mountains, crying and cutting himself with stones. He was a demoniac.

Seeing Jesus afar off, he ran to Him, and, falling down, adored Him. And, crying out with a loud voice, he said:

"What have I to do with Thee, Jesus Son of the most High God? I beseech Thee do not torment me."

And Jesus asked him: "What is thy name?"

"And he said, "Legion."

"For many devils were entered into him," says St. Luke. And the spirits besought Him that He would not command them to go into the abyss. And there was

Casting out Demons

"The devils therefore went out of the man, and entered into the swine"
(Luke 8:33)

there near the mountain a great herd of swine feeding, in number about two thousand. And the devils said:

"If Thou cast us out, send us into the swine."

And He said to them: "Go!"

And they going out went into the swine, and the whole herd ran violently down a steep place into the sea and were stifled in the waters. And the men in charge of them fled into the city and told the news—how the fierce demoniac, the terror of the country, had been healed, and how the swine had perished. Strange to say, it was the last event that seemed to make the most impression on the townsfolk, for instead of rejoicing at the cure of the poor man, "they were taken with great fear. And the whole city went out to see what was done. And they came to Jesus, and saw him that had been troubled with the devils sitting at His feet, clothed and well in his wits."

And—poor, foolish people—all the multitude being seized with terror, besought Jesus to depart from them. And He went up again into the ship. The man who had been troubled with the devils begged earnestly that he might be with Him. It seemed to him that only in our Lord's presence could he be safe and happy. But Jesus told him that he had a work for him to do among his countrymen:

"Return to thy house," He said, "and tell how great things God hath done to thee."

And he went through the whole city publishing the great things Jesus had done for him.

On reaching the western side of the Lake, they saw the shore thronged with people. Here at least our Lord was welcome. "The multitude received Him gladly, for they were all waiting for Him." He came among them and was surrounded at once by petitioners of every kind.

Presently the crowd made way with pitying words for a man whose face was sad and troubled. He was Jairus, the ruler of the synagogue. He had a little daughter, his only one, about twelve years old, and she was dying, and he had come to see if our Lord would go home with him and cure her.

The poor father fell down at the feet of Jesus, and his voice was broken by sobs:

"My daughter is at the point of death, but come, lay Thy hand upon her that she may be safe and may live."

Our Lord went with him, accompanied by the multitude, curious to see what would happen. They went fast, for the father knew every moment was precious. But as they neared the house one of the servants came up to Jairus and his face told his tale:

"Thy daughter is dead," he whispered, "trouble not the Master farther."

But Jesus hearing said kindly: "Fear not, believe only and she shall be safe."

It was a dismal scene around the house. The relatives, musicians and hired mourners had already arrived in preparation for the burial that would take place before night. From the room where the child lay came sounds of wailing mingled with the doleful music of the flute. Our Lord went in, and, finding the minstrels and the mourners making a rout, He said:

"Give place, for the girl is not dead but sleepeth."

And they laughed Him to scorn, "knowing that she was dead," says St. Luke. He put all out of the room except Peter, James and John and the father and mother of the child. There, on a low pallet she lay, white and still, her little hands joined upon her breast, fragrant spices strewed about her. Jesus took one of the small, chill hands in His, and in tones low and tender as her mother's, when she waked her from sleep, said:

"*Talitha cumi!*"—Little maid, arise.

And her eyes opened, and, when she saw Him she smiled. And she rose up and began to walk about before them all; father and mother, beside themselves with joy, watching her in silence. Then our Lord told them to give her something to eat. And, leaving the happy three together, He went out with His disciples.

Think how miracles, following fast upon one another like this, must have strengthened the faith of the Twelve. Within a few hours they had seen the wind and the sea, the devils, and death itself obey Him whom they called "Master." And along with their faith grew their admiration and veneration, their love and their trust. For He whose word nothing could resist lived among them as one of themselves. When they journeyed together, exposed to cold, rain, and sun, when they stopped by the wayside to take their scanty meal, He fared no better than the rest. Humble and kind, ready to answer all their difficulties and to defend

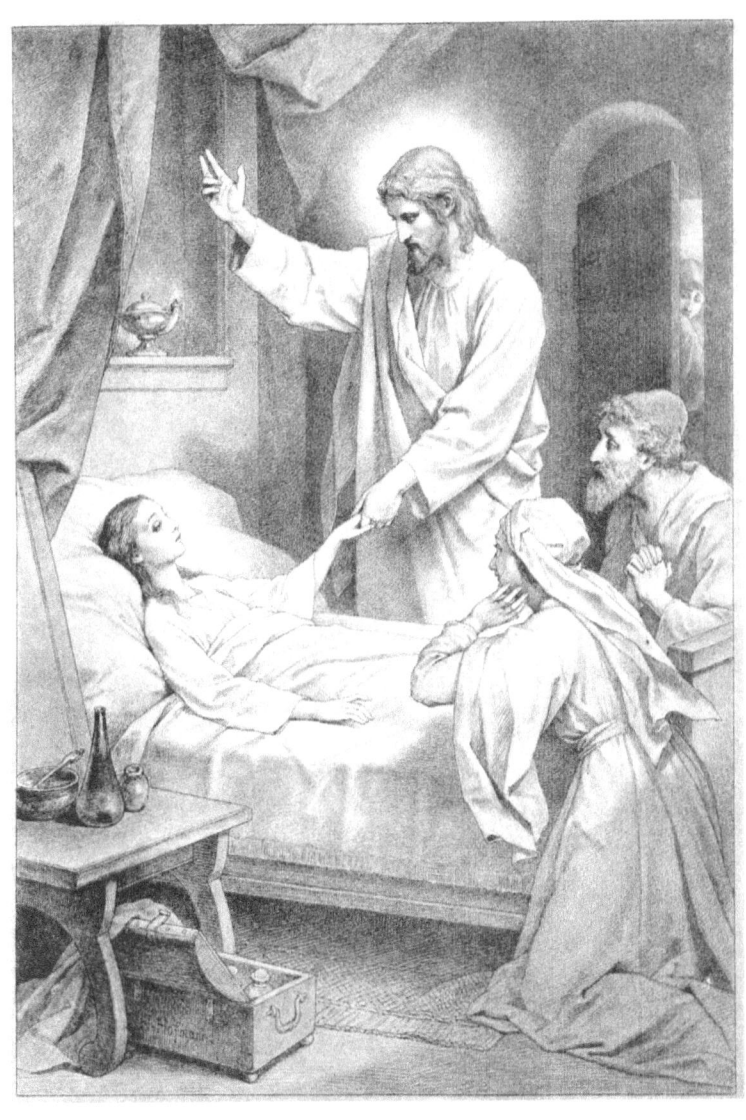

Jairus' Daughter

"And taking the damsel by the hand, he saith to her: Talitha cumi"
(Mark 5:41)

them against their enemies, patient with their slowness and their mistakes, watchful to see that nothing should hurt them, and to provide for all their wants—such was the Master to whom they had given themselves.

He did not spoil them. He corrected their faults and let them share the hardships of His Life, for they were to carry on His work amidst all kinds of sufferings when He was gone, and they had to be trained for this. But He would not let things be too hard for them. St. Peter, it is said, used to tell how, when they spent the night with Him on the mountain side, sleeping around Him whilst He prayed, He would rise from His prayer and go amongst them, and if the night was chill and He found any of them slightly covered, He would wrap them up better against the cold.

Is it wonderful that these poor, rough men loved Him as they did?

When He told them one day that He was going to send them out to preach, they were not frightened, for they knew that with His help they could do all things. They were to spread the good tidings that the Kingdom of Heaven was at hand. They were to go without money or provision for their journey, but with the wonderful powers He would give them:

"Heal the sick," He said, "raise the dead, cleanse the lepers, cast out devils: freely have you received, freely give."

And they went two and two through the towns, preaching the Gospel and healing everywhere.

"Talitha Cumi"

It was at this time that St. John the Baptist's wonderful life came to a close. For twelve months he had been imprisoned in the gloomy fortress of Machaerus for declaring the king's marriage with Herodias, his brother's wife, to be unlawful. It was a terrible place that underground dungeon for one who had lived all his life in the free air of heaven. And there was other pain as well.

His life had been spent in making ready the road for our Blessed Lord. And now he was left alone in his prison, seemingly abandoned. Our Lord did not go to see him and did nothing for him. But he never complained, his patience was not exhausted, his faith remained unshaken. He did not want to be released, but only to do God's Will, and to carry on as long as he could the work for which he was sent. Even in prison he went on preparing his Master's way. For, finding that some of his disciples who were allowed to visit him did not yet believe in Jesus, he sent them to Him with this question:

"Art Thou He that art to come or look we for another?"

He knew quite well that Jesus was the Messiah, but he wanted his disciples to know and follow Him. He must have been aware that his own death could not be far off. Herodias would never rest till she had got rid of him, and he wanted his faithful followers to be safe among our Lord's disciples before the end came. Jesus, who knew St. John's motives in asking this question, answered, not by words but by deeds. As the messengers stood around Him, He cured many sick, and to many that were blind He gave sight:

"Go," He said, "and relate to John what you have heard and seen."

And they went away believing in Him.

Meanwhile the wicked Herodias, who could not feel safe so long as John lived, was casting about for some means of bringing about his death. Herod's birthday brought her chance. The king kept the day with the utmost magnificence, and in the evening made a great supper for the chief men of his kingdom. The castle palace of Machaerus was brilliantly lighted up, and the sound of music mingled with the shouts of the revellers penetrated even into the dungeon where the holy Baptist lay.

When the merriment in the banqueting hall was at its height, Salome, the daughter of Herodias, came in to amuse the guests. She danced before them and was loudly applauded by all who sat at table. Then Herod, half intoxicated, and scarcely knowing what he was saying, swore to her:

"Whatsoever thou shalt ask I will give thee, though it be the half of my kingdom."

The girl, delighted, slipped out of the hall and said to her mother:

"What shall I ask?"

"The head of John the Baptist," was the answer.

Salome returned with haste to the king:

"I will," she said, "that thou forthwith give me in a

dish the head of John the Baptist."

What a demand from the lips of one little more than a child! All who heard it shuddered. But what would the king do? Every eye was turned upon him. Every eye saw upon his face the signs of the struggle going on within. He was struck sad, for he reverenced John and had often heard him gladly. Yet because of his oath—an oath wicked to make, more wicked still to keep—and to appear honourable in the sight of those who sat at table with him, he granted the horrid petition. One of his bodyguard was standing behind him with a naked sword in his hand. He was despatched to the prison with orders to bring the head into the hall.

There was silence now in that scene of revelry, and suspense, horrible but short. Presently the door reopened, and the gory head was brought in upon a dish. Then, in the sight of all, the king gave it to the unflinching girl, who bore it off in triumph to her mother.

When the disciples of John heard what had befallen their beloved master, they took the body and buried it, "and came and told Jesus," says St. Matthew.

The royal murderer never had another peaceful hour. That ghastly sight in the banqueting hall was constantly before his mind. When he heard of the wonderful works of Jesus, he cried out: "John the Baptist is risen from the dead," and he wanted to see our Lord. He did see Him one day, and on that day the measure of his wickedness was filled up.

XXIX.
A Holiday

On their return from their little mission, the Twelve told our Lord all things that they had done and taught.

"Come aside into a desert place and rest a little," He said, for they were tired.

It was a welcome invitation. The Lake, which they must cross to reach the desert place, was about the only spot where they could have Him all to themselves, and they had much to tell Him. So they were soon on their way. Look at them all in the boat with Him, bending forward on their oars to catch all He says; speaking to Him, first one, then another; telling Him of their success or failure. See how kindly He looks at them as they speak, how interested He is in all they say.

But look! One of them points to the shore. A great crowd is moving slowly round the head of the Lake. The people see the boat is steering for Bethsaida Julius on the eastern side, and are following it on foot along the beach. They will be there first, many of them, for it is only a couple of hours' walk from Capharnaum. The Apostles grumble. The multitude never leaves Him

A Holiday

alone, and they had come out for rest. But their Master tells them His disciples must not be selfish. These poor people need Him badly; the sick are being carried all that way, and there are many sad hearts in the crowd. They are ashamed of themselves now as they look at Him, more tired a great deal than they are, yet so kind, so thoughtful for others, so self-forgetting. There is no more murmuring. The boat is run into a little creek, and they get out and follow Him up a mountain side. He sits down, and they seat themselves in a circle on the ground at His feet and listen to Him.

They will not have Him long to themselves, the people are coming up in thousands—men, women and children "flocking after Him from all the cities." He watches them from this height and has compassion on them, for they are like sheep without a shepherd. Now He goes down to them and is surrounded at once.

All day He is among them, teaching, healing, comforting. See Him going in and out of the crowd, asking for the sick, laying His hands on them, seeking out those in sorrow and getting them to tell Him their troubles. He has such a tender way of listening. His kind eyes look so interested as the poor and the sick tell their sad tales. And they know by His questions that He really cares to hear and wants to help.

What a happy multitude it is around Him all day! The newly cured exulting in the use of eyes and ears and healthy limbs; their friends taking them about, showing them off before the astonished neighbours who had helped to bring them in the morning; the children following our Lord about like a bodyguard, crowding round to watch Him as He heals, so eager, so intent, especially when the blind and the maimed are brought to Him. They love to see the dull, vacant eyes fill with brightness and fix themselves with adoring love and thankfulness on Him who gives them light and sight, and the crippled and the palsied come from under those mighty hands straight and strong. They are His heralds, as well as His guards, these joyous children, for at every fresh cure their shouts and their cheering go out over the crowd and tell where He is. Yes, it has been a happy time; how many hearts have been lightened to-day for having poured their heaviness into His!

But evening is drawing on and the Apostles think it is time to see about food and rest. The crowds have lost count of time, of distance from home, of everything but Jesus. But they cannot stay here for ever. They have had nothing to eat and will have a good two hours' walk before they can find shelter for the night. So the Twelve come to Jesus and say:

"This is a desert place and the hour is now past. Send them away, that going into the next villages and towns they may buy themselves meat to eat."

Jesus says to them: "They have no need to go, give you them to eat."

It was like Him to say that, but how can they provide for such a multitude?

"Let us go and buy bread for two hundred pence," they say, "and we will give them to eat."

THE FEEDING OF THE FIVE THOUSAND

"But Jesus said to them, They have no need to go: give you them to eat."
(Mt 14:16)

"How many loaves have you? He asks. "Go and see."

Andrew says to Him: "There is a boy here who has five barley loaves and two fishes, but what are these among so many?"

Jesus answers: "Bring them hither to Me."

See the boy being led by St. Andrew to our Lord; the pride and pleasure of the little fellow as he gives Him his loaves and his fishes; our Lord thanking him for them.

A great miracle is going to be wrought, the type of another still greater. It is a solemn moment, and our Lord will have all in order.

"Make the men sit down," He says to the Twelve.

They sit down in ranks, by hundreds and by fifties, looking in their bright, many-coloured garments on the green grass like flowerbeds on the turf. And the eyes of all are on the hillock where Jesus stands, the twelve Apostles round Him.

He takes the loaves, and, looking up to Heaven, with indescribable majesty, blesses and breaks them, and gives them to the Apostles to be set before the people. And the two fishes He divides among them all. Up and down among the ranks go the Twelve, giving into the eager hands on every side, hearing such cries of wonderment, getting such grateful thanks. Our Lord watches all from His little height, directing the distribution with His hand—an old couple here have been missed; those children over there are ready for more.

A Holiday

When all have had enough, He says to the Apostles:

"Gather up the fragments that remain lest they be lost."

And they fill twelve baskets with what is left after that multitude is satisfied—five thousand hungry men, besides women and children. Our Lord and the disciples take some of the fragments for their own meal. Whilst they are eating, a great cry is heard and taken up by the whole multitude:

"This is the Christ! This is of a truth the Prophet that is to come into the world! Hosanna to the King of Israel!"

The Apostles are delighted. The long-expected Kingdom is coming at last! And they join in the joyful shout. But their rejoicing is short. Their Master tells them to go home now across the Lake whilst He stays behind to dismiss the crowd. What a woeful disappointment! Their faces show their dismay. It is such a pity to go just now when the people are in such good dispositions. May not some of them stay—Peter and James and John—to help Him with the crowd? No, they must all go. Very reluctantly they obey, all the more so as there is a storm-cloud gathering and the wind is rising. They have not forgotten that storm when they came from Gadara. However, there is no help for it, so they get into the boat and push off.

Waving their arms and shouting, the people come round our Lord. He must be their King, and they will fight for Him and die for Him if need be. But He tells them He does not want to be an earthly King, and they must be quiet and go back to their homes and think of all He has taught them. There is no resisting the gentle gravity and authority with which He speaks; the cries die down, and before long they are all on their way home, a joyful, peaceful army, but the King and Leader left behind.

Where?

When the crowds have all gone, He goes with weary feet up the mountain side again—to pray. Before choosing His Apostles He spent the night in prayer. And now, on this night, before the great Promise He is to make on the morrow, He prays. This is His custom always. He teaches, heals, comforts, makes Himself all to all. And then He seeks a quiet time and place for prayer, to teach us that however busy our lives may be, however full of work for others, we must keep time for being alone with God in prayer. We notice when and where He prays, and find another lesson for ourselves. We cannot indeed pray at night under the quiet stars on a still mountain side; but as far as possible we should choose an hour and a spot where we shall not be distracted, and where we shall not distract ourselves.

As He prayed the wind rose higher and higher, and at length the storm broke in all its fury upon the Lake. Woe to the fishing craft out that night! Peter's boat in the midst of the sea was tossed about and could not make head against the violence of the wind and waves. In vain did its crew furl the sail and bale out the water and row their best. It was plain to them that they would never see land. Oh, why had the Master sent

A Holiday

them away from Him! It was foolish to be frightened the other day with Him in the boat, but now they were alone and He had forgotten them. St. John, who was there, wrote long after of that dreadful night: "It was now dark and Jesus was not come unto them."

They were clinging to the sides of the boat as the sea rose and fell, when, suddenly—a Form was seen in the distance, a human Form, and It was coming towards them. Seamen are very superstitious, easily frightened by what they take to be spectres, or evil omens. But here was no imagination. It was plainly a Man and He was walking on the sea.

"It is an apparition!" they said, and they cried out for fear. For they all saw Him and were troubled. And immediately He spoke with them across the waves, saying:

"Be of good heart; it is I, fear ye not."

Oh, what a change, what joy and peace and comfort came to them with those words: "It is I!" A few moments and He would be with them. But Peter could not wait. His Master was there; he must go to Him at once.

"Lord," he cried, "if it be Thou, bid me come to Thee upon the waters."

And Jesus said: "Come!"

In an instant Peter's foot was over the side of the boat and down on the waves that grew firm beneath his tread. Up and down he walked on the heaving sea, his eyes fixed on Jesus, the Eleven leaning over the side of the boat watching him in breathless silence. He is only a few steps from our Lord when a tremendous wave

Walking on the Water

"Be of good heart: it is I, fear ye not."
(Mt 14:27)

A Holiday

almost overthrows him. He looks round, loses sight of Jesus, gets afraid and begins to sink.

"Lord, save me!" he cries, and flings out his arms towards his Master.

And Jesus immediately stretching out His hand takes hold of him and says:

"O thou of little faith, why didst thou doubt?" And Peter, clinging to Jesus, comes safe to the boat, and as soon as they are inside the wind ceases. The disciples come up and fall at our Lord's feet and adore Him, saying:

"Indeed, Thou art the Son of God!" And He works yet another miracle, "for presently the ship was at the land to which they were going."

XXX.
"Will you also go away?"

That land was Capharnaum. We can scarcely picture to ourselves the excitement and enthusiasm which greeted our Lord when His boat drew up on the strand. Whilst the Apostles had been battling with the storm on the Lake, the people had gone round along the beach and got home before nightfall. The wonderful news they had brought of their day in the desert—the teaching and the healing and the evening feast—was now the talk of the city. Everyone wanted to see the mighty Wonderworker, and the crowd on the shore was so great that our Lord and His disciples with difficulty made a passage through. He did not stop to speak there, but led the way to the synagogue of the good centurion. His words on this day were to be more solemn than any He had yet spoken, and the synagogue was the fittest place wherein to speak. The ruler Jairus would be there, so pleased to receive Him and show Him honour, and no doubt the little daughter, too, and her mother.

The lintel above the door of the synagogue—which has been found lying among the ruins—had carved on it a pot of manna with vine leaves and clusters of grapes. As He passed beneath, our Lord will have looked up and thought how fitly it was there that day. For He was going to speak for the first time of that Gift of gifts to us, His own Real Presence in the Blessed Sacrament under the appearances of bread and wine.

The Church calls this Sacrament an abridgment of all God's wonderful works. Everything about it is so marvellous that men had to be prepared for it by other marvels and by types. There was the manna in the wilderness, the food of their fathers on their way to the Promised Land. There was Melchisedech's sacrifice of bread and wine. There was the food of Elias given to strengthen him in his flight from his enemies. There was the changing of water into wine at the marriage feast of Cana. And there was that miraculous multiplication of bread in the desert the day before, of which all minds were full.

The congregation crowded into the synagogue till it was a closely packed mass of heads. The Twelve took up their position near their Master. Our Lord mounted the platform, or *bima*, and sat down. All eyes were fixed upon Him. Looking around with His heart-searching gaze, He said:

"Amen, amen, I say to you, you seek Me because you did eat of the loaves. Labour not for the meat which perisheth, but for that which endureth unto life everlasting, which the Son of Man will give you."

Some from the crowd called out: "What sign dost

Thou show that we may see and may believe? What dost Thou work?"

And this after the miracle of yesterday!

"Our fathers did eat manna in the desert," they went on, "as it is written: 'He gave them bread from Heaven to eat.'"

Jesus said to them: "Amen, amen, I say to you: Moses gave you not bread from Heaven, but My Father giveth you the true Bread from Heaven. For the bread of God is that which cometh down from Heaven and giveth life to the world."

They said to Him: "Lord, give us always this bread."

Jesus said to them: "I am the Bread of life; he that cometh to Me shall not hunger, and he that believeth in Me shall never thirst."

Wayward and fretful, they murmured at Him now because He said: "I am the Living Bread which came down from Heaven." And they said to one another:

"Is not this Jesus, the son of Joseph, whose father and mother we know? How then saith He: 'I came down from Heaven?'"

Jesus answered and said to them: "Murmur not among yourselves... I am the Bread of Life. If any man eat of this Bread he shall live for ever, and the Bread that I will give is My flesh for the life of the world."

The discontent and murmuring increased. It was a repetition of the scene in the synagogue at Nazareth, the same enthusiastic reception of our Lord, the same eager listening at the beginning of His discourse, the same indignation and rejection before the end.

The Bread of Life

"Labour not for the meat which perisheth, but for that which endureth unto life everlasting."

(John 6:27)

"How can this man give us his flesh to eat?" they asked.

Tens of thousands have asked this question since that day: "How can Christ be present whole and entire in the Host?" The answer is that we do not know *how*. Our Lord did not tell the Jews to understand the mystery, but to believe it—to believe Him who for years had been working among them the signs for which they asked, signs such as no other man had ever wrought. They ought to have believed His word and waited humbly to see how He would accomplish it. But instead of this many even of His disciples among the crowd said:

"This saying is hard, who can hear it?"

And they went back and walked no more with Him.

Let us stop a moment to ask what this wonderful Promise really meant, and why so precious a Gift was left us.

When our Divine Lord took a body and soul like ours and the Word was made Flesh and dwelt amongst us, He did not mean this dwelling in our midst to be merely for the time of His mortal life, and for the few who were able to approach Him then. It was to be for all time and for all mankind. His blessed body, whose touch gave life and healing to the sick of Galilee and Judea, was to be our life and healing, too. Nay, we were to be allowed a closer union with Him than were those whose sores He touched and healed. He promised a Divine Bread that should give life to the world. This

Bread was to be His Flesh and the food of all who should believe in Him:

"My Flesh is meat indeed and My Blood is drink indeed," are His solemn, earnest words.

When our Lord spoke in parables, He explained their meaning clearly, at least to the Apostles. But there was no parable here. He meant just what He said, and when some of His hearers, refusing to believe, went away, He let them go. He would have let the Twelve go, had they refused to take His words as He meant them, in their simple, literal meaning. The way in which He was going to make this Gift to men and the manner in which His Body and Blood were to be received, He did not at this time explain.

He watched the disciples going away, and, turning to the Twelve, said sadly:

"Will you also go away?"

Simon Peter, his face aglow with love and loyalty, replied for all:

"Lord, to whom shall we go? Thou hast the words of eternal life. And we have believed and have known that Thou art the Christ, the Son of God."

Our Lord accepted from their spokesman, Peter, this solemn confession of faith from eleven among the Apostles. But not from the twelfth. For He saw among His Twelve one who for some time past had followed Him in body only, whose heart was far away. Judas was now full of anger and vexation because his Master had refused the earthly kingdom which the people had pressed upon Him. He did not care to be His disciple any longer, and He was annoyed at His teaching and at the marks of reverence shown Him.

The heart of Christ our Lord, then, was full of sadness this day at Capharnaum. Though nothing disturbed His peace or tried His patience, unkindness, distrust and ingratitude wounded Him sensibly. He felt keenly the rejection of His best Gift, the desertion of His disciples, the gradual hardening of heart and falling away of one of the Twelve. For of all hearts His was the most faithful, the most tender and affectionate.

XXXI.
"*Lord, Help me!*"

We are drawing near to the end.
Not Judas alone but all those who looked for a Messiah who should be the temporal Ruler and Liberator of His people, were grievously disappointed when our Lord declared that He had not come to be a king of the world. It was an earthly kingdom that they wanted, not the Kingdom of Heaven of which He spoke.

According to the rabbis, the Messiah was to march at the head of His people against all heathen nations, to make them subject to the Jews, and to rule from Jerusalem over the whole earth. There was to be a reign of a thousand years, a reign of prosperity, glory and pleasure for the people of God. The fruit trees and the harvest fields were to yield their produce continually, and every product of every clime was to be found in Palestine in an abundance such as the wildest imagination only could conceive. Jewish children were brought up from their earliest years with these expectations, and even our Lord's disciples were full of such earthly hopes. So that when, about this time, their Master began to break gently to them that He was going to redeem the world, not by fighting against the Romans, but by shedding His Blood, they could not understand what He meant.

His enemies—the priests, the Pharisees, the Sadducees and the Herodians—were glad to see the people disappointed, and their enthusiasm for Jesus of Nazareth cooling. They told them that a poor, unlearned man, the son of a carpenter, could never be the glorious Messiah of whom Moses and the Prophets had spoken. They reproved the poor sick people who came to Him on the Sabbath to be cured. They followed Him about, watching Him, laughing at Him, putting difficult questions to Him in the hope of puzzling Him.

For a long time our Lord bore meekly with the Pharisees, who were among the most violent of His enemies. He answered their questions, though He knew they were only asked to entrap Him, and gently pointed out to them the sins which made them displeasing to God. But when He saw that they continued to shut their eyes to the light, and that they were leading the people away from Him, He fearlessly and publicly rebuked them for their hypocrisy and pride, and warned them of the terrible punishment they were preparing for themselves. One day He told the people this parable:

"Two men went up into the Temple to pray, the one a Pharisee and the other a publican. The Pharisee, standing, prayed thus with himself: 'O God, I give Thee thanks that I am not like the rest of men, extortioners,

The Proud Pharisee

"O God, I give thee thanks that I am not as the rest of men"
(Luke 18:11)

unjust, adulterers, as also is this publican. I fast twice in a week, I give tithes of all that I possess.' And the publican, standing afar off, would not so much as lift up his eyes towards Heaven, but struck his breast, saying: 'O God, be merciful to me a sinner.' I say to you this man went down to his house justified; 'that is, pleasing to God,' rather than the other, because everyone that exalteth himself shall be humbled, and he that humbleth himself shall be exalted."

How the pride of the Pharisees must have been stung by this parable! To think of anyone daring to compare a Pharisee with a publican, and preferring the publican! From this time their rage against our Lord knew no bounds, and they leagued with their enemies, the Sadducees and the Herodians, to bring about His destruction.

He knew all their plots, but went calmly on His way, teaching and healing, casting out devils, and training His Apostles, knowing that His enemies could do nothing against Him until His hour should come. On a certain day, when He had been telling the people that in the Kingdom of God the last should be first and the first last—a prospect very unwelcome to the Pharisees—some of these came and said to Him:

"Get Thee hence, for Herod hath a mind to kill Thee."

He answered: "Go and tell that fox: Behold, I cast out devils and do cures to-day and to-morrow, and the third day I am consummated." "No man," He said another day, "taketh My life away from Me, but I lay it down of Myself, and I have power to lay it down, and I have power to take it up again."

One day our Lord crossed the northern border of Palestine and came into the heathen land of Phœnicia. "He would that no man should know it," says St. Mark, "but He could not be hid." His fame had gone beyond the limits of His own little country, and a poor pagan woman came to Him in her distress. Her daughter was possessed by an evil spirit, and the mother, who had heard of the cures in Palestine, hoped that Jesus of Nazareth would have pity on her child. So she came after Him crying out:

"Have mercy on me, O Lord, Thou Son of David, my daughter is grievously troubled by a devil."

But He answered her not a word. "What an unheard of thing is this!" says St. John Chrysostom. "He helped those who were undeserving; He would not send away those who came to tempt and hurt Him, but for one who ran after Him and humbly implored His aid He had not a word."

The disciples, annoyed at the disturbance she was making, came to Him, saying:

"Send her away, for she crieth after us."

But she would not be sent away, and, paying no heed to them, she besought Him that He would cast forth the devil out of her daughter.

And He, answering, said: "I was not sent but to the sheep that are lost of the house of Israel."

What a disappointment! And she had been told He

was so kind to those in trouble. Anyone but a mother would have lost heart and gone away disconsolate; but she did not give in, she was not discouraged. She came and fell down at His feet and adored Him, saying:

"Lord, help me!"

And He said: "It is not good to take the bread of the children and to cast it to the dogs."

To this poor woman these words sounded harsher than they do to us, for the dogs of the East are not the companions and pets we make them, but starving, wretched creatures for which nobody cares. It is not fit, our Lord meant, that the favours granted to the children of God, that is, to the Jews, should be given to pagans like her.

Will she go away now, hurt or brokenhearted?

No, she is too humble to be hurt, too resolute to be brokenhearted. She will turn His words against Him and make them plead her cause.

"Yes, Lord," she says eagerly, "for the whelps also eat under the table of the crumbs of the children. What Thou sayest is true. It is not fit to take the children's bread for the dogs, but it is fit to give just the crumbs to the little dogs waiting under the table for them. This will not hurt the children. I am only a dog, but a little one to whom some broken bits might perhaps out of kindness be given."

How could our Lord hold out any longer! He had determined to set this poor heathen before His followers to the end of time as a model of the humble, persevering prayer that wins reward at last. Therefore

The Canaanite Woman

"Then Jesus answering, said to her: O woman, great is thy faith: be it done to thee as thou wilt."
(Mt 15:28)

He was obliged to try her by seeming hard. It was all seeming. From the first He was full of compassion for her and her unhappy child. He longed to help her, and had to hold back the tender, pitying words His heart was prompting Him to say. They came at last as an outburst of admiration that He could no longer restrain:

"O woman, great is thy faith, be it done unto thee as thou wilt!"

He who rebuked His disciples for their little faith was delighted with what He found in this Canaanite. He liked, too, the way in which she turned His words about the dogs against Him. St. Mark says it was this sharpness of hers that in the end gained her cause. And Jesus said:

"For this saying, go thy way, the devil is gone out of thy daughter."

And, when she was come into her house, she found the girl lying upon the bed, and that the devil was gone out. Was it worth while to have waited patiently and humbly, and to have persisted in spite of weariness and delay?

XXXII.
At Caesarea Philippi

In the north of Palestine at the foot of snowy Hermon stood the magnificent city of Cæsarea Philippi. Philip, the tetrarch, had enlarged and beautified it and called it Cæsarea, in honour of Tiberias Cæsar. Philippi, from Philip, was added to distinguish it from another Cæsarea on the coast. The city is interesting to us, not for its heathen memories, but for the presence of Christ our Lord in its neighbourhood, and for the events that took place there one memorable day.

It was now about ten months before the Passion, and the Apostles had been in the company of our Blessed Lord for nearly three years. During those years their knowledge of Him had been gradually growing. At the time of their call it was very imperfect indeed, and even later, when, from His teaching and wonderful works, they had come to acknowledge Him as the Messiah, their belief as to who He was remained very vague. Like the rest of their nation they knew that the Messiah was to be a great Deliverer; they did not clearly understand that He would be God. And by minding only the glorious things foretold of Him by the Prophets, they had lost sight of the prophecy that He would be a Man of Sorrows.

It was time for our Lord to test the faith of the Twelve, to prepare them for His coming Passion and Death, and to lay the foundations of that Church by which men were to be brought to the knowledge of Him and of what they must do to save their souls.

All this was to be done at Cæsarea Philippi. What wonder that on the morning of the eventful day of which we are speaking He was found alone in prayer!

When He rose from His prayer He said to the Twelve:

"Who do men say that I am?"

And they said: "Some, John the Baptist, and other some, Elias, and others Jeremias or one of the Prophets."

Jesus said to them: "But who do you say that I am?"

Peter, foremost as usual, answered: "Thou art Christ, the Son of the Living God."

Here was a glorious profession of faith, proclaiming Christ to be true God, equal to the Father in all things.

Jesus said to him: "Blessed art thou, Simon Bar-Jona, because flesh and blood hath not revealed it to thee, but My Father who is in Heaven. And I say to thee that thou art Peter, and upon this rock I will build My Church, and the gates of hell shall not prevail against it. And I will give to thee the keys of the Kingdom of Heaven, and whatsoever thou shalt bind upon earth it shall be bound also in Heaven, and whatsoever thou shalt loose on earth it shall be loosed also in Heaven."

Thus, in reward for his grand confession, was Peter made the Vicar of Christ on earth. The other Apostles understood now why, on seeing him for the first time, their Master had called him a rock. As a rock keeps the house firm that is built upon it, so was Peter to keep steady and united the Church founded by Christ on him.

And the gates of hell—the power of the devil—shall not prevail against it. Because by the gift of infallibility, Peter and his successors, when they speak to the whole Church on matters of faith or morals, will be preserved from teaching what is false.

But Peter is to be not the foundation only, but the Governor and Head of the Church. Therefore, as the governor of a city has the keys put into his hands, so has Peter received full power over the Church to give orders and make laws as he shall see fit. And Christ, the invisible Head of the Church, promises to confirm in Heaven the acts of His Vicar on earth.

Moreover, as the Church is not to pass away with Peter, but to last as long as the world, what is promised to Peter is promised to his successors to the end of time.

Now that through their spokesman the Apostles had confessed their faith in our Lord's Divinity, He began to show them that sin requires expiation, and that this can be made only by suffering. Gently and gradually He broke it to them that He would have to redeem the world by bitter pains and a cruel death, but that He would rise again the third day. "And He began to teach them that the Son of Man must suffer many things, and be rejected by the ancients and by the high priests and the scribes, and be killed, and after three days rise again."

They were horrified. It was so different from what they had expected. Why, it was only the other day that He was nearly being made King! To be the Messiah and to suffer! To be the Son of the Living God and to be killed! It was more than Peter, with his faith in our Lord's Divinity, his reverence, his intense affection for Him, could bear. And—oh, what boldness!—he took Him aside and began to rebuke Him.

"Lord, be it far from Thee, this shall not be unto Thee."

"Go behind Me, Satan! because thou savourest not the things that are of God but the things that are of men."

What tremendous words! and from the lips that had just said: "Blessed art thou." Poor Peter fell back, dismayed, among his fellow-Apostles. It was a severe reproof, and showed the Twelve that no one must venture to dissuade the Master from going through the terrible sufferings that lay before Him. His Heart was full of His coming Passion. From this time He spoke of it often, and each time with greater fullness:

"The Son of Man shall be betrayed into the hands of men, and they shall mock Him, and kill Him, and the third day He shall rise again." Always at the end those comforting words. He never separated the Passion from the Resurrection, that the thought of our

At Cæsarea Philippi 275

resurrection and of the joys of Heaven may support us in the troubles of this short life.

But the poor disciples could not take in either the trouble or the comfort that He foretold: and "they were afraid to ask Him," says St. Luke, so they used "to question among themselves what these things might mean."

And there was more yet. Not only did our Lord foretell His own sufferings, but He now made it clear that the disciples must be like their Master and that through labours and trials of every kind they must follow Him into the Kingdom of Heaven—they and all who professed themselves His disciples. He was so resolved that there should be no mistake on this point that He called the multitudes together with His disciples and said to all:

"If any man will come after Me, let him deny himself and take up his cross and follow Me."

These words sorely distressed the Twelve. To think of all their expectations coming to this—a suffering Messiah, and no end of troubles for all who followed Him! Their Master had pity on them, and to strengthen their faith and courage He gave them a proof of His Divinity and a foretaste of the reward prepared for them in Heaven when their trials here were over. It happened in this way:

One evening, a week after Peter's confession at Cæsarea Philippi, He took Peter and James and John and went up into a mountain to pray. He loved the mountains. They lifted Him for a little while above this sad earth. He loved the majesty of their solitude, their stillness, their strength. He loved the tranquil glory of the midnight skies into which they rose. He was the Creator of the starry heavens above Him. He knew and controlled all that they contain. If one of His Saints exclaimed: "How dull does earth appear when I look up to Heaven," how did His glorious Soul pour Itself forth in admiration and praise as He knelt there amid the wonders of His own creation through those eastern nights!

And so this evening He went up the mountain, probably Thabor or Hermon, with His chosen three. It was getting dark when they reached the top and knelt down to pray. His companions watched with Him awhile, then, wearied with the labours of the day and the steep ascent, and drowsy in the strong mountain air, they fell asleep.

A dazzling light falling on their faces roused them. They woke and looked around. The Mount, the surrounding heavens, the earth beneath were lit up by a supernatural splendour. And there in the midst—the Source from which all that glory streamed—was their Master, so transfigured that His face shone as the sun, and His glittering garments were white as no fuller on earth can make white. The glory of the Divinity within poured Itself out upon His Face and Form with a brilliancy so intense as to transfigure even His raiment. He had laid aside the form of a servant and taken to Himself the majesty and splendour that

The Transfiguration

"And his face did shine as the sun: and his garments became white as snow. And behold there appeared to them Moses and Elias talking with him."

(Mt 17:2-3)

became the Son of God. The Sacred Humanity was like a lantern enclosing a light too brilliant to be seen without a shade. In the Transfiguration the shade was withdrawn, and, for an instant, the Light of Light in its transplendent beauty was seen by men.

And, behold! two men, Moses and Elias, appeared in majesty, and they were talking with Jesus of His decease which He should accomplish in Jerusalem. Here was a new wonder, Moses, the Lawgiver of the Jews, and Elias, the most marvellous Prophet of the Old Law, coming to pay homage to the Founder of the New Law, and speaking to Him, even in this scene of glory, of His coming sufferings and death. One of the accusations of our Lord's enemies was that He did not respect the Law of Moses. What would His accusers have said had they seen Moses on this night humbly waiting on Jesus of Nazareth as a servant on his lord!

The glorious scene before them so captivated the Apostles that they could only enjoy it in silent awe and intense delight. They listened to Moses and Elias speaking in admiration and gratitude to our Lord of His coming Passion. They heard His tender words in reply. How long this lasted we do not know, but when the Saints seemed to be going, Peter, in his vehement desire to keep them, cried out:

"Lord, it is good for us to be here, if Thou wilt let us make here three tabernacles, one for Thee, one for Moses, and one for Elias!" "not knowing what he said," adds St. Luke. Truly, not knowing what he said. It was a simple thought at which he must have wondered afterwards, that those three, resplendent with heavenly glory, could need a dwelling made with hands!

And as he was yet speaking, behold, a bright cloud overshadowed them, and lo! a Voice out of the cloud saying:

"This is My Beloved Son in whom I am well pleased: hear ye Him."

And the disciples, hearing, fell upon their faces and were very much afraid. Overwhelmed by the awfulness of so much glory, they did not dare to look up till Jesus came and touched them and said to them:

"Arise, and fear not!"

And they, lifting up their eyes and looking about, saw no one but only Jesus. The bright cloud had disappeared. The sky was dark as before, lit only by the distant stars. Moses and Elias were gone, and Jesus, gentle and lowly as usual, was bending over them and telling them not to be afraid. And, as they came down from the mountain, He charged them saying:

"Tell the vision to no man till the Son of Man be risen from the dead."

St. Mark adds: "And they kept the word to themselves, questioning together what that should mean 'when He shall be risen from the dead.'"

Poor Apostles! not their Master only, but now Moses and Elias had spoken of the Death that was at hand. And still they could not understand. Peter had wished that night of glory to last for ever. It was good for them to be there on the Mount of Transfiguration, he said. He did not know that this glimpse of Heaven was to prepare them to tread the Way of the Cross, and he little dreamed of another hill, a hill of shame, on which one of the three was to stand beside his Master before many months were passed.

The memory of that glorious night was graven deep in the minds of the Apostles. St. Peter, writing to the faithful thirty-five years later, speaks of what he had heard "when we were with Him in the holy Mount." And in the Last Gospel we hear St. John saying: "And we saw His glory, the glory as it were of the Only-Begotten of the Father, full of grace and truth."

His glory was shown to them that their faith might not falter at the sight of His shame, and that all who believe in Him may know that the Way of the Cross is the Way to Heaven, and that the sufferings of this short life are not worthy to be compared with the glory that is to come.

Coming down from the mountain next morning our Lord found the nine Apostles who had been left behind, surrounded by a great crowd, and in a difficulty. A poor, possessed boy had been brought to them for cure, and they could not cast out the devil. How glad they were to see their Master coming to their help. And there was another glad, too. The father of the boy came running to Jesus, and, falling at His feet, cried out:

"Lord, have pity on my son, because he is my only one. And, lo! a spirit seizeth him and he suddenly crieth out, and he throweth him down and teareth him, so that he foameth, and bruising him he hardly departeth from him. And I desired Thy disciples to cast him out and they could not."

And Jesus said: "O unbelieving and perverse generation, how long shall I be with you, how long shall I suffer you? Bring him hither to Me."

And as he was coming to Him the spirit troubled him, and being thrown down upon the ground, he rolled about foaming.

And Jesus asked his father: "How long is it since this hath happened unto him?"

But he said: "From his infancy. And oftentimes hath he cast him into the fire and often into waters to destroy him. But if Thou canst do anything, help us having compassion on us."

And Jesus said to him: "If thou canst believe, all things are possible to him that believeth."

And immediately the father of the boy, crying out with tears, said:

"I do believe, Lord, help my unbelief."

And Jesus said: "Deaf and dumb spirit, I command thee, go out of him and enter not any more into him."

And, crying out and greatly tearing him, he went out of him, and he became as dead, so that many said: "He is dead." But Jesus taking him by the hand lifted him up; and he arose and was cured from that hour.

And when He was come into the house, His disciples secretly asked Him: "Why could not we cast him out?" And He said to them: "This kind can go out by nothing but by prayer and fasting."

XXXIII.
With the Children

In spite of all our Lord could do and say, the minds of the Apostles were still full of the coming Kingdom and of the first places there. Whether it was the favour shown to the three who had been taken into the room of Jairus' little daughter when the rest were left outside, and had been with the Master on the Mount, where it was plain they had seen something wonderful and heard some secret which they would not tell the nine; or whether the great promise made to Peter after his confession at Cæsarea Philippi had aroused jealousy among the others, there was a dispute among the Twelve at this time as to which of them was the greatest. Andrew was the first called; James and John were cousins, or, in Jewish language, "brothers" of the Lord; and John was plainly His best beloved. On the other hand, Peter was the most noticed by the Master and was the Rock; Judas came from the south, and spoke the best, and was better off than the rest. Which of them, then, was the greatest? This was the kind of talk among them as they walked one day behind our Lord on the way to Capharnaum.

When they came to the house He said quietly:

"What did you treat of in the way?"

"But they held their peace," says St. Mark, "for in the way they had disputed among themselves which of them should be the greatest."

At length, one bolder than the rest answered the Master's question after a fashion by putting another:

"Who, thinkest Thou, is the greater in the Kingdom of Heaven?"

It shows their confidence in our Blessed Lord, and their habit of taking all difficulties to Him, that ashamed as they were of being caught in this dispute, they yet appealed to Him to settle it and to satisfy their curiosity.

Our Lord sat down and made them all come round Him. A little child happened to be near. Jesus called him, and, when He had embraced him, He set him in the midst. See the Twelve looking at the child, wondering what was coming and why he was put there. See the child looking round innocently at them all, standing there at our Lord's knee because he was bid, asking no questions.

And Jesus said to them: "Amen, I say to you unless you be converted and become as little children you shall not enter into the Kingdom of Heaven. Whosoever therefore shall humble himself as this little child, he is the greater in the Kingdom of Heaven."

What a surprise! They had been disputing about the first place, and He threatens them with not getting in at all unless they change.

Our Blessed Lord goes on to speak of the preciousness of these little ones in the sight of God, of the reward those will have who do them good, and of the terrible punishment those deserve who teach them what is wrong, or neglect or harm them in any way:

"He that shall receive one such little child in My Name receiveth Me. But he that shall scandalise one of these little ones that believe in Me, it were better for him that a millstone should be hanged about his neck and that he should be drowned in the depth of the sea. See that you despise not one of these little ones, for I say to you that their Angels in Heaven always see the face of My Father who is in Heaven."

We must not think that these solemn promises and threats are for grown up people only. They are for children too. Children help or harm one another very much. Wherever they meet—in the playground, in the street, in church, at school, at home, they are doing good or doing mischief, pleasing or displeasing the Good Angels of their brothers, or sisters, or companions. The Holy Angels watch with the greatest care over the little ones entrusted to them. Happy those who make friends of these blessed spirits by helping their little charges. But woe to any who by word or example harm a little child. Its powerful friend and protector who stands always in the Presence of God will accuse them there.

Children are very dear to Our Blessed Lord, and He loves to see them near Him. He was resting one

With the Children

day when some Jewish mothers, who had watched their opportunity, brought a whole flock of little ones, infants in arms many of them, that He might touch them and lay His hands on them and pray.

The Apostles were not at all kind to the visitors and went about rebuking both mothers and children: "Get away, children," they said, "the Master is tired and cannot do with you." They had soon forgotten the lesson He had given them at Capharnaum and the small teacher He had set over them there. They thought, no doubt, that to be worthy of their Master's attention, all should be important people like themselves. He had to teach them for the second time that they must become like children if they were to be near and dear to Him. A child is—or ought to be—simple and innocent, content to be little, to depend on others, to obey. This is why he is great in God's sight and worthy to be set as an example even to Apostles.

Jesus, seeing the children being driven away, was much displeased and said to the Twelve:

"Suffer the little children to come unto Me and forbid them not, for of such is the Kingdom of God."

From these words we see that the children were eager to come to Him, and were not simply brought by others. How gentle and inviting must have been His look, that encouraged the little troop to make their way up to Him in spite of the rough ways and words of the Twelve! They clustered round His knees. They held out their arms to be taken into His. They cried out "me! me!" as they saw first one and then another

Jesus, Friend of Children

*"Suffer the little children to come unto me, and forbid them not;
for of such is the kingdom of God."*
(Mark 10:14)

folded in His embrace. They prattled round Him. They nestled on His breast. They took His hand and held it fast. Happy little children, who shall tell the graces that came to them that day from their Saviour's blessing and caress!

XXXIV.
With the Twelve

No one must keep the children from Him, and no one must hinder His coming Passion. Only when the disciples did these things was their Master angry with them. He was patient with their dullness—and, oh! they were dull—and with their many faults.

He had taught them to be kind and forgiving. But when a Samaritan city refused Him a passage through, because He was going to Jerusalem, James and John, filled with indignation, said: "Lord, wilt Thou that we command fire from Heaven to come down and consume them?" "You know not of what spirit you are," He answered quietly; "the Son of Man came not to destroy souls but to save."

People who did not do as they did were sure to be in the wrong. "Master," said John to Him, "we saw one casting out devils in Thy Name who followeth not us, and we forbade him." "Do not forbid him," Jesus answered; "he that is not against you is for you."

He had been telling the Twelve to try to gain by gentleness a brother who might have offended them. "How often shall my brother offend against me and

I forgive him? till seven times?" said Peter, thinking this a great stretch of generosity. "I say not to thee till seven times," Jesus answered, " but till seventy times seven times."

One day a young man came running up to Jesus, and, kneeling before Him, said:

"Good Master, what shall I do that I may receive life everlasting?"

Our Lord told him that he must keep the Commandments.

"All these have I kept from my youth: what is yet wanting to me?" he said, and looked up with innocent eyes into the face of Jesus.

He spoke truly, his soul was beautiful in the sight of God. And Jesus looking on Him loved him and said to him:

"One thing is wanting to thee; if thou wilt be perfect, go sell all whatsoever thou hast, and give to the poor, and thou shalt have treasure in Heaven, and come, follow Me."

When the young man heard this he went away sad, for he had great possessions. And Jesus, seeing him become sad, looking round about, said to His disciples:

"Children, how hard it is for them that trust in riches to enter into the Kingdom of God. It is easier for a camel to pass through the eye of a needle than for a rich man to enter into the Kingdom of God."

Then Peter answering, said to Him: "Behold, we have left all things and have followed Thee: what therefore shall we have?"

Christ and the Rich Young Man

"If thou wilt be perfect, go sell what thou hast, and give to the poor, and thou shalt have treasure in heaven: and come follow me."
(Mt 19:21)

Instead of reproving this fisherman for talking about leaving all things, Jesus said to him:

"Amen, I say to you, that you who have followed Me, when the Son of Man shall sit on the seat of His majesty, you also shall sit on twelve thrones judging the twelve tribes of Israel."

Perhaps it was this promise of thrones that made James and John ask a little later for the first place in the Kingdom that was coming. Our Lord was not angry with them, but wonderfully indulgent and patient. He saw that the faults of His Apostles were on the surface only, so much on the surface, indeed, that they were very visible. But their hearts were right. They were simple and straightforward, having no secrets from Him, coming out with all that they felt without caring whether it might meet with a reproof. And when He did reprove, they were docile and saw their fault, and were sorry and began to try again. There was no sulking, no keeping away from Him after a rebuke. And often there was something good and generous even in their failures. If James and John were hard upon the Samaritan city, it was because they could not bear to see their Master treated with disrespect. If they asked for the first places in His Kingdom, it was that they might be near Him. And if Peter inquired whether he should forgive seven times, it was from the fear that such generosity might perhaps be excessive. They spoke of having left all for Christ because they had left willingly the little they had, and would have left palaces and all the wealth of this world had it been theirs.

Dear Apostles of our Lord! With all their shortcomings, how delightful they are, how charming in their simplicity and in the devotedness of their rough, tender hearts. We could not spare one single word they say, one act of loving ambition, or faulty zeal. But for them we should never have known our Blessed Saviour as we do. It is encouraging to find that in spite of His teaching and blessed example always before their eyes, they remained for a long time so imperfect. It helps us to see them struggling with the same passions we have to fight, and falling again and again into the same faults.

One—one only—among His Twelve disappointed the Master and lay like a dead weight on His Heart, that one on whom all His teaching and deeds of mercy and of power were thrown away, who hardened himself more and more now that the prospects of an earthly kingdom seemed to be vanishing. Judas remained indeed in the little company and followed his Master still, but in body only. He had long since ceased to care for Him who had called him. His life was all pretence; his prayers with the others, his teaching of the people, his conversations with our Lord when he was obliged to speak—all this was acting. We never find him asking questions like the rest when their Master was instructing them. He did not care to learn, for he did not mean to improve. There was only one thing he really cared for now, and that was—money. Little by little he had let this love of money take possession of him, till at last all his thought was to get it, no matter how. He had charge of the purse which contained the alms given for the support of our Lord and the Apostles, and the poor. He began to steal from this purse. The first time his conscience reproached him terribly and made him very unhappy. He was afraid, too, that our Lord, who of course knew of his theft, might reprove him for it before his fellow-Apostles. But as time went on and his Master said nothing, at least in public, he grew bolder and took more and more.

Jesus loved him tenderly still. He had called him to be an Apostle because He loved him and saw in his soul what pleased Him, and He warned him again and again to beware of the covetousness which, like poison, was killing all the good that was there. He kept him in His company, He treated him like the rest, sent him out to preach, gave him power to cast out devils and to cure, spoke to him kindly, tried to win him—but all in vain. The agony He felt at the gradual falling away of His poor, miserable Apostle comes out when He speaks of His coming Passion. He mentions a few only of the sufferings that were in store for Him, the sharpest, and chiefly the pains of the soul—mocking, spitting, betrayal. This last was the worst. He could bear insult and cruelty from the Gentiles who knew Him not, but betrayal from one of His own! Oh, the anguish there is in those words at the Last Supper: "Amen, I say to you, one *of you* shall betray Me!"

Our Lord was praying one day whilst His disciples stood at a little distance watching Him. They never tired of seeing Him at prayer. His stillness, His profound reverence, the fervour of soul that appeared on His countenance filled them with admiration and the desire to pray like Him. This day one of them said when His prayer was finished:

"Lord, teach us to pray, as John also taught his disciples."

The Prophets had taught them; the rabbis had taught them. Their prayers began with one or other of the Names by which God was known to the Jews: "the Strong One," "the Adorable," "the great Lord," "the God of Hosts," "the Most High," "the Almighty." One Name out of reverence they might never pronounce—*Jehovah*, "He who is and will be." How will their Master have them speak to God? by what dread Name must they call Him? See them gather round Him, eager, reverent. Watch their faces as He makes answer:

"When you pray say: Father, hallowed be Thy Name; Thy Kingdom come; give us this day our daily bread; and forgive us our sins as we also forgive our debtors; and lead us not into temptation."

What a surprise, what a relief! No terrible Name, but "Father." They may speak to the God who made them as children to the most loving of fathers, and ask, not for great things only, but for little things, for the least things, for everything. They remember how long ago He said to them: "Thus, therefore shall you pray: Our Father who art in Heaven, hallowed be Thy Name; Thy Kingdom come; Thy Will be done on earth as it is in Heaven." It was a little shorter now, but the

Teach us to Pray

"Our Father, who art in Heaven..."
(Mt. 6:9)

same prayer. "Father, Our Father"—the prayer for all. He makes no exception; the poorest, then, the most ignorant, the most guilty have a right to look up and say: "Our Father who art in Heaven."

Yes, there is nothing our Lord has more at heart than this—to see us go to our Heavenly Father with great confidence and ask again and again for all we want, persisting if we do not obtain at once. To show how we should persist, He told the people a parable of a man who goes at midnight to his friend and says to him: "Friend, lend me three loaves, for a friend of mine has come off his journey and I have nothing to set before him." He from within answers: "Trouble me not, the door is now shut, and my children are with me in bed, I cannot rise and give thee." "Yet," our Lord goes on, "if he shall continue knocking, I say unto you, although he will not rise and give him, because he is his friend, yet because of his importunity he will rise, and give him as many as he needeth. And I say unto you, Ask, and it shall be given you; seek, and you shall find; knock, and it shall be opened to you."

We are to knock again and again, and louder and louder by persevering prayer till at last the door is opened. Any other friend would be annoyed at such persistence, but God loves it and delights to reward it, as He rewarded the perseverance of the Canaanite. And here we may notice in passing what beautiful prayers—prayers we can all feel and say, prayers of sinners and needy ones like ourselves, the Gospel gives us:

"Lord, help me!"
"Lord, if Thou wilt Thou canst make me clean."
"Lord, save me, I perish!"
"O God, be merciful to me, a sinner!"

It was about this time that our Lord chose seventy-two of His disciples and sent them two and two to preach. It was now, too, that He spoke that most beautiful parable of the Prodigal Son, to encourage all who have wandered from their Father's Home to return to the open arms and the welcome that await them there.

A certain man had two sons, and the younger of them said to his father: "Give me the portion of substance that falleth to me." He had all he needed to make him happy in that home of his—all but the spirit of contentment and gratitude. But, wanting these, he wanted everything. He was restless and dissatisfied. He thought he would be happier away from his father's eye, in some far off country where he would be his own master and could do just as he liked—no rules, no duties, no reminders, nothing but pleasure all day and all night, a good time always.

His share of his father's wealth would have come to him on the old man's death, but he could not wait. So he went to his father and said: "Give me now what I shall have when you die." There was no reproach at the heartless words; the father divided all he had between his sons; and, not many days after, the younger, gathering all together, left home and set out for the far country. Many places that he passed on his way looked bright and tempting, but they were too near home; his father might come to hear of him and try to get him back. At last he was far enough. From the gay city here no news of him would ever reach his home. So he settled down and soon found himself surrounded by a number of young fellows, only too glad to make friends with a rich stranger, and be treated at his expense.

All went merrily for a while—as long as the money lasted. Then came a change. One by one his new friends left him, famine brought distress upon the country, and he began to be in want—the spoilt child of that wealthy home, in want! He hired himself to a man who sent him into his farm to feed swine. There, day after day he sat among them, cold, hungry, friendless, coveting the husks they ate. Then in the misery of his need came the memory of his home and of the plenty there:

"How many servants in my father's house abound with bread," he said to himself, "and I here perish with hunger."

He thought of his willfulness and ingratitude, and—oh, well for him that it was so! of the goodness of his father's heart.

"I will arise," he said, "and will go to my father and say to him: Father, I have sinned against Heaven and before thee; I am not now worthy to be called thy son, make me as one of thy hired servants." To be back again under the old roof and earn his bread there as a

THE PRODIGAL SON

*"Father, I have sinned against heaven, and before thee,
I am not now worthy to be called thy son."*
(Luke 15:21)

hired servant was more than he deserved, but he would ask it of his father's charity.

And he arose and set out on his way home. There was weariness to be faced, for the way was long. There was shame, too, as he drew near the old, familiar places. But no one knew him. No one recognized in the ragged, miserable boy, starved and ill, the sprightly young fellow who had turned his back on home and gone far away and been lost sight of.

No one? Yes, there was one who knew him, one who had never lost sight of him, who had watched for him daily, who was watching now. When he was yet a great way off his father saw him and was moved with compassion, and, running to him, fell upon his neck and kissed him. The poor boy fell on his knees, and, covering his face with his hands, sobbed out:

"Father, I have sinned against Heaven and before thee, I am not now worthy to be called thy son."

No more; for his father's kiss had sealed his lips, and his father's arms were round him. And the servants were bidden to make haste lest any should see him in his disgrace—make haste to clothe him once more as a son, and put a ring on his hand and shoes on his poor, blistered feet, and prepare a feast with music and dancing that they might make merry and be glad because he had been dead and was come to life again, he had been lost and was found.

Perhaps we think God Himself could hardly be kinder than the father of the prodigal? Our Lord did not think so; He knew He is much kinder, for after all the father did not go out into the far country to look for his son and bring him back. Yet this is what God has done for us. He has come all the way from Heaven into this world to seek us, and, when we are sorry for our sins and want to be better, it is the voice of God our Father calling us back to Him.

So our Lord made another parable of a good shepherd who left his ninety-nine obedient sheep to go after one that had strayed away from the fold and got lost in the mountains, where wild beasts live and prowl about at night in search of such foolish wanderers. The good shepherd goes after his sheep in the cold wind and the darkness and the rain, not minding his bleeding feet, cut by the sharp stones of the way. He gets upon a little height, and stands, and listens! And, when at last he hears its far off bleating cry, he hastens to where, over the side of the precipice, it stands on a narrow ledge, ready to fall into the depths below and be dashed to pieces. At the risk of his life he leans over and lifts it up and sets it in safety by his side. He does not beat, or scold it, or drive it back to the fold, but speaks to it tenderly, and strokes it, and lifts it on his shoulder rejoicing, and so carries it home, and, when he gets back to the fold, calls together his friends and neighbours, saying:

"Rejoice with me because I have found my sheep that was lost."

"I am the Good Shepherd," said our Lord, "and I lay down My life for My sheep." When He told this

The Good Shepherd

"I am the Good Shepherd; and I know mine, and mine know me."
(John 10:14)

story the day was drawing near when He was going to give His life for His sheep. He was always thinking of that day and longing for it, because by His cruel death we, whom He loved so dearly, were to be saved.

XXXV.
With His Friends

The hatred of our Lord's enemies was growing in intensity day by day. They were now fully resolved upon His death, but they feared the people. And well they might. He had been amongst them now nearly three years, "curing every disease and every infirmity." Thousands of poor sufferers—demoniacs, lepers, the blind, the paralyzed, the deaf, the dumb, had been made happy by His kind word or His gentle touch. Would the people suffer harm to come near Him? This was the question the rulers asked somewhat anxiously when they met together, priests and scribes, Pharisees, Sadducees, Herodians, all united for once by their common hatred of Him "who went about doing good." How was His death to be brought about? How, without danger to themselves, could they get Him into their power? Alas! there was one at hand ready to help them.

Meantime our Lord, who knew every word spoken in their secret councils, was on His way to Jerusalem. His hour was now nearly come, and He went forth bravely to meet it. St. Mark tells us that He walked so fast, on this His last journey to the Holy City, that the Twelve "were astonished and following Him were afraid." Some vague apprehension of coming trouble frightened them, though they did not understand that the redemption of the world was to be wrought by means of the sufferings and death of which their Master had now so frequently spoken. The Kingdom! the Kingdom! this was the cry of their hearts still.

The hatred of the rulers was too plainly expressed to be any secret to the people, and many who would have liked to show our Lord gratitude and hospitality were hindered from doing so by their fear of those in power. No one wanted to get into trouble with the Sanhedrin, that formidable council which could pass and carry out any sentence excepting only that of death.

There was one house, however, where our Lord was always welcome, one family that counted the happiness of having Him under its roof to be worth any risk and any penalty. Let us make the acquaintance of this blessed family.

To the south-east of Jerusalem, separated from the City by the brook Kedron, lay the Mount of Olives, so called from the number of olive trees with which it was covered. On its eastern side the Mount sloped down to a village about a mile and a half from Jerusalem, named Bethany. Here the sisters Martha and Mary lived with their brother Lazarus, a quiet, happy little household, united by the closest affection, and having as their intimate Friend and frequent

Guest the Son of God Himself.

In character the sisters were very different, and each had her own way of entertaining our Blessed Lord. Martha, the mistress of the house, was a practical woman, full of activity and energy. She went here and there seeing herself to all the preparations. No trouble must be spared to make the house look nice; the setting out of the table, the flowers and brightness everywhere, must testify to the heartiness of her welcome and her sense of the honour done to her by His visit.

Of Mary we know something already, for, though it is not certain that she is the same as Mary Magdalen, this is the common opinion. We are not surprised, therefore, to find her sitting at the feet of Jesus, so absorbed by His Presence and conversation as to be unmindful of all beside.

What joy there was in this little home when He was expected! As evening fell the three would go up to the flat roof of the house to watch for the white Figure coming slowly over the brow of the hill, sometimes with the Twelve, sometimes alone. Then they would go out on to the road to meet Him and reverently bring Him within and give Him of their best. Martha never thought she had done enough by way of preparation, and so it was with dismay she found one day that He had come without warning and lovingly taken them by surprise. Things were not ready, and there was no time to provide. However, she set to work with hearty good will, hurrying here and there, and beholding, not without displeasure, Mary seated as usual silent and still

AT BETHANY

*"Mary hath chosen the best part,
which shall not be taken away from her."*
(Luke 10:42)

at the Master's feet. Could she not see how much there was to do? It was selfish of her to sit there thinking of her own satisfaction only. So thought poor Martha as she passed and repassed the two sitting apart, and heard the low tones of the Master's voice, and saw Mary's rapt and reverent face. At last she turned round and spoke:

"Master, hast Thou no care that my sister hath left me alone to serve? Speak to her, therefore, that she help me."

Our Lord looked up:

"Martha, Martha," He said, "thou art careful and art troubled about many things. But one thing is necessary. Mary hath chosen the best part, which shall not be taken away from her."

He was not displeased; how should He be? He who had noticed the want of hospitality in the house of Simon the Pharisee, could He blame His eager hostess here? He had watched her loading the table with meats, and fruit, and flowers, and had accepted the love and generosity of her heart. But there was a little too much fret and fuss, and this He gently corrected. She need not have been put out because her sister's way of entertaining the Master was different from her own, and it was almost like blaming His indulgence with Mary to have found fault with her in His Presence. "Martha, Martha!" He repeated her name twice, a mark of great affection, and there was more of love than of rebuke in His tone. Both the sisters were very dear to Him. Martha was something like Peter, an ardent, eager soul, and, as we shall see presently, she has the glory of making her profession of faith in the same words as those at Cæsarea, which won for Peter the Headship of the Church.

Now it happened that Lazarus fell ill, and, of course, the first thought of his sisters was to send word to Jesus.

"Lord, behold he whom Thou lovest is sick!"

This was the message. No mention that the danger was great, no prayer that He would come quickly. What need for this? He who hastened when a stranger called Him, what would He not do for them! The sick man grew worse and they saw the end must come even before their messenger could reach the Master who was across the Jordan in Perea. But what of that! He knew it all before, and no doubt was even now on His way to them. So, whilst one sat by the deathbed, the other from the roof watched the road for the first sign of His approach.

But He did not come, and Lazarus died. Up to the last moment they had hoped, and each time the door opened they had turned to welcome their Lord. Now all was over, and, when that same day, having left their dearly loved brother in his cave sepulchre, they returned to the desolate home, who shall tell the anguish of their hearts!

During the days of mourning they sat upon the ground, their heads veiled, their feet bare, silent and lonely amid the lamentations of the hired mourners and the noise of friends and comforters coming and going. If Jesus is not our Comforter in trouble, we are exceedingly sad and desolate as were these poor sisters. People, meaning to be kind, expressed surprise at His absence; thought He was such a Friend of theirs who would have been the first to hasten to them in their distress; but, of course, He did not know how ill Lazarus was. Every word was agony to the mourners. And they could say nothing in reply. It was indeed strange. But they struggled bravely with temptation and would not let His absence or His silence shake their trust in Him. Then their messenger returned, saying that on hearing of their trouble the Master had merely said the sickness was not unto death, and had turned again to His teaching. They heard and bore their anguish in silence, and trusted still.

Now, why did our Lord try them so sorely? The words of St. John sound strange to us: "Now Jesus loved Martha and her sister Mary and Lazarus. When He had heard, therefore, that he was sick, He still remained in the same place two days." God's ways are not like ours. But His ways are always best, as we shall see clearly some day.

After two days our Lord said to His disciples: "Let us go into Judea again."

The disciples said to Him: "Rabbi, the Jews but now sought to stone Thee, and goest Thou thither again?"

Jesus said to them: "Lazarus, our friend, sleepeth, but I go that I may awake him out of sleep."

His disciples said: "Lord, if he sleep he shall do well."

But Jesus spoke of his death, and they thought He spoke of the repose of sleep.

Then Jesus said to them plainly: "Lazarus is dead, and I am glad for your sakes that I was not there, that you may believe. But let us go to him."

Thomas said to his fellow-disciples: "Let us also go that we may die with Him."

Jesus, therefore, came and found that he had been four days already in the grave. And many of the Jews were come to Martha and Mary to comfort them concerning their brother. Martha, therefore, as soon as she heard that Jesus was come, went to meet Him, but Mary sat at home.

Martha, therefore, said to Jesus: "Lord, if Thou hadst been here, my brother had not died."

It was not lament, still less complaint—only that plaintive word that the sisters had said again and again to one another during those days of watching and waiting.

She went on: "But now also I know that whatsoever Thou wilt ask of God, God will give it Thee."

She asks nothing, but holds up her faith and her trust to Him, a silent prayer, to be heard as He shall see best.

Jesus saith to her: "Thy brother shall rise again."

Martha saith to Him: "I know that he shall rise again in the resurrection at the last day."

Jesus said to her: "I am the resurrection and the life; he that believeth in Me, although he be dead, shall live. . . . Believest thou this?"

She saith to Him: "Yea, Lord, I have believed that Thou art Christ the Son of the living God, who art come into this world."

The grand confession of Cæsarea Philippi over again!

And, when she had said these things, she went and called her sister Mary secretly, saying: "The Master is come and calleth for thee."

She, as soon as she heard this, riseth quickly and cometh to Him. The Jews, therefore, who were with her in the house and comforted her, when they saw Mary that she rose up speedily and went out, followed her, saying: "She goeth to the grave to weep there."

When Mary, therefore, was come where Jesus was, seeing Him, she fell down at His feet and saith to Him: "Lord, if Thou hadst been here, my brother had not died."

Jesus, therefore, when He saw her weeping, and the Jews that were come with her weeping, groaned in the spirit, and troubled Himself, and said: "Where have you laid him?"

They say to Him: "Lord, come and see."

And Jesus wept.

The Jews, therefore, said: "Behold how He loved him."

But some of them said: "Could not He that opened the eyes of the man born blind have caused that this man should not die?"

Jesus, therefore, again groaning in Himself, cometh to the sepulchre. Now it was a cave, and a stone was laid over it.

Lazarus raised from the Dead

"And presently he that had been dead came forth, bound feet and hands with winding bands"

(John 11:44)

Jesus saith: "Take away the stone."

Martha saith to Him: "Lord, by this time he stinketh, for he is now of four days."

Jesus saith to her: "Did not I say to thee that if thou believe thou shalt see the glory of God?"

They took, therefore, the stone away.

And Jesus, lifting up His eyes, said: "Father, I give Thee thanks that Thou hast heard Me. And I know that Thou heareth Me always, but because of the people that stand about have I said it, that they may believe that Thou hast sent Me."

When He had said these things, He cried with a loud voice: "Lazarus, come forth."

And, presently, he that had been dead came forth, bound feet and hands with winding-bands, and his face was bound about with a napkin.

Jesus said to them: "Loose him and let him go."

Many, therefore, of the Jews who were come to Mary and Martha, and had seen the things that Jesus did, believed in Him.

We have had the account of this wondrous scene in the words of St. John who saw it. He does not go on to tell us what followed—of the trembling hands that unloosed the graveclothes, of the awe and the thankfulness with which the sisters and their brother fell at the feet of Jesus. But he says that some who witnessed that stupendous miracle went to the Pharisees and told them the things that Jesus had done, and that the chief priests and the Pharisees gathered a council of the Sanhedrists and said:

"What do we, for this Man doth many miracles? If we let Him alone so all men will believe in Him, and the Romans will come and take away our place and nation."

But Caiaphas, being the High Priest of that year, said to them: "You know nothing, neither do you consider that it is expedient for you that one man should die for the people, and that the whole nation perish not."

From that day, therefore, they devised to put Him to death. Wherefore Jesus walked no more openly among the Jews, but went to a city called Ephrem, and there abode with His disciples till the time came for His final journey to Jerusalem.

He can do no more. He has filled the land with the "signs" demanded of Him. He has fulfilled the prophecies and proved Himself the Promised One who was to be sent. It only remains for Him to show Himself the Man of Sorrows, foretold by the prophets, and, as the High Priest had prophesied—to die for the people.

XXXVI.
The Beginning of the End

At last His hour was come. It was time to go up to Jerusalem for the offering of the Great Sacrifice.

Before setting out, He took the disciples apart and said to them:

"Behold, we go up to Jerusalem, and the Son of Man shall be betrayed to the chief priests and the scribes, and they shall condemn Him to death, and shall deliver Him to the Gentiles to be mocked, and scourged, and crucified, and the third day He shall rise again."

St. Luke tells us that "they understood none of these things." Accustomed to see Him followed by admiring crowds, untouched by the hands raised to stone Him, and by the officers sent to make Him prisoner, they would not believe that harm could come to Him. On the contrary, they thought He was going up to Jerusalem to take possession of His throne and begin His glorious reign as the Messiah-King. He had promised them that they too should sit on thrones. It was time to remind Him of this and to secure the first places in the new Kingdom. So at least thought James and John. They slipped away from the rest and returned

The Beginning of the End

presently with their mother, who came with them to our Lord, adoring and asking something of Him:

"Master," they said, "we desire that whatsoever we shall ask Thou wouldst do it for us."

"What would you that I should do for you?" He replied.

"Grant to us that we may sit, the one on Thy right hand and the other on Thy left in Thy glory."

What a time for such a petition! When He had scarcely finished speaking of His bitter sufferings that were at hand—then to come begging for honours! Yet their gentle Master did not reproach them.

"You know not what you ask," He said. "Can you drink of the chalice that I drink of?"

They said to Him: "We can."

He said to them: "Of My chalice indeed you shall drink, but to sit on My right hand or on My left is not Mine to give to you, but for them for whom it is prepared by My Father."

And the ten hearing it began to be much displeased with James and John. Jesus called them all round Him and told them that in His Kingdom those who want to be first must make themselves the servants of the rest. This settled the dispute for the time. He knew the day would come when, by the grace of His Holy Spirit, these jealousies, quarrels and desires of earthly greatness would cease—and He waited.

On His way to Jerusalem our Lord was accompanied by a multitude of pilgrims going up for the Passover, and as they approached Jericho the crowd around Him became enormous. Past the gardens of roses, for which the city was famous, past the orchards of figs and dates, it moved slowly along till He suddenly stopped beneath a sycamore tree growing by the wayside, and looked up. The crowd came to a standstill. Zaccheus, the chief of the tax gatherers, had climbed up there because he wanted to see Jesus, who, he had been told, was the Friend of publicans and sinners. He was too short to see over the shoulders of others, and no one would make way for him. He had made himself rich at the expense of his fellow-countrymen and in the service of the Romans, and, therefore, was hated and despised by all. But he was determined to see Jesus, and, without minding the laughter of the passers by, had climbed up into the tree beneath which the Lord must pass. What was his astonishment to see Him stop, look up, and call him by his name:

"Zaccheus, make haste and come down, for this day I must abide in thy house."

His house! the house of a publican! He of all that crowd to have the honour of entertaining the Master! "He made haste and came down," says St. Luke, "and received Him with joy. And, when all saw it, they murmured, saying that He was gone to be a guest with a man that was a sinner." Zaccheus took the harsh judgment humbly; his heart was too full of gladness to mind it, and he was ready to pay any price for the favour shown him. He came and stood before our Lord

ZACCHEUS

*"Looking up, he saw him, and said to him: Zaccheus,
make haste and come down; for this day I must abide in thy house."*
(Luke 19:5)

to make his confession and purpose of amendment and satisfaction:

"Behold, Lord," he said, "the half of my goods I give to the poor, and if I have wronged any man of anything, I restore him fourfold."

Jesus said to him: "This day is salvation come to this house. For the Son of Man is come to seek and to save that which was lost."

Here was the absolution.

Next morning our Lord set out again on His way, "a very great multitude" going before, following, thronging Him as before.

Blind Bartimeus, the beggar, sat by the wayside, and hearing the tramping past of many feet, he asked what it meant, and was told that Jesus of Nazareth was passing by. An intense desire to recover his sight sprang up within him:

"Jesus, Son of David," he cried, "have mercy on me!"

And many rebuked him that he might hold his peace, but he cried a great deal more: "Son of David, have mercy on me!"

And Jesus standing still commanded him to be called. The people were kinder then: "Be of better comfort," they said, "arise, He calleth thee."

He leaped up, cast aside his outer garment that he might move the faster, flung out his arms for some one to lead him. And, trembling with hope, came and fell down at our Lord's feet, his hands clasped, his sightless eyes lifted to the face of Jesus.

Bartimeus The Blind Man

"Jesus son of David, have mercy on me!"
(Mark 10:47)

"What wilt thou that I do for thee?" Jesus asked.

"Rabboni, that I may see!"

"Go thy way, thy faith hath made thee whole."

And immediately he saw and followed Him in the way glorifying God. And all the people, when they saw it, gave praise to God.

Accompanied by the crowd, our Lord went on to Bethany, where He arrived on Friday, "six days before the Passover," says St. John, for Thursday, when the Paschal lamb was slain, was regarded as the first day of the Festival. With the Twelve He went to the house of His friends, leaving the multitude to go on to Jerusalem. The excitement there was intense, both among rulers and people, for the chief priests had now given commandment that if anyone knew where Jesus of Nazareth was he was to tell them, that they might apprehend Him. On every side inquiries were being made for Him. Standing in the Temple men said to one another:

"What think you that He has not come to the festival day?"

Presently word was brought by the crowds from Jericho that He was at Bethany. At once a great multitude flocked out there, not for Jesus' sake only, but that they might see Lazarus whom He had raised from the dead. Numbers came back believing in Him. Enraged beyond measure at the enthusiasm spreading on every side, the chief priests thought of killing Lazarus also. From this time forward it is these priests who take

The Beginning of the End

the lead in all the plots for bringing our Lord to death. The people, in Galilee especially, believed in Him, but the rulers—the Scribes and Pharisees, the ancients, the wealthy Sadducees, the Herodians, the Sanhedrin, and the priests, who had been against Him from the first, were only hardened by His miracles. The resurrection of Lazarus at the very gates of Jerusalem brought their fury to a climax. But nothing could be done as long as He had these huge crowds as a bodyguard. His reputation, then, must be destroyed and the people turned against Him.

In and out, then, among the crowds went the rulers stirring the people up against Jesus of Nazareth, declaring in words of fierce indignation that He was a blasphemer, who gave Himself out to be the Son of God, a friend of publicans and sinners, an impostor who pretended to be the Messiah, and would get them all into dreadful trouble with the Romans, as other impostors had done, a dealer with the Evil One, by whose help He cast out devils. The people were puzzled; they saw that all the respectable part of the nation was against Him; they were terrified of the Romans, and they began to waver.

This was the state of things in Jerusalem.

On Friday and Saturday our Lord remained quietly with His friends at Bethany. They were always glad to have Him under their roof, and now more than ever when others whom He had loved and comforted were afraid to harbour Him or show Him gratitude.

On Saturday evening He was at the house of Simon the Leper, in the same place, and St. John says they made Him a supper there. It was a wealthy home, and everything provided was of the best. Our Lord was in the place of honour, and, as the guests reclined round the tables, every eye turned in wonder and admiration to the calm face of Him who lay there upon His couch, so grave yet so attractive, the Man whom the rulers were hunting to His death. Beside Him was His friend Lazarus, whom He had raised from the dead. The presence of those two made the supper a time of solemn thought; the guests spoke quietly, noise and merriment were felt to be out of place.

Martha did the honours and served, more quietly than once before, but eager still, delighted to be near our Lord, to show reverence to Him and His, waiting on the disciples herself that their awkward ways might pass unnoticed, and by her kindness and heartiness making them feel at home.

During the supper Mary came in carrying in an alabaster box a pound of ointment of precious spikenard. She anointed the feet of Jesus as before and wiped them with her hair, and, breaking the box, poured it out upon His head, and the house was filled with the fragrance of the ointment. At this Judas, usually so cautious and silent, could not conceal his vexation, and, unmindful both of the reverence due to his Master and of what was becoming in a guest, called out:

"Why was not this ointment sold for three hundred pence and given to the poor?"

The Alabaster Box

*"She hath done what she could:
she is come beforehand to anoint my body for burial."*
(Mark 14:8)

"Now he said this," says St. John, "not because he cared for the poor, but because he was a thief, and, having the purse, carried the things that were put therein." The other disciples, some of them at least, followed his example, and, filled with indignation, said:

"To what purpose is this waste?"

"Let her alone, why do you molest her?" said our Lord. "She hath wrought a good work upon Me. For the poor you have always with you, and whensoever you will you may do them good, but Me you have not always. What she had she hath done; she is come beforehand to anoint My body for the burial. Amen I say to you, wheresoever this Gospel shall be preached in the whole world, that also which she hath done shall be told for a memory of her."

XXXVII.
"Jerusalem! Jerusalem!"

We have come to the last week of our Lord's Life. The Evangelists could not set down all the wonders of that Life, for St. John tells us every day was filled with marvels. But when they come to this last week they follow their Lord, as it were, with slower and more reverent step, giving a fuller and more minute account of His actions day by day.

There are many reasons for this. It is not only that in this week He accomplished the great work He came to do; redeemed us from sin and hell; reconciled us with His Father; opened the gates of Heaven to us, and set up the New Law, the New Sacraments, the New Priesthood in place of the Old; but it is because in this week the tenderness of His love comes out more wonderfully than ever. His words and acts and prayers are so brimming over with love and sweetness that the Evangelists could not bear to pass them over in silence. We owe these blessed writers more for their account of this week than for all beside. And we should come to the history of these last days of our dear Lord's Life on earth with hearts more reverent, more full of love and gratitude than hitherto, that we may believe and understand and feel about them as is pleasing to Him and helpful to our own souls.

The day after the supper in Simon's house was chosen by Christ for His solemn entry into the City in which such great things were to be done. Accompanied by the Twelve and by a crowd going up for the Feast, He left Bethany. When they had reached Bethphage, a village on the eastern slope of Olivet, He sent two of His disciples, saying to them:

"Go ye into the village that is over against you, and immediately you shall find an ass tied and a colt with her, on which no man hath ever sitten; loose them and bring them to Me. And if any man shall say anything to you, say ye that the Lord hath need of them, and forthwith he will let them go."

"Now all this was done," says St. Matthew, "that it might be fulfilled which was spoken by the prophet saying: "Tell ye the daughter of Sion: Behold, thy King cometh to thee meek, and sitting on an ass, and a colt, the foal of her that is used to the yoke." Every prophecy concerning Him was clearly before the mind of our Blessed Saviour, and, at the proper time, He fulfilled each even to its smallest circumstances. This exact fulfilment of prophecy was one of the marks by which the Jews ought to have known Him to be the Messiah, but they would not notice what they did not want to see.

The disciples found the colt and its mother tied to the gate just as Jesus had said, and they began to loose them.

"What are you doing loosing the colt?" cried out the owners.

They answered as Jesus had told them, and the owners let the animals go.

The disciples brought them to Jesus and laid their long cloaks upon the colt by way of trappings, and He sat upon it. The procession formed about Him and began its march, the solemn entry of the Messiah-King into His capital, solemn and yet so humble, the King riding on a little creature not yet broken in, and followed, not by the royal guards, but by a joyous throng, men, women, and children, chiefly the poor, who crowded round Him and filled the air with their shouts of gladness. "A very great multitude," we are told, "spread their garments in the way, and others cut boughs from the trees and strewed them in the way."

When, following the steep footpath up the Mount, they had reached the summit, they halted, for another multitude from Jerusalem was making its way up the western slope. News had spread through the City that Jesus of Nazareth, who had raised Lazarus to life, was on His way thither, and the people were pouring out to meet Him and take Him back in triumph. The two multitudes met and mingled at that point of the road from which the City first bursts full on the view. Jerusalem in all its majesty appeared beneath, and at the sight the whole concourse of His disciples, they

JESUS ENTERS JERUSALEM

"Hosanna to the son of David:
Blessed is he that cometh in the name of the Lord"
(Mt 21:9)

that went before and they that followed, began with joy to praise God with a loud voice for all the mighty works they had seen, saying:

"Blessed be the King who cometh in the name of the Lord, peace in Heaven and glory on high! Hosanna to the Son of David! Blessed be the Kingdom of our father David that cometh, Hosanna in the highest!"

There were some Pharisees in the vast procession, and at their old occupation of faultfinding. Having tried in vain to stop the shouts of joy, they made their way up to our Lord and said to Him:

"Master, rebuke Thy disciples."

He said to them: "I say to you that if these shall hold their peace, the stones will cry out."

The disciples were beside themselves with delight. "It has come at last!" they said to one another as they walked proudly by their Master's side. And right heartily did they wave their palms and join in the cry:

"Blessed be the Kingdom of our father David that cometh, Hosanna in the highest!"

There, on the summit of Olivet, stood the procession facing the City. Palaces, towers, battlements, gardens, lay bathed in the warm glow of the afternoon sun; and, towering above all, appeared the snowy marble and glittering gold of the gorgeous Temple, the pride and the joy of every child of Israel. The people were bringing her King, her long-expected Messiah, to Jerusalem, and at the sight of the City rising there in all her glory, their joyous shouts broke out afresh.

And the King Himself—how did He look upon Jerusalem?

St. Luke tells us: "And when He drew near the City He wept over it, saying:

"If thou also hadst known and that in this thy day the things that are to thy peace! but now they are hidden from thy eyes. For the days shall come upon thee, and thy enemies shall cast a trench about thee, and compass thee round, and straiten thee on every side, and beat thee flat to the ground and thy children who are in thee; and they shall not leave in thee a stone upon a stone, because thou hast not known the time of thy visitation."

He knew what was coming—that in five days He would be hanging in agony on a cross outside the walls, forsaken by all. But it was not this that brought the tears to His eyes. It was the misery of the guilty City that was about to reject Him and pray that His Blood might be upon her and upon her children. He looked forward forty years and thought of the horrors of that awful siege when, at just such a Passover as this, the Roman army would close round the walls and the starving millions within; when the Temple would be burnt to the ground; when there would not be wood enough for the numbers to be crucified, nor purchasers for the thousands sold into slavery. He knew what was coming upon poor Jerusalem, and His tears were for her.

Amid cries of joy and waving of branches, the children running on before shouting "Hosanna, blessed

JERUSALEM

"And when he drew near, seeing the city, he wept over it"
(Luke 19:41)

be He that cometh in the name of the Lord!" He entered Jerusalem. And the whole City was moved. Men, women and children swarmed on to the roofs and out into the streets to ask:

"Who is this?"

Those who were bringing in our Lord answered triumphantly:

"This is Jesus, the Prophet of Nazareth."

Under their breath the Pharisees muttered to one another: "Do you see that we prevail nothing? Behold the whole world has gone after Him."

The crowds dispersed, our Lord dismounted, and followed by the Twelve entered the Temple. Let us see Him going in at the Beautiful Gate.

His form is slender and delicate. His hair falls over His shoulders beneath the handkerchief that binds His brow and covers the back of His neck. Over the tunic, a long robe girt in at the waist, is a wide cloak, or *abba*, blue bordered and tasselled at the corners. It falls over one shoulder, reaching nearly to the bottom of the tunic. The sandals, much worn, are merely soles strapped to the feet. Everything is simple, poor, travel-stained. Yet He is truly kingly as He moves forward among the throng. In His look, His bearing, His gestures, there is a marvellous mingling of majesty and humility. The charm of His Person, the graciousness of His ways, captivates the people and attracts even the little children, who crowd about Him. Yet those who love Him most worship Him with deepest awe. Never have men felt as they feel in the Presence of this Man. And no wonder, for He is not only truly Man—He is God!

Still singing "Hosanna!" which means "Save now!" the children followed Him into the Temple. They called upon the Levite children of the Temple choir to join them, and presently there rose up from the marble Court into the blue sky overhead the exquisite voices of the little choristers, welcoming our Blessed Lord in the *Hallel*, or hymn of praise they had ready for the Messiah's coming. The priests and the rulers disowned Him, but the children received Him with songs of gladness. Sweeter far and more pleasing to God than all the solemn chants of the Temple's magnificent worship, was that afternoon's Benediction service of the little children.

He needed their comfort, for His Heart was saddened by the same sights and sounds that had dishonoured His Father's House three years before. Up from the Court of the Gentiles came the cries of traders, the bleating of sheep, the wrangling of the money-changers—all the noise of a market, and a greater uproar than usual, for on this day the Paschal lamb was chosen, to be kept apart till the hour of sacrifice.

Our Lord said nothing. He had come to the Temple to offer Himself as the Lamb chosen from all eternity for sacrifice, and He would spend these last peaceful hours in the Temple Courts quietly with the children.

The blind and the lame came to Him and He healed them as the children stood around. Then, as evening fell, He went out to Bethany with the Twelve. The short triumph was over. Not one out of those multitudes who had hailed Him as Messiah in the morning had offered Him a shelter for the night. He climbed the path down which the procession had passed a few hours before, and came to the house at Bethany and was welcomed there.

Early next morning, Monday, on His way to Jerusalem, He saw a fig-tree in the distance. He went up to it, for He was hungry, And finding nothing on it but leaves, He said to it: "May no fruit grow on thee any more for ever." Coming into the Temple, He found in the Court of the Gentiles the same disgraceful scene as before—oxen, sheep and lambs huddled together by thousands, or being dragged hither and thither, traders shouting to one another, pilgrims from distant countries disputing in many languages with the money-changers.

Suddenly, above the confusion and the din, was heard a loud, clear Voice:

"My House shall be called the House of prayer, but you have made it a den of thieves."

Every head was turned to the Speaker. He stood upon a step looking down upon the scene. There was no scourge in His hand now; the Divine majesty that shone in His human face—this did the work of cleansing. The birdsellers caught up their cages as

The Barren Fig Tree

"And seeing a certain fig tree by the way side, he came to it, and found nothing on it but leaves only, and he saith to it: May no fruit grow on thee henceforward for ever."
(Mt 21:19)

best they might; the money-changers, the traders of every kind, fled before Him, content to drop and lose their wares rather than meet the indignation of that glance.

Not a word had the priests to say in self-defence. It was they who allowed this unholy trading, it was to them the profits went. They were stung to the quick by being thus disgraced, and consulted together how they might destroy Jesus. If only He in His turn could be put to shame before the people, their credit might be restored. And at last they hit on a plan for bringing this about.

Everyone knew that the scribes, whose task it was to interpret the Law, were only ordained after long study, and empowered to teach by the delivery of a tablet and a key. Now, where had this carpenter of Nazareth studied? Let Him answer that and show His tablet and key before the people. If He should avoid this trap, they had another ready from which it would be impossible to escape. Some of the Herodians should go up to Him when He was teaching and pretend to have a difficulty of conscience about the tribute which every Jew had to pay to Caesar. Was it lawful to pay it or not? If He said it was not lawful, they would at once give Him over to Pontius Pilate and to the vengeance of Rome. If He should say it was lawful, the people would turn upon Him as a traitor to His country. Now, then, they had Him safe. They were so delighted with their scheme that they were impatient for His hour of teaching on the morrow.

As our Lord with the Twelve came over Olivet on Tuesday morning they passed the fig-tree, or rather the place where it had stood, for it was withered away to the very roots. "And the disciples seeing it wondered," says St. Matthew. Our Lord entered the Temple and made His way through the crowd already waiting for Him to the Court of the Women, the common meeting place of worshippers. He was walking in one of the Porches there when a number of chief priests, scribes and ancients were seen advancing. They were Sanhedrists, and the people respectfully made way before them. Coming up to Jesus, they addressed Him in a lofty tone:

"Tell us by what authority Thou dost these things, and who hath given Thee this authority."

Jesus answering said to them: "I also will ask you one word, which, if you shall tell Me, I will also tell you by what authority I do these things. "Was John the Baptist a prophet sent from God or not?"

They were silent and thought within themselves: If we say he was a prophet from God He will ask: Why, then, did you not believe in Him? If we say he was no prophet we are afraid of the people. And they said:

"We know not."

He said to them: "Neither do I tell you by what authority I do these things."

He went on to tell them a parable of a householder who sent servant after servant to the husbandmen in charge of his vineyard to receive the fruits from them. And the husbandmen beat, and wounded, and killed

The Coin of the Tribute

"Render therefore to Caesar the things that are Caesar's: and to God the things that are God's."
(Luke 20:25)

them. Having yet one son most dear to him, He also sent him unto them last of all, saying: "I will send my beloved son; it may be when they see him they will reverence him." And the husbandmen said: "This is the heir, let us kill him and we shall have his inheritance." And, taking him, they cast him forth out of the vineyard and killed him.

After this our Lord told the parable of a king who made a marriage for his son, and those who were invited would not come. So the king gave their places to others. His enemies knew that in these parables He spoke of them, and they were filled with rage; but the people were there and they could do nothing.

A party of the Herodians now came up, and one of them, bowing low before Him, said:

"Master, we know that Thou art a true speaker and teachest the way of God in truth. Tell us, therefore, is it lawful to give tribute to Cæsar or not?"

But Jesus, knowing their wickedness, said: "Why do ye tempt Me, ye hypocrites? Show Me the coin of the tribute."

And they offered Him a penny.

Jesus said to them: "Whose image and superscription is this?"

They say to Him: " Cæsar's."

He said to them: "Render therefore to Cæsar the things that are Cæsar's and to God the things that are God's."

What could they say? By their own law he was the owner of a country whose image and inscription were found on its coins. They were so filled with wonder at His answer, that they could neither reply nor hide their confusion. The best thing to do was to get away as fast as possible. And this they did.

Thus did His enemies come up one after another, to have their plots overthrown as easily as a child's house of cards. The people watched Him with admiration. They saw Him interrupted continually in His teaching by His malignant foes, yet bearing Himself with a royal dignity and calmness that neither insult nor cowardly cunning could disturb.

Will the people keep faithful to Him when the hour of trial comes? We shall see.

Our Lord had borne long and patiently with the Pharisees. But, seeing that they were hardening their hearts more and more and doing grievous harm to others, He at length pronounced against them those terrible condemnations which make us tremble as we hear them. Again and again came the fearful words:

"Woe to you Scribes and Pharisees, hypocrites!"

He rebuked their pride, their avarice, their cunning. He would still send His servants to teach them and warn them of the judgments that were at hand, but they would persecute and scourge and crucify them.

"Jerusalem! Jerusalem!" He cried, "thou that killest the prophets and stonest them that are sent to thee, how often would I have gathered together thy children as the hen gathers her chickens under her wings and thou wouldst not. Behold, your house shall be left to you desolate. For I say to you, you shall not see Me henceforth till you say: 'Blessed is He that cometh in the name of the Lord.'"

Leaving the rulers, He went and sat down near the Treasury and watched the people dropping their offerings into the trumpet-shaped chests that stood there. Many that were rich cast in much. And there came a certain poor widow, and she cast in two mites, which make a farthing. And, calling His disciples together, He said to them:

"Amen, I say to you this poor widow hath cast in more than all. For all they did cast in of their abundance, but she of her want hath cast in all she had, even her whole living."

He took His final leave of the Temple that Tuesday. The disciples, struck by His sadness, followed Him in silence down into the valley and across the brook Cedron and up the slope of Olivet. But He could not leave the city without another farewell glance. He loved Jerusalem, and His heart was breaking at the thought of what it was, what it might have been, what in a few years it was to come to.

Arrived at the summit of the Mount, He turned and faced the City. So beautiful it looked in the quiet glow of evening, its massive walls, palaces, terraces, the snowy colonnades and golden roofing of the Temple, all lit up by the setting sun, that one of the disciples said to Him:

"Master, behold what manner of stones and what buildings are here."

The Widow's Mite

"Amen I say to you, this poor widow hath cast in more than all."
(Mark 12:43)

And Jesus answering said to him: "Seest thou all these great buildings? There shall not be left a stone upon a stone that shall not be thrown down."

He seated Himself on a ledge of rock facing the Temple, and seemed lost in thought. Peter, Andrew, James, and John came and asked Him apart:

"Tell us when shall these things be, and what shall be the sign of Thy coming and of the end of the world?"

Then He told them what would happen before the destruction of Jerusalem and before the Last Day. The way to Heaven for His followers would be through troubles of every kind. "But he that shall persevere to the end," said Jesus, "he shall be saved."

As the awful Day of Judgment draws near, there will be signs in the sun and in the moon and in the stars, earthquakes and pestilence and famine, and roaring of the sea and of the waves, men withering away for fear and expectation of what shall come upon the whole world.

And yet, in spite of these signs and terrors, the Great Day will come suddenly at last and find men in the midst of their enjoyments and sins. Like a flash of lightning, seen by all, startling all—so will He come, His servants must be always ready, not so much for the Last Day of the world as for the day of their death, which will be the Last Day for each one of us. He told them the parable of the Ten Virgins who had to meet the Bridegroom with lighted lamps. And five were foolish and took no oil with them. And when at midnight came the sudden cry: "Behold, the

Bridegroom cometh, go ye forth to meet Him!" they were not ready and were shut out.

"Watch ye, therefore," He said, "for you know not when the lord of the house cometh. And what I say to you I say to all: 'Watch!'"

He went on to tell them what will happen at the end of the world when He comes to judge all men:

"They shall see the Son of Man coming in the clouds of Heaven with much power and majesty. And He shall send His Angels with a trumpet and a great voice; and they shall gather together His elect from the four winds, from the farthest parts of the heavens to the utmost bounds of them. And all nations shall be gathered together before Him, and He shall separate them one from another as the shepherd separateth the sheep from the goats, and He shall set the sheep on His right hand, but the goats on His left.

Then shall the King say to them that shall be on His right hand:

Come, ye blessed of My Father, possess you the Kingdom prepared for you from the foundation of the world.

Then He shall say to them also that shall be on His left hand:

Depart from Me, you cursed, into everlasting fire which was prepared for the devil and his angels.

And these shall go into everlasting punishment, but the just into life everlasting."

THE LAST JUDGEMENT

"They shall see the Son of man coming in the clouds of heaven with much power and majesty."

(Mt 24:30)

XXXVIII.
The Night in which He was Betrayed

Our Lord had foretold His Passion again and again, but vaguely, naming no time. Now, on the Wednesday of this week, He said to the Twelve:

"You know that after two days shall be the Passover, and the Son of Man shall be delivered up to be crucified."

His enemies, too, were preparing for the end. On Wednesday the Sanhedrists met at the house of Caiaphas to make their final plans. They dared not take Jesus by force nor in the Temple; for this would provoke the people and draw down their anger upon themselves. If only they could seize Him secretly and get the Romans to make away with Him!

Whilst they were considering how this could be brought about, they were told that a man, one of the common sort, craved admittance. He entered with signs of profound reverence, having come, he said, in obedience to their command that whoever should know where Jesus of Nazareth was should declare it to them.

Judas agrees to betray Jesus

"What will you give me, and I will deliver him unto you?"
(Mt 26:14-15)

"What will you give me," he asked, "and I will deliver Him unto you?" He told them that as one of His disciples he was constantly with Him, knew His secrets, and would be able to do the business for them quietly and securely.

Bad as these men were, and delighted at this unexpected succour, they could scarcely disguise their contempt for the traitor. They accepted his services, however, and for thirty pieces of silver, about $19.50 of our money,[1] he agreed to deliver his Master into their hands as soon as he should find a convenient opportunity when there was no one about to help Him. Thus were the words of the prophet Zacharias fulfilled: "And they weighed for my wages thirty pieces of silver, a handsome price that I was prized at by them."

How had Judas come to this?

Because of that one evil passion which he did not try to conquer. His fall was not sudden. At the time of his call he would have been horrified at the thought of such a crime. But his heart had hardened gradually, and at last, when temptation came, he betrayed and sold for a few pieces of silver the Master for whom he had left all things.

Whilst Judas in Jerusalem was plotting with the Sanhedrists, our Lord in the quiet home of Bethany was preparing His disciples for His coming Passion and Death. Probably His Blessed Mother was there, too. He had told her what was to happen to Him, and

---

1   This is roughly $500 in today's money.

though her heart was breaking, she did not try like Peter to save Him from suffering and a cruel death, but bravely and generously accepted the Will of God.

On Thursday morning the disciples came to Jesus, saying:

"Where wilt Thou that we prepare for Thee to eat the Passover?"

Judas quietly drew near to hear the answer.

Jesus said: "Go ye into the city, and there shall meet you a man carrying a pitcher of water. Follow him into the house where he entereth in. And you shall say to the good man of the house: The Master saith to thee, Where is the guest-chamber where I may eat the Passover with My disciples? And he will show you a large dining-room furnished, and there prepare."

Judas was baffled, but, as keeper of the purse, be would probably be sent, and he stood forward ready. No, Peter and John were to go, and he was foiled again. That Supper Room was to be the scene of holiest mysteries; our Lord was not going to have them disturbed nor the house of His entertainer invaded by Judas' armed band. At His own time and in another place He would suffer Himself to be taken, and in the meantime the traitor was kept in the dark.

Entering the City, Peter and John see the man with the pitcher on his head, and follow him, not without difficulty, through the narrow, thronged streets. Jews out of every nation under heaven, nearly three millions of them, are here—too many by far to be housed within the walls, though every house is taxed to its utmost.

Late comers are camping out on Olivet and all the country round as far as Bethany.

What variety of costume, and what a Babel of tongues! Here, in bright armour, come a body of Roman soldiers, for the Governor has come from Cæsarea as usual and taken up his quarters in the Prætorium. And in the fortress of Antonia, overlooking the Temple Courts, is a strong garrison of troops ready to swoop down upon the people at the least sign of disturbance—the Passover is wont to be a troublesome time. There go some courtly Herodians and wealthy Sadducees and despised publicans. Over there, above the heads of the crowd, appear the high turbans of rabbis. Priests, traders, Gentile strangers, slaves—through what a motley throng the two Apostles made their way!

They have come to a house on Mount Sion in the south-western quarter of the City. Here their guide stops, and they go in and give their message. The owner's face brightens at the first words: "The Master saith," and whilst Peter goes off to buy the lamb, he helps John to make everything ready in the upper chamber which he puts at our Lord's disposal. The Apostles wonder why he is so willing—he is a secret disciple, perhaps.

Peter buys the victim, a lamb without blemish of a year old, and takes it to the Temple, where it is killed. In preparing it for cooking the greatest care must be taken that no bone shall be broken. This lamb is a type of Him of whom the prophet had said: "They shall not break a bone of Him." Before being roasted it is

Betrayal

fastened to two pieces of wood, the front feet being stretched out in the form of a cross.

When Peter returns he finds all ready—on the tables the thin cakes of unleavened bread, the bitter herbs, the wine mixed with water, and a red sauce called *charoseth*. Round the low tables, forming a semi-circle, John had so arranged the couches that he would be on one side of his Master and Judas on the other, at one end of the tables, Peter opposite at the other end, the rest in pairs around, as he knew they would like. Pitchers of water and basins for washing hands were about the room, and the whole was lit up by festive lamps.

As evening drew on Jesus came with the other Apostles. When they had taken their places He said to them:

"With desire I have desired to eat this Pasch with you before I suffer."

Then John, as the youngest present, asked the meaning of this night's solemn service, and our Lord told the story of the deliverance from Egypt, of the sprinkling of the blood of the Paschal Lamb, of the Manna in the desert, and of the lifting up of the Brazen Serpent, by which their fathers of old were saved from death. As He looked upon the lamb stretched crosswise before Him, He thought of the morrow, when, after fifteen hundred years of types, the fulfillment would come, and the Lamb of God by His Death would take away the sins of the world.

During the Paschal Supper Jesus rose from the table, laid aside His upper garment, and, having taken

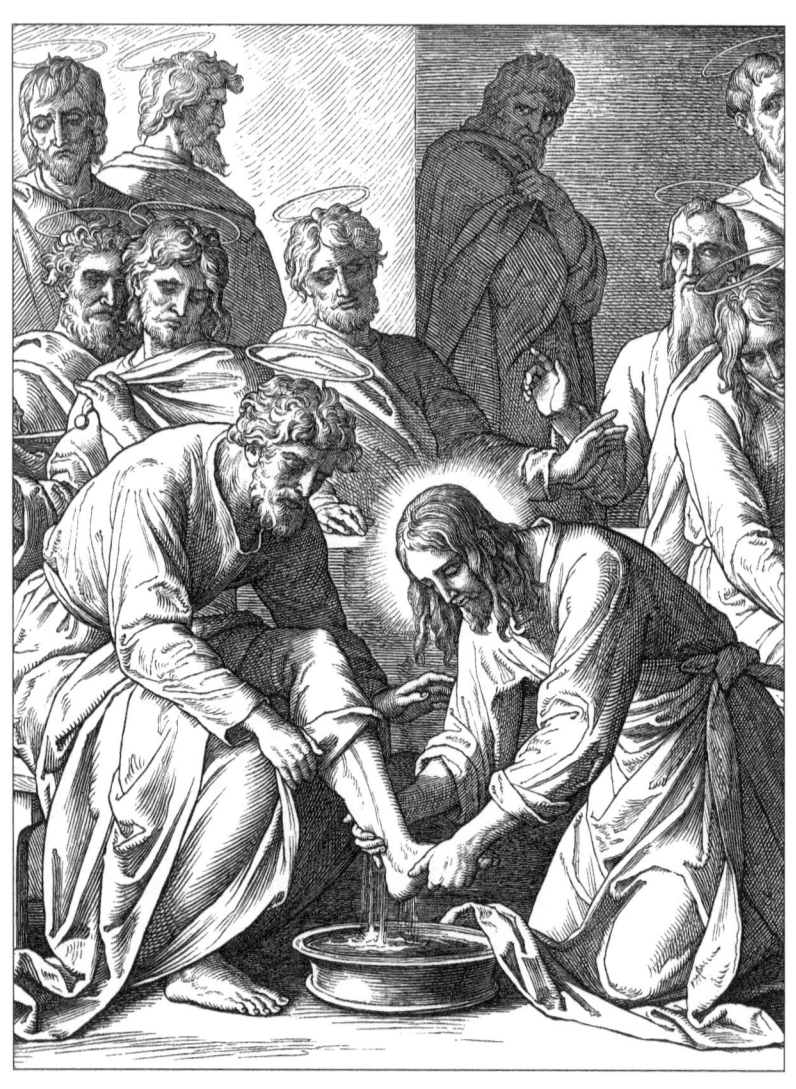

JESUS WASHES THE DISCIPLES' FEET

*"If then I, being your Lord and Master, have washed your feet;
you also ought to wash one another's feet."*
(John 13:14)

a towel, girded Himself. Then, pouring water into a basin, He came and knelt before Peter to wash his feet. Peter, all amazement, drew them up, exclaiming:

"Lord, dost Thou wash my feet?"

Jesus said to him: "What I do thou knowest not now, but thou shalt know hereafter."

Peter said to Him: "Thou shalt never wash my feet."

Jesus answered him: "If I wash thee not thou shalt have no part with Me."

Peter said to Him: "Lord, not only my feet but also my hands and my head."

Jesus said to him: "He that is washed needeth not but to wash his feet, but is clean wholly. And you are clean, but not all."

Then after He had washed their feet and taken His garments, being sat down again, He said to them:

"Know you what I have done to you? You call Me Master and Lord, and you say well, for so I am. If then I, being your Lord and Master, have washed your feet, you also ought to wash one another's feet. For I have given you an example that as I have done to you, so you do also."

Then He said to them sorrowfully:

"Amen, amen, I say to you, one of you shall betray Me."

The disciples in consternation looked upon one another, "doubting of whom He spoke," says St. John. And being very much troubled they began to say to Him one by one:

"Is it I, Lord?"

And He answering said: "One of the Twelve whose hand is with Me on the table, he shall betray Me. The Son of Man indeed goeth as it is written of Him, but woe to that man by whom the Son of Man shall be betrayed; it were better for him if that man had not been born."

Terrified at these awful words, the disciples were silent. But presently Judas, afraid of being noticed if he did not ask with the rest, said:

"Is it I, Rabbi?"

Jesus answered him in a whisper: "Thou hast said it."

How careful our Lord must have been of the good name of Judas, that not one of his fellow-disciples thought of suspecting him. Even now the miserable man was not afraid of his Master betraying him, or he would never have dared to put that question. What would have happened if Peter or the sons of Zebedee had heard those words: "Thou hast said it?"

The Heart of Jesus was wrung with anguish at the thought of the misery to which one of His chosen Twelve was rushing. Again and again during the supper He speaks of the betrayal, now in tender, now in terrible words, striving by fear when love had failed to save him before it is too late.

But now for a brief space the heavy cloud that overshadowed them all seemed lifted. For, as they looked upon the Master, they saw His countenance glow with a love and fervour so intense as to appear transfigured. He had cleared a little space in front of Him and taken into His holy and venerable hands one of the loaves of unleavened bread. And, whilst they looked on in wonder, He lifted up His eyes to Heaven, and, giving thanks, blessed, and broke, and gave to them, saying:

"Take ye and eat, this is My Body which is given for you. Do this for a commemoration of Me."

And they received from His hand what He gave—His true Body under the appearance of bread. Here, then, was the meaning of those mysterious words at Capharnaum: "The bread that I will give is My flesh for the life of the world." They did not understand even now, but He had the words of eternal life; they believed, and adored.

During the Paschal supper three cups of wine mixed with water were passed round from one guest to another. Standing before Jesus was the third cup, "the chalice of benediction," which had to be taken before the last hymns were sung. Jesus took it into His hands, and, giving thanks, blessed it and passed it to them, saying:

"Drink ye all of this. For this is My Blood of the New Testament which shall be shed for many unto the remission of sins."

And again they received what He gave them—His true Blood under the appearance of wine. They received not more than before, not more than we receive in Holy Communion, but under another appearance. And because it was Himself whole and

The First Eucharist

*"For this is my blood of the new testament,
which shall be shed for many unto remission of sins."*
(Mt 26:28)

entire, together with His Body and Blood were His Soul and Divinity, all that He has and is. Truly might the Beloved Disciple say of Jesus, instituting this Sacrament of Love, that "having loved His own, who were in the world, He loved them unto the end." Love, even such as His, can go no further. It is because it has gone so far that men refuse to believe.

The first Mass had been said; the first Consecration wrought; the first Communicants fed in the greatest of the Sacraments with the true Bread from Heaven; the first priests ordained. For Christ, as David had foretold, was to be a Priest, not once only, on Calvary, but "for ever," a Priest like Melchisedech, whose offering was bread and wine. The New Sacrifice was to be the Sacrifice of the Gentiles, as the prophet Malachy had foretold, offered in every land, at every hour, from the rising to the setting of the sun, not lessening but magnifying the first and bloody Sacrifice from which its virtue flows. Where but in the Sacrifice of the Mass shall we find these prophecies fulfilled? To carry on His office when He was gone, the great High-Priest had to ordain other priests, and this He did in these words: "Do this in commemoration of Me."

With bowed heads the first Communicants made their thanksgiving. When they looked again into their Master's face, the glow of exultation with which He had made us the greatest of His gifts had passed away, and once more there had settled on His brow the anguish of a friend betrayed. Peter could bear the dreadful suspense no longer. Being directly opposite to John, he beckoned to him and said:

"Who is it of whom He speaketh?"

John, leaning back on his couch, was resting his head on his Master's breast. He looked up into His face and said:

"Lord, who is it?"

Jesus answered: "He it is to whom I shall reach bread dipped."

And when He had moistened the bread, He gave it to Judas Iscariot. Then, seeing every warning lost on the traitor, He said to him: "What thou doest, do quickly."

No one at the table, St. John tells us, knew why this was said. They thought our Lord had sent Judas to buy something, or to give an alms to the poor. Judas at once rose and went out. And it was night.

The white light of the Paschal moon shone into the room and fell full on the Master's face. It was pale and troubled. And its trouble was reflected on all the faces round. The disciples were so accustomed to lean on Him, to cast all their care on Him, that they could only see with blank dismay the cloud upon that brow hitherto serene in every storm. A dim apprehension of coming sorrow, of parting from Him who was all in all to them, weighed heavily on them, and they looked at Him helplessly for comfort.

He did not disappoint them. Never before had His words been so tender:

In the Supper Room

"Amen I say to you, that one of you is about to betray me."
(Mt 26:21)

"Little children," He said, looking round upon them, "yet a little while I am with you. You shall seek Me, but whither I go you cannot come."

Peter said to Him: "Lord, whither goest Thou?"

Jesus answered: "Whither I go thou canst not follow Me now, but thou shalt follow hereafter."

Peter said to Him: "Why cannot I follow Thee now? I will lay down my life for Thee."

Jesus answered him: "Wilt thou lay down thy life for Me? Amen, amen, I say to thee, the cock shall not crow till thou deny Me thrice."

Peter deny his Master! The disciples were astonished. Of all the surprises to-night this was the greatest. But, if Peter is to fall away, some one else must be first. Who will it be? And at once they begin the old dispute—which of them is the greatest. But Peter, in spite of his fall, was not to lose the place to which his Master had raised him.

Our Lord went on: "Simon, Simon, behold Satan hath desired to have you that he may sift you as wheat; but I have prayed for thee that thy faith fail not, and thou being once converted confirm thy brethren."

Peter said to Him: "Lord, I am ready to go with Thee both to prison and to death."

And He said: "I say to thee, Peter, the cock shall not crow this day till thou thrice deniest that thou knowest Me."

Every act, every word of our Blessed Lord's at the Last Supper speaks of love. He is taking leave of

His dearly beloved disciples. He is giving them His farewell instructions. And now He gives them that Commandment which, because it is so dear to His Heart, He calls His own.

"A new commandment I give you that you love one another. This is My commandment that you love one another as I have loved you. By this shall all men know that you are My disciples, if you have love one for another. Let not your heart be troubled. I go to prepare a place for you. And I will come again and will take you to Myself, that where I am you also may be. And I will ask the Father to give you another Comforter. Peace I leave with you, My peace I give unto you. You now indeed have sorrow, but I will see you again and your heart shall rejoice, and your joy no man shall take from you."

Then, lifting up His eyes to Heaven, He prayed for them to His Father that they might be kept safe amid the dangers of the world, and that where He was going they too might come and be with Him. After this they said a hymn and went out. It was late, but the moon was flooding the City with light. The Temple roof was one sheet of silver. They crossed the brook Cedron, and began to go up the Mount of Olives.

And Jesus said to them: "You will all be scandalized in Me this night, for it is written: 'I will strike the shepherd and the sheep shall be scattered.' But after I shall be risen again, I will go before you into Galilee."

Peter said to Him: "Although all shall be scandalized in Thee, yet not I."

Jesus said to him: "Amen, amen, I say to thee, to-day, even in this night, before the cock crow twice, thou shalt deny Me thrice."

But he spoke the more vehemently: "Although I should die together with Thee, I will not deny Thee."

And in like manner also said they all.

A few paces above the brook was a garden called Gethsemane. It was a quiet place, and our Lord often went there to pray; sometimes He spent the whole night in prayer beneath the olive trees. On this night He left eight of the Apostles at the gate, and took inside only Peter, James and John.

"My soul is sorrowful even unto death," He said to these three, and He begged them like good and faithful friends not to leave Him alone in His trouble, but to watch and pray with Him.

Bright moonlight lit up the Garden, but beneath the trees all was dark and gloomy. Our Lord went forward alone and knelt down. Presently He fell on His face and prayed in an agony of terror that He might be spared the awful sufferings that were at hand.

"Abba, Father," He said, "all things are possible to Thee; remove this chalice from Me; but not what I will, but what Thou wilt."

He had offered Himself to take away the sins of the world, and now they all came distinctly before Him, every sin and every sinner. And He was to be punished as if He had done all those wicked things. He saw the punishment—the spitting, the scourging, the nailing to the cross, the hanging there for three long hours. He saw, too, that all He was going to suffer would be of no use to many souls that He loved.

The pain of all this was so dreadful that He went to His three disciples to get a little comfort from them. But they were asleep! Gently waking them, He said to Peter:

"What! Could you not watch one hour with Me? Watch and pray that ye enter not into temptation."

Again He went and prayed saying the same words! His trouble of mind became so awful that it was like the agony of a dying man. He was bathed in a sweat of blood, which, after soaking His garments, trickled down upon the ground. Then an Angel came from Heaven to comfort Him by showing Him the good that from His bitter pains would come to us. And He said:

"O My Father, if this chalice cannot pass away unless I drink it, Thy Will be done."

He did not give up prayer on this dreadful night, but taught us by His example to pray more earnestly when we are in trouble; for "being in an agony He prayed the longer."

About midnight lights appeared behind the trees, and our Lord went to rouse His disciples, who had fallen asleep again.

"Rise," He said, "behold, he that will betray Me is at hand."

A band of soldiers and servants from the chief priests, with lanterns, torches and weapons, were

The Garden of Gethsemane

"Rise up, let us go. Behold, he that will betray me is at hand."
(Mark 14:42)

coming stealthily into the Garden, led by a man who looked about here and there as if in search of someone. He had given the party a sign, saying: "Whomsoever I shall kiss, that is He; lay hold on Him and lead Him away carefully." And, going up to Jesus, he said:

"Hail, Rabbi!" and kissed Him.

Jesus said to him: "Friend, whereto art thou come? Judas, dost thou betray the Son of Man with a kiss?"

It was the last warning—a tender word, and a solemn one—and both thrown away.

Then, knowing all things that were to come upon Him, He went forward and said to the soldiers:

"Whom seek ye?"

They answered: "Jesus of Nazareth."

Jesus answered: "I am He."

As soon as He had said this they went backward—Judas, the soldiers, the priests—and fell on their faces before Him. He let them rise, and asked again:

"Whom seek ye?"

They answered: "Jesus of Nazareth."

Jesus answered: "I have told you that I am He; if, therefore, you seek Me, let these go their way."

He pointed to His disciples, and forbade the soldiers to touch them. Then His enemies came up and bound Him fast.

"Lord, shall we strike with the sword?" cried Peter.

And without waiting for an answer, he drew a sword he had with him, and striking one of the servants of the High-Priest, cut off his right ear.

But Jesus said: "Put up thy sword into its place. The chalice which My Father hath given Me, shall I not drink it?"

And bending forward, He touched the servant's ear and healed him.

Then the disciples all leaving Him fled away. But Peter and John, ashamed of their cowardice, soon returned and followed their Master as He was led to the palace of the High-priest. This was Caiaphas, though many of the Jews who would not acknowledge a man appointed by the Romans regarded Annas, his father-in-law, as the High-priest. The palaces of the two were separated by a courtyard only. All was astir there when the soldiers arrived with the Prisoner. Annas, a cruel and wicked old man, the chief contriver of the plots against our Lord, had sent for Him that he might enjoy the sight of his enemy now helpless and humbled; and at the house of Caiaphas the members of the Sanhedrin were arriving for the trial that was to be held there immediately.

Annas questioned our Blessed Lord about His doctrines and His disciples, in the hope of getting Him to say something that could be turned against Him. Our Lord who saw into his heart bade him ask those who had heard His teaching. On this, a servant of Annas, thinking to please his Master, struck Jesus a heavy blow on the face, saying:

"Answerest Thou the High-priest so?"

Jesus said gently: "If I have spoken evil, give testimony of the evil, but if well, why strikest thou Me?"

BEFORE CAIAPHAS

"And the high priest said to him: I adjure thee by the living God, that thou tell us if thou be the Christ the Son of God."
(Mt 26:63)

The Sanhedrists were now assembled at the house of Caiaphas, and seated in a semi-circle on cushions, Caiaphas, as president, on a platform. Our Lord was brought in by His guards and placed standing before His judges for trial. It was a strange trial, for the death of the Prisoner was already decreed, and all that was wanted was some evidence against Him to give an appearance of justice to the sentence. But His life had been so holy that there was no hope of finding anything amiss in it; false witnesses were therefore brought in, but their testimony did not agree.

Jesus heard all and was silent. The prophet Isaias had said of Him: "He shall be dumb as a lamb before His shearer, and He shall not open His mouth." At length Caiaphas, flushed with anger, rose up and exclaimed:

"Answerest Thou nothing to the things that are laid to Thy charge by these men?"

But He answered nothing.

What was to be done? How could He be made to speak? The crafty president sees a way. He will put a question to which the Accused will be bound to answer, and on that answer He can be condemned.

See them standing there face to face—the High-priest in his robes of office, the Son of God with His hands bound behind His back.

"I adjure Thee by the Living God," said Caiaphas, "that Thou tell us if Thou be the Christ, the Son of God."

Jesus said to him: "Thou hast said it. And, hereafter, you shall see the Son of Man sitting on the right hand of the power of God and coming in the clouds of Heaven."

This was all they wanted. Transported, as it were, with holy indignation, the High-priest seized His garment and tore it from the neck down.

"He hath blasphemed!" he cried; "behold, you have heard the blasphemy; what think you?"

And they answering said: "He is guilty of death."

A disgraceful scene of insult and cruelty followed, in which the priests themselves seem to have set the example. "The men that held Him mocked Him and struck Him. And they did spit on His face and buffeted Him. And they blindfolded Him and smote His face with the palms of their hands, saying:

Prophesy unto us, O Christ! who is he that struck Thee?"

While all this was going on before Annas and Caiaphas, another scene was taking place in the courtyard below where the servants were waiting to hear the result of the trial. The night was cold and they had made a fire and were standing round it warming themselves. Peter, who had come into the court, was warming himself with the rest. The light was full upon his face, and the portress, who had let him in, after looking at him attentively, said:

"Thou also wast with Jesus of Nazareth."

Peter was frightened and denied before them all: "Woman, I know Him not."

And the cock crew.

Peter's Denial

*"And Peter remembered the word that Jesus had said unto him:
Before the cock crow twice, thou shalt thrice deny me."*
(Mark 14:72)

A little later another maid saw him and said to the standers by:

"This man was with Jesus of Nazareth."

Again he denied and with an oath: "I know not the Man."

An oath this time, and his Master is "the Man."

About an hour after, when it had got about among the servants that one of the disciples of the Galilean had dared to come in amongst them, they came about Peter and said:

"Surely thou art one of them, for even thy speech doth betray thee."

Even the commoner sort in Jerusalem made fun of the pronunciation and talk of the north country folk, and Peter had only to open his mouth to prove that he was unmistakably from Galilee. Poor Peter, he had been getting more and more frightened. Thoroughly terrified now, he began to curse and to swear, saying:

"I know not this Man of whom you speak."

The cock crew again, and at the same moment our Lord passed through the court. He was suffering cruelly from the hands of His tormentors, but more cruelly from the lips of His chosen disciple who had denied Him. Yet there was no indignation in His Heart. Rather was It full of pity for one who after all had followed Him into danger out of love.

And the Lord turning looked on Peter. And Peter remembered the word that Jesus had said unto him: "Before the cock crow twice thou shalt thrice deny Me." And, going forth, he wept bitterly.

XXXVIII.

"It is Finished."

It was early morning, about four o'clock. Already the Sanhedrists were hastening to a second meeting to confirm the condemnation passed during the night, and to discuss the best means of extorting from the Roman Governor the sentence of death which they were not allowed to carry out themselves. Being a Gentile, Pilate would not take much notice of the charge of blasphemy, but his well-known dread of falling into disgrace with Cæsar could be turned to account.

By this time it had spread all over the City that Jesus of Nazareth had been taken and found guilty of death. Everyone was talking of Him. Some were surprised that a man who had spent his days in doing good should be so persecuted. Others said it had been found out that his wonderful works were done by the power of the devil. The priests had declared—and surely they should know best—that he was a dangerous man, who must be got out of the way, or he would bring ruin on the nation.

And what were his feelings who had betrayed Him? Perhaps Judas had persuaded himself that our Lord would escape unharmed from His enemies as He had often done before. At all events, the tidings that He had been condemned to death, and was being taken to Pilate that the sentence might be confirmed, filled him with unspeakable horror. What could he do to still the remorse of conscience that was torturing him? People said the priests were even now entering the Temple on their way to the Prætorium. He would hasten thither and give them back the hateful pieces of silver which had brought him to this.

A few minutes later the worshippers in the Temple were startled by seeing a wretched-looking man rush past them after the priests, who with their Prisoner were passing through the Courts.

"I have sinned," he cried, "in betraying innocent blood," and he held out both hands to them with the money.

They looked at him with contempt. "What is that to us?" they said; "look thou to it."

The cruel words filled up the measure of his misery. He might have been saved yet had he thrown himself at the feet of Jesus, or gone away and wept like Peter. But though his heart was full of a fierce hatred of himself, there was no true contrition for his sin, no hope of forgiveness. He gave himself up to despair, and, casting down the money in the Temple, went into a lonely place near the Garden where he had betrayed his Master, and hanged himself.

The Governor had been told that the chief priests, followed by an immense crowd, were bringing Jesus of Nazareth to the Prætorium for judgment, and he prepared for one of his stormy interviews with the rulers of the people. Pilate disliked and despised the Jews, and was severe—often cruel—in his dealing with them. But he had no prejudice against our Blessed Lord, of whom he had heard, not from public report alone, but from Claudia Procula, his wife. How she had come to hear of the young Teacher from Galilee, we are not told, but His gracious words and ways, the hatred of the rulers, the dangers that hedged Him round, had come to her knowledge, and her heart was drawn to Him. Whilst He was suffering in the Garden, Procula, too, was suffering in a dream on His account. Terrified now lest her husband should do anything against Him, she determined to follow the proceedings as far as possible from one of her apartments where she could see without being seen. Here, at the window, she stood watching with alarm the masses of excited people now approaching the Prætorium.

Knowing that the chief priests were delivering up Jesus of Nazareth out of envy, Pilate was resolved to hear the cause himself and give the Prisoner a fair chance. He therefore gave orders that the priests should present themselves before his tribunal. But they would not defile themselves at this holy Paschal time by crossing the threshold of a Gentile, and the Governor had to go out and meet them in the great

Brought before Pilate

*"And Pilate asked him, saying: Art thou the king of the Jews?
But he answering, said: Thou sayest it."*
(Luke 23:3)

square in front of the Prætorium, called *Lithostrotos*, or the Pavement, from the coloured stones with which it was laid.

"What accusation do you bring against this Man?" he asked.

They answered haughtily: "If He were not a malefactor we would not have delivered Him up to thee." And in loud, angry voices they began to accuse Him, saying:

"We have found this man perverting our nation, and forbidding to give tribute to Cæsar, and saying that He is Christ the King."

It was something new to Pilate to find this sudden zeal for Cæsar, and he could not repress a sneering smile. But he was not going to condemn a man on no better evidence than their word, as they seemed to expect. Serious charges had been brought against Him, and Roman justice required that they should be seriously examined. He would see the Accused in private, and two of his guards were sent out to bring our Lord into the hall.

"Art Thou a King?" inquired the Governor.

Jesus answered: "Thou sayest that I am a King. For this was I born and for this came I into the world . . . but My Kingdom is not of this world."

It was as Pilate had been informed. The Man was no danger to Rome. He had always spoken peacefully to peaceful crowds. If His enemies had anything against Him, it was on account of some Jewish superstition that was beneath his notice. Satisfied, therefore, as to

His innocence, Pilate brought Him out to the people and said:

"I find no cause in Him."

The chief priests began to cry out, and to bring charge upon charge against Him.

The Governor waited for His reply. But He answered nothing. Pilate was struck by this silence and looked well at the Man before him. Never had he had to do with so noble a prisoner; never had he seen such majesty and serenity, and such contempt of death. Wondering exceedingly he said again:

"I find no cause in this Man."

But the priests only exclaimed more vehemently: "He stirreth up all the people, beginning from Galilee to this place."

Pilate was naturally just. He saw through the accusations of the Jews. He knew that our Lord was innocent of all these crimes, and that He ought to be released at once. But Pilate was weak. He was afraid that the Jews might report him to the cruel Emperor Tiberias, and that disgrace, or something worse, might befall him if he declared himself openly in favour of One who claimed to be a King. He tried therefore to strike a middle course, and began the wretched shuffling, which was the cause of so much shame and agony to our Lord and of such perplexity to himself.

The name Galilee brought up by the priests seemed to show a way out of the difficulty. Galilee belonged to Herod, who was in Jerusalem for the Passover. Jesus of

Nazareth as his subject should be tried by him. Greatly relieved at having thus shifted the responsibility on to another, Pilate sent our Lord to Herod, and congratulated himself on having brought to a successful conclusion an important and awkward case.

Herod was as much pleased to see our Lord as Pilate was to get rid of Him. For a long time he had wanted to get a sight of this extraordinary Man, and to see some of the marvels of which he had heard. His opportunity had come, for the Prisoner would surely be only too glad to gratify him and win his favour. On His appearance, therefore, before the courtiers assembled as for an entertainment, Herod treated Him with respect, showed an interest in His case, and asked Him many questions. But He who had answered Pilate would not deign to speak to this vicious prince, the murderer of St. John the Baptist, the man whom for his cunning He had called a "fox."

Herod's conscience told him the reason of this silence, and, provoked at being thus put to shame before his court, he took his revenge by mocking his Prisoner. He had Him dressed up in a white garment as a fool, and in this guise sent Him back to Pilate.

Now, at last, the persistent efforts of the priests to dishonour Christ before the people were rewarded. The crowds that had flocked to Him in the Temple and poured out of Jerusalem six days ago to bring Him in triumph into the City, the crowds that He had loved and taught and healed, turned against Him. As He came out of Herod's palace in the fool's garment, He

Before Herod

*"And Herod with his army set him at nought, and mocked him,
putting on him a white garment, and sent him back to Pilate."*
(Luke 23:11)

was received with hisses, jeers, and all the wonted insults of an Eastern mob.

It was an hour or two after Pilate had sent our Lord to Herod that He was told the soldiers were bringing Him back. The weak, cowardly judge was terribly perplexed. He knew what he ought to do, but he was afraid. He could not in justice condemn Jesus; he dared not release Him. A sudden thought struck him: the people might come to his help. There was a custom by which they were allowed at the time of the Passover to have any prisoner they should choose released to them. They were beginning now to cry out for the grant of their annual privilege. Pilate saw his chance. He had then in prison a bandit and murderer called Barabbas. The people should choose between this man and Jesus—the people, not the envious priests, the people who would be terrified to see Barabbas let loose again.

He mounted the platform in the Lithostrotos and seated himself in his chair of gold and ivory. His soldiers and servants took up their position behind him and the Prisoner was again summoned. All around was the multitude thronging every part of the enclosure.

"Whom will you that I release to you," cried the Governor, "Barabbas, or Jesus who is called Christ?"

At this moment he turned aside to hear a message from his wife:

"Have thou nothing to do with that just Man, for I have suffered many things this day in a dream because of Him."

"It is Finished."

His Apostles were hiding; His friends in the Sanhedrin, Nicodemus, and Joseph of Arimathea, were afraid to plead His cause; His priests were clamouring for His death. One alone in the holy City was found to speak for Him—the Gentile woman, who, from her splendid apartment, was looking down upon Him with reverence and with pity, Claudia Procula, Pilate's wife.

Her words agitated her husband greatly, and confirmed him in his resolution of saving this Just One from the fury of His enemies. But what might have been done with ease two hours ago was a difficult matter now. The chief priests were steadily making way, even the few minutes' interruption caused by Procula's message had not been lost by them; and when the Governor put his question a second time, the people, whom they had worked up to a state of frenzy, were ready with their reply.

"Whom will you that I release to you," he cried, "Barabbas, or Jesus who is called Christ?"

A shout as of one voice went up: "Away with this Man and release unto us Barabbas."

Astounded and disgusted, Pilate called out: "What will you, then, that I do to the King of the Jews?"

They cried out: "Crucify Him! Crucify Him!"

"Why, what evil hath He done?" demanded the Governor. "I find no cause in Him. I will chastise Him, therefore, and let Him go."

But again rose up that howl: "Crucify Him! Crucify Him!"

THE SCOURGING AT THE PILLAR

"For he shall be delivered to the Gentiles, and shall be mocked, and scourged, and spit upon."
(Luke 18:32)

Weary of the struggle, Pilate called for water and washed his hands before the people, saying: "I am innocent of the blood of this Just Man, look you to it."

Oh, the awful shout that went up from the whole multitude there:

"His blood be upon us and upon our children!"

In vain did the cowardly judge wash his hands, the guilt was upon his soul. On him depended the life or the death of Jesus Christ. Therefore will all Christians to the end of time say in their Creed: "suffered under Pontius Pilate."

The rage of the people was becoming more and more ungovernable; they were thirsting like wolves for the blood of this innocent Lamb, and now nothing less would satisfy them. Again Pilate yielded, and, to appease them and save Christ without harming himself, he had recourse to the shameful expedient of ordering Him to be scourged.

Scourging was a punishment so cruel and so degrading that it was reserved for slaves. The poor victim often died under it, and, in itself, it was far worse than death. Trembling with fear, for He was truly man, our Lord was fastened by His wrists to a low pillar. Then the executioners, standing on a step to deal their blows more surely, struck Him unmercifully with their horrible iron-spiked lashes, which tore the flesh to the very bones. His sacred body was soon one wound; "from the sole of the foot to the top of the head there was no soundness therein, wounds and bruises and swelling sores," as the prophet had said. And not a friendly face anywhere, none of all He had healed and comforted to help Him now! Gasping for breath, He sank at last to the ground, but only to be dragged off to a fresh torment.

He had wanted, it was said, to be a King; well, the soldiers would have the coronation in their barrack room. They tore off His garments, which they had put on roughly after the scourging and which clung to His wounded body; threw over His shoulders an old, scarlet cloak, and put a reed into His hand for a sceptre. Then they plaited a crown of hard, sharp thorns, and beat it down with sticks upon His head and forehead, so that streams of blood trickled through His hair and ran down His face. Then they got into line and marched before Him, kneeling as they passed, and with shouts of laughter and cries of "Hail, King of the Jews!" came up to Him, some spitting on Him, some striking Him on the head, all trying who could ill treat Him most.

Our Lord was a king, and He felt, as only a king could feel, the shame as well as the pain He had to endure. But He sat there bearing all meekly as the prophet had foretold: "I have given my body to the strikers, I have not turned away my face from them that spit upon me."

Accustomed as he was to cruel sights, Pilate was struck with horror and compassion when our Lord appeared again before him. The face so beautiful an hour ago was quite disfigured, swollen, bruised, besmeared with blood. His limbs trembled, He could scarcely stand. The half closed eyes were dim

Crowned with Thorns

"And platting a crown of thorns, they put it upon his head, and a reed in his right hand. And bowing the knee before him, they mocked him, saying: Hail, king of the Jews."
(Mt 27:29)

with tears and blood. The scourging must have been horrible, thought the Governor, but at least it has saved His life; a sight so piteous would melt hearts of stone. There was a balcony built over the archway that overlooked the thronged entrance to the Prætorium. Here, where He could be seen by all below, Pilate placed our Lord, still clothed with the old, red cloak, thrown over His bleeding shoulders, His eyes half blind with pain.

"Behold the Man!" he cried. "I bring Him forth to you that you may know I find no cause in Him."

"Crucify Him! Crucify Him!" they shouted. "He ought to die because He made Himself the Son of God."

"Son of God!" Pilate was filled with a new and terrible fear. Innocent this Man certainly was. But what if He were something more, what if He were a God! Never, surely, had man borne himself like this Man, with such calm dignity, such invincible patience in the midst of torments and shame. He dared not leave this awful question unsolved. He must see Him again in private.

"Whence art Thou?" he asked, when they were again alone. But Jesus gave him no answer. Pilate, offended, said to Him:

"Speakest Thou not to Me? Knowest Thou not that I have power to crucify Thee and I have power to release Thee?"

Jesus answered: "Thou shouldst not have any power against Me unless it were given thee from above."

Ecce Homo

"Behold the Man."
(John 19:5)

It was between ten and eleven o'clock when the poor, irresolute judge again appeared with his Prisoner in the Lithostrotos. He was greeted with the shout:

"If thou release this Man, thou art not Cæsar's friend."

"Behold your King," was his reply.

"Away with Him! Away with Him!" they shouted. "We have no king but Cæsar."

Pilate's courage gave way. He had to choose between Cæsar and Christ, and to keep Cæsar's favour "he released unto them him who for murder and sedition had been cast into prison, whom they had desired," says St. Luke, "but Jesus he delivered up to their will."

All over the City was heard the howl of triumph with which the sentence was received. No time was lost in carrying it out, lest Pilate should repent and recall it. The cross, already prepared, was brought out, and the title Pilate had ordered to be fixed to it:

"JESUS OF NAZARETH, KING OF THE JEWS."

The procession formed and set out in all haste. First came on horseback the centurion, whose duty it was to preside at the execution and to maintain order in the crowd; next a herald bearing the title of the cross and proclaiming the crimes of the condemned. Then two thieves to be crucified. Last of all, our Lord, weak and tottering, yet laden with His heavy cross. On each side of Him the soldiers who were to fasten Him to the cross and guard Him till death. Running on in front, shouting and laughing, children who had sung

"Hosanna!" six days before. All around and behind, an immense multitude hooting and jeering, those nearest throwing mud and stones at Him after the fashion of an Eastern crowd.

What a spectacle was Jerusalem that Friday morning nineteen hundred years ago!—a mass of men, women, and children choking up every thoroughfare, pouring along under the arches that cross the narrow roadways, climbing and descending in endless procession the steep streets of the hill-built City; all going the same way, all talking excitedly, rejoicing that justice had at length overtaken "the seducer" and "blasphemer." Roofs, windows, doorways, filled with eager sightseers; rabbis and priests hurrying about among the people, in a fever of anxiety lest anything should happen to prevent the execution.

The way to Calvary was long and painful, now up hill, now down, sometimes a series of steps. Our Lord struggled on slowly; three times His little remaining strength gave way, and, gasping for breath, He sank beneath His load. Fearing He would die before He could reach Calvary, the soldiers forced a countryman, Simon of Cyrene, to carry His cross.

At a street corner was a little group waiting to see Him pass—His Blessed Mother with the Beloved Disciple, Magdalen, Mary of Cleophas, and Salome. The Mother's face would have moved a heart of stone; but hearts in Jerusalem were harder than stone that day, and there was no more pity for the Mother than for the Son. She saw the ladders, the ropes, the cross.

The Women of Jerusalem

*"Daughters of Jerusalem, weep not over me;
but weep for yourselves, and for your children."*
(Luke 23:28)

"It is Finished." 393

And then, staggering along, she saw Him coming. Their eyes met, and He looked pityingly at her. They did not speak, but He strengthened her breaking heart, that she might be able to endure to the end. There were many hard things to bear on the road to Calvary, but to the tender Heart of Jesus the hardest of all was the sight of His Mother's face.

A little further on He stopped to speak to the weeping women of Jerusalem. All through His life of hardship and persecution women were faithful to Him and showed Him reverence. A woman's voice from the crowd had been raised to bless Him as He preached; women ministered to His wants, received Him into their houses when all other doors were closed against Him, lavished upon Him costly gifts which even His own disciples grudged Him. In His hour of need a woman's voice alone was raised in His defence. And now, heedless of the rough soldiers and the hooting rabble, a crowd of women pressed round Him and filled the air with their lamentations. What wonder that He could not leave them without a parting word! But it was a word of solemn warning, for He knew what was coming upon them and upon the little ones they carried in their arms.

"Daughters of Jerusalem," He said, "weep not for Me, but weep for yourselves and for your children."

About twelve o'clock Calvary was reached. It was a mound outside the walls, the place of public executions—a place of horrors. Our Lord was quite spent. The priests who crowded round Him could see He was dying. "Quick, quick," they cried, "or it will be too late!" And whilst the soldiers kept the ground clear, He was thrown down upon the cross and ordered to stretch out His arms. His terror was indescribable, for He was truly man. Yet He obeyed without a word. One strong blow, and a long nail was driven through the right hand into the wood. The left arm had to be drawn with ropes to the hole drilled for it in the cross. Then it too was nailed fast. They dragged the feet till the sinews broke and the bones were out of joint. The torture was beyond what we can even think. Yet it was not able to turn His thoughts from us and our needs. He must make haste to appease His Father's anger, aroused by this awful crime, to pray for His executioners and for all who have crucified or will crucify Him again by sin.

"*Father, forgive them,*" He said, "*for they know not what they do.*"

St. John, who was there, tells us that "when they had crucified Him, the soldiers took His garments and made four parts, to every soldier a part, and also His coat. Now, the coat was without seam, woven from the top throughout. They said then one to another: 'Let us not cut it, but let us cast lots for it whose it shall be,' that the Scripture might be fulfilled, saying: 'They have parted My garments among them, and upon My vesture they have cast lots.' And the soldiers indeed did these things."

Nailed to the Cross

"Father, forgive them, for they know not what they do."
(Luke 23:34)

Meantime the thieves, shrieking and blaspheming, had been crucified, and the three crosses raised into position and firmly fixed with wedges driven in all round. Then at last the enemies of Jesus were satisfied. The priests came up and stood before His cross and cried:

"Vah! Thou that destroyest the Temple of God and in three days dost rebuild it, save Thy ownself. If Thou be the Son of God, come down from the cross and we will believe."

The people came and stared, blaspheming like their rulers. One of the thieves cried out:

"If Thou be Christ, save Thyself and us."

But the other rebuked him and said: "We, indeed, receive the due reward of our deeds, but this Man hath done no evil."

And he said to Jesus:

"Lord, remember me when Thou shalt come into Thy Kingdom."

And Jesus said to him:

"*Amen, I say to thee, this day thou shalt be with Me in Paradise.*"

Our Lord had always loved sinners. And now He gave these poor men grace to know that He who shared their disgrace and was put between them as the most guilty was the long-expected Messiah, the King of Heaven and earth. One of them—alas! only one—opened his heart to grace, was sorry for his sins, took his punishment humbly, and, for the simple remembrance which he asked, received the forgiveness of his sins and

THE GOOD THIEF

"Lord, remember me when Thou shalt come into Thy Kingdom."
(Luke 23:42)

the promise of Heaven in the company of his Saviour before the sun had set.

Sinners first, sinners even before His Mother. But His next thought was for her. She was losing all in losing Him; He must provide her with a home. Brave and patient she was standing beside His cross, and, except for her companions and the centurion and his men, almost alone. A strange darkness creeping over the heavens had frightened away the crowds; there was room now by the cross; John had brought her up to it, and she had taken her stand there beside her Son to stay with Him until the end. His eyes were dimming fast. He could scarcely see. But He turned them painfully to her and then to John, and said to her:

"*Woman, behold thy son.*"

After that He said to John: "*Behold thy Mother.*"

And from that hour the disciple took her to his own. She was given to the Beloved Disciple, and in him to all disciples. Mary, the Mother of God, became the Mother of us all that day.

And now there was darkness over the whole earth, not that of a dark day, but the darkness of night. Our Lord had hung in silence a long time, when, suddenly, a loud cry broke from His lips:

"*My God, My God, why hast Thou forsaken Me?*"

How hard it is to understand that cry! We should

have thought His Heavenly Father would have leaned in tenderest pity over that cruel cross and have filled with consolation the soul of His dying Son. It was to win back for His Father our perishing souls that He had come down from Heaven; all His life through He had sought, not His own glory but his Father's; He had done everything His Father asked of Him—why was He forsaken? Because He was being treated as a sinner. Sinners deserve to be forsaken by God in this world and in the next. He would take their place, and suffer this most dreadful pain and punishment in our stead, that we may know we are never, never forsaken by God in this life, no matter how lonely or how sinful we may be.

Of all the pains of crucifixion, the most terrible is thirst. It is so awful that the crucified seem to forget every other, and, as if there were nothing more to ask, beg only of the passers by a drink of water in their intolerable pain. It is loss of blood that brings this thirst. What must His thirst have been after the sweat of blood in the Garden, after the scourging, and now the draining of His sacred body on the cross? But it was not to get relief that Jesus cried:

"*I thirst*," but that David's prophecy of Him might be fulfilled: "In My thirst they gave Me vinegar to drink." On hearing His cry, a soldier ran, and filled a sponge with vinegar from a vessel that stood by, and, fixing it on a reed, put it to His mouth.

It Is Finished

"Indeed this was the Son of God."
(Mt 27:54)

"It is Finished."

And now at last, after three hours of agony, the end was come.

When He had taken the vinegar Jesus said:
"*It is finished.*"

All He had come to do was done—the world redeemed; a perfect example set us in each stage of His blessed Life; every prophecy concerning Him accomplished; His Church founded, by which His followers in every age were to be taught what He had done for them, and how they must save their souls. He had spared Himself in nothing; He had sacrificed for our sakes, all He could give up—home, friends, reputation—He had loved us to the end—all was finished.

And again, crying with a loud Voice, He said:
"*Father, into Thy hands I commend My spirit.*"

The eyes closed; the head fell forward on the breast; the body sank low on the nails—He was dead.

And the veil of the Temple that hid the Holy of Holies from the sight of men was rent from top to bottom. And the earth quaked, and the rocks were rent, and the graves were opened, and many of the bodies of the saints that had slept arose, and, coming out of the tombs after His Resurrection, came into the holy City and appeared to many. And the centurion and they that were with him watching Jesus, having seen the earthquake and the things that were done, were sore afraid, saying:

"Indeed this was the Son of God."

And all the multitude of them that were come together to that sight and saw the things that were done returned striking their breasts.

In vain did the priests try to quiet the people, Jerusalem was beside itself with terror; the rocking earth, the opening graves, the midnight darkness at midday—all this spoke plainly for Him whose lifeless body hung upon the cross.

There was no question of Feast or holiday. What they had done to Jesus of Nazareth was the one absorbing thought. All His goodness and gentleness and compassion, His teaching and His healing, came back to them; their cry of long ago: *"He hath done all things well,"* their cry six days ago: *"Hosanna to the Son of David!"* their cry of this day: *"Crucify Him! Crucify Him! His blood be upon us and upon our children!"* They felt that an awful crime had been committed, and a dreadful sense of the anger of God enkindled against them weighed upon every heart.

Meantime evening was drawing on, and the Mother on Calvary had seen the last outrage to her Son. Soldiers had broken the legs of the thieves and taken the dead bodies away that they might not hang there to cast a gloom over the rejoicings of the morrow. When they saw that Jesus was already dead they did not break His legs, but one of them with a spear opened His side and so fulfilled the prophecy of Zacharias: "They shall look on Him whom they pierced."[1]

---

[1] Zacharias 12:10

She had no grave wherein to lay Him, but God, she knew, would provide. And, presently, there came up to the cross two men who up to this time had been disciples in secret for fear of the Jews. But now, when all Jerusalem was in fear, their hearts were filled with a new courage, and they had come to give honourable burial to their Master. Joseph of Arimathea had been boldly to Pilate and begged the body of Jesus, which he was going to lay in his own monument in the garden close by. Nicodemus came with him, and they brought fine linen and spices for the burial according to the custom of the Jews. Helped by their servants, they gently took down the sacred Body from the cross and laid it on the ground, the head on the Mother's knee. The Soul was not there but in Limbo, rejoicing all the holy ones from Adam to the good thief, and turning that place of weary waiting into a very Heaven. The Divinity was with the Soul and with the lifeless Body too, and both were to be worshipped with the honour due to God.

The preparations for burial had to be hastened, because of the Sabbath rest, which would begin when the first stars came out. With the help of Magdalen and John, Mary swathed Him in the long linen bands, and covered the white, disfigured face. Then they formed in sad procession and bore Him through the garden into the rocky tomb. There they left Him, and, rolling the great stone to the entrance, went their way.

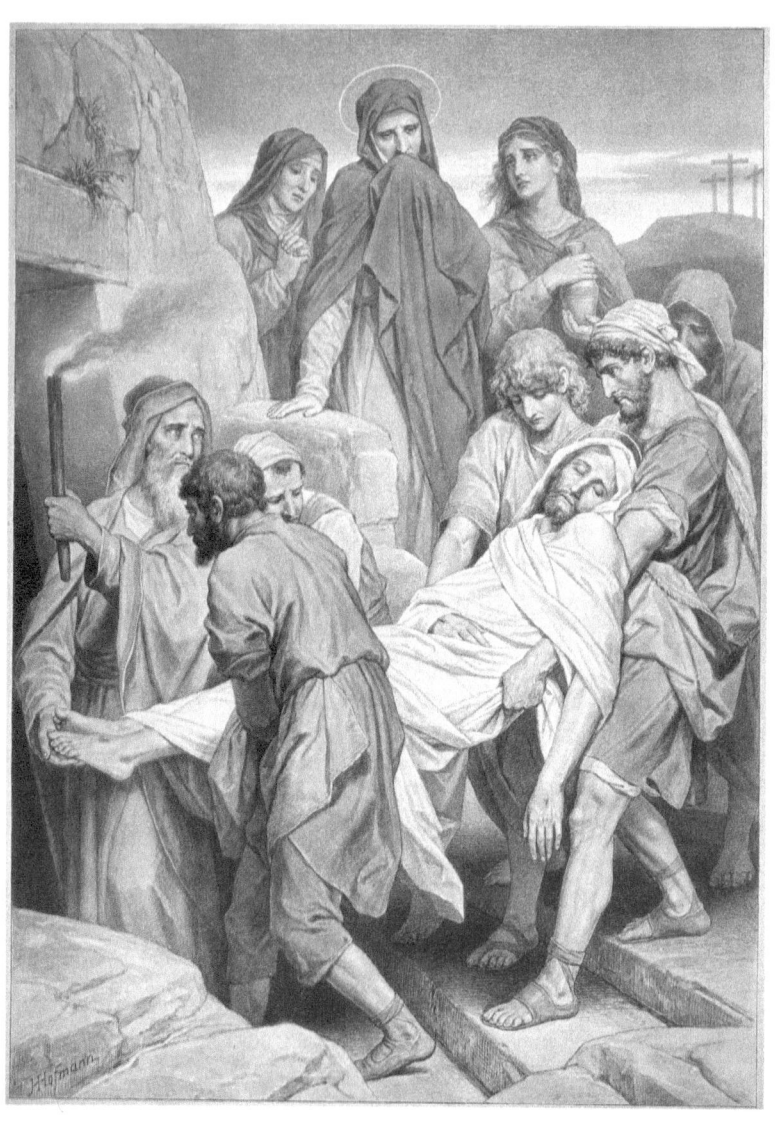

Jesus is laid in the Tomb

*"There, therefore, because of the parasceve of the Jews,
they laid Jesus, because the sepulchre was nigh at hand."*
(John 19:42)

As darkness fell for the second time that awful day, the disciples left their hiding places and crept back one by one to the Upper Chamber on Mount Sion, which now became their ordinary place of meeting. There they gathered round John to hear all that had befallen the Master since they had left Him in the Garden. They listened in trouble and in shame, poor Peter's tears running fast down his rugged face, all sorrowing over their cowardly desertion of their Master, all envying John who had stood by Him to the last.

Then they talked of the past, of the happy days in Galilee, of their nights with Him on the mountain side, of His gentle, patient teaching, of His tenderness to them at the Supper in this very room. And now all was over, and had ended in this! There was nothing more to live for. They remembered how clearly He had foretold to them all that had come to pass—the betrayal, the scourging, the crucifixion; but not one of them called to mind that last word with which He always ended: "the third day He shall rise again." Far into the night they talked; then, weary and comfortless, broke up the meeting and went back to their homes. On the festival day they were together again in the same place, going over all anew. Others came in, but there was no comfort from any. All was over, they said again and again to one another as they mourned and wept.

His friends, then, were weighed down by hopeless sorrow. But what about His enemies? They were rejoicing, surely? The priests had promised themselves a quiet evening after their anxious day. All had gone better than they had dared to hope. Through the cowardice of Pilate, insult and torment beyond what they could have desired had been heaped upon "the seducer," and now He was safely in His grave, and all was over.

But was it? This, in their hour of triumph, was the question they kept asking themselves. The darkness, and the earthquake, and the rent veil in the Holy Place, were being taken as signs of His innocence and of the wrath of God upon His enemies; and not by the common people only but by men of note and their fellow-councillors in the Sanhedrin. Word had been brought to them how the centurion and his soldiers had proclaimed the Crucified to be the Son of God, and how Nicodemus and Joseph of Arimathea had given Him honourable burial.

Of course they themselves had no further fears. He was certainly dead, and His disciples were far too timid to give cause for alarm. And yet there was that word of His about rebuilding the Temple in three days. What if there should be anything in it! What if anything should happen on the third day! It would be well to guard against such a calamity. No precautions could be too great to prevent a reappearance which would at once mark all His words and works as divine and prove Him to be in very deed what He had given Himself out to be. They would make all safe by applying to Pilate for a guard until the third day.

"It is Finished."

It was the afternoon of the Sabbath when the Governor was told that a party of priests craved an audience. Tortured by his conscience, and terrified by all that had followed upon the Crucifixion, Pilate was in no mood to receive visitors, and least of all these hateful men who had forced on him the deed of yesterday. Very unwillingly he gave orders for their admission.

"Sir," they said, bowing low before him, "we have remembered that that seducer said while he was yet alive: 'After three days I will rise again.' Command, therefore, the sepulchre to be guarded until the third clay, lest perhaps his disciples come and steal him away, and say to the people that he is risen from the dead, and the last error shall be worse than the first."

"You have a guard, go guard it as you know," was the curt reply. And they, delighted to have gained their point so easily, departed and made all secure by sealing the stone of the Sepulchre and setting four Roman soldiers to guard it.

Our Risen Lord

*"I am the way, and the truth, and the life.
No man cometh to the Father, but by me."*

(John 14:6)

THE RISEN LIFE

The Resurrection

"And for fear of him, the guards were struck with terror, and became as dead men."
(Mt 28:4)

XL.
"Jesus Christ Yesterday, Today, and the Same For Ever."

The darkness of that Sabbath night was just giving place to day. It was beginning to dawn towards the first day of the week. Within the sealed sepulchre all was stillness and gloom. The mangled Body in its wrappings lay motionless, stiff and cold.

Suddenly a blaze of glory filled the rocky chamber, and in the midst was Jesus—Jesus risen from the dead to die no more! The Soul had returned from Limbo and re-entered the Body, and He rose, Body and Soul reunited for ever, in a majesty and beauty befitting the Son of God.

He was the very same, but oh! how changed; all the marks of His suffering and humiliation gone, only in hands and feet and side five Wounds, not disfiguring, but glorifying Him by their dazzling beauty. As He rose by His own power, so by His own power He left the tomb; no angel rolled back the stone to let Him pass, but, with the subtility that belongs to a glorified body, He passed through, leaving the guards still sleeping and the seal untouched. But the next instant Jerusalem was shaken to its foundations by a great earthquake, for an Angel of the Lord descended from Heaven, and, coming, rolled back the stone and sat upon it. And his countenance was as lightning, and his raiment as snow. And for fear of him the guards were struck with terror and became as dead men.

One—one only—of those who believed in Him was preparing to welcome Him back from the grave. She who kept all His words, pondering them in her heart, held fast the promise: "and the third day He shall rise again." She knew He would return to her. She was counting the hours all that sad Saturday, and, when night fell, she was keeping watch and turning continually to the East for the first streaks of the coming day. We wonder, perhaps, that with hope such as hers, sorrow could have been so crushing. But, whilst her Son was absent and the memory of His sufferings was allowed to overwhelm her, there could be no consolation for that stricken Mother. She could only make her acts of faith and hope, and wait patiently till He should come.

And He came! More swiftly than the lightning flashing from East to West, He passed from His rocky tomb to her chamber on Mount Sion, and as swiftly came the change in that desolate heart from midnight darkness to midday brightness and joy. The dawn was only breaking, the third day scarcely come, when He returned from the grave, eager to comfort those who mourned for Him, and His Mother first of all. The Scripture, indeed, does not mention His visit to her, but can we think that the best of sons would refuse this honour and consolation to His Mother? St. Ignatius of Loyola says that anyone who could doubt that Christ's first visit was to her, would deserve to hear His own word of reproach: "Are you also without understanding?"

The meeting between the Mother and the Son was for themselves alone. It will be one of the joys of Heaven to know what passed between them in those first moments of His Risen Life. All we know now is that Mary could say with greater truth than David: "According to the multitude of my sorrows in my heart, thy comforts have given joy to my soul."[1]

Both were eager for the glad surprises of this blessed day to begin soon. He must hasten to comfort those who on His account were in such bitter trouble. And so He left her to go on His errands of love, to do that work of comforting which is always the delight of His Sacred Heart.

Who could come next but Magdalen? After His Blessed Mother's, no heart was so desolate as hers. She had stayed by Him to the end, had helped to lay Him in His grave, had sat at the door weeping when all had gone away. As long as there was anything she could do for Him, even after death, her love was restless, and so she set out very early on the first day of the week, with the holy women her companions, to finish

---
1 Psalm 93.

Mary Magdalen

"Woman, why weepest thou? whom seekest thou?"
(John 20:15)

the embalming of the sacred Body. On the way to the Sepulchre they remembered the huge stone at the entrance and wondered how they would get in. But the difficulty did not stop them, and on their arrival they found the stone rolled away and the entrance to the tomb wide open.

Without waiting to see anything further, Magdalen in dismay ran off to Peter and John and said to them:

"They have taken away the Lord out of the Sepulchre, and we know not where they have laid Him."

In the meantime the other women went into the Sepulchre and saw a young man sitting at the right-side clothed with a white robe, and they were astonished. And he said to them:

"Fear not you, for I know that you seek Jesus who was crucified. He is not here, for He is risen as He said. Come and see the place where the Lord was laid. And going quickly tell His disciples and Peter that He is risen, and, behold, He will go before you into Galilee, there you shall see Him as He told you."

And they going out fled from the Sepulchre, for a trembling and fear had seized them. And they went quickly with fear and great joy, running to tell His disciples.

What running there was that morning! For Peter and John, on hearing Magdalen's tale, both ran together to the Sepulchre. They saw the stone rolled back, and the linen cloths in which our Lord had been swathed folded together, but there was no angel there now to explain what it all meant. Full of wonder and perplexity they had gone home again, when Magdalen, who had followed them, arrived and went in. There she stood before the empty tomb weeping.

Now, as she was weeping, she stooped down and looked into the Sepulchre: and she saw two Angels in white, sitting one at the head and one at the feet where the Body of Jesus had been laid.

They said to her: "Woman, why weepest thou?"

She said to them: "Because they have taken away my Lord, and I know not where they have laid Him."

When she had said this she turned herself back, and saw Jesus standing; and she knew not that it was Jesus.

Jesus said to her: "Woman, why weepest thou? whom seekest thou?"

She, thinking that it was the gardener, said to Him: "Sir, if thou hast taken Him hence, tell me where thou hast laid Him, and I will take Him away."

Jesus said to her: "Mary."

She, turning, said to Him: "Rabboni," which is to say: Master.

Jesus said to her: "Do not touch Me, for I am not yet ascended to My Father; but go to My brethren and say to them: I ascend to My Father and to your Father, to My God and to your God."

Mary Magdalen went and told the disciples, who were mourning and weeping:

"I have seen the Lord and these things He said to me."

And they, hearing that He was alive and had been seen by her, did not believe.

Her two companions were on their way to Jerusalem

to deliver the Angel's message, when Jesus met them, saying:

"All hail!"

And they came up and took hold of His feet and adored Him.

And Jesus said to them: "Fear not, go tell My brethren that they go into Galilee, there they shall see Me."

But Magdalen's radiant face and joyful words: "I have seen the Lord," and the assurances of her companions that they had kissed His feet, failed to cheer the disciples. Only the women had seen Him, they said, and who could believe such idle tales as theirs!

Two of them were so weighed down with sorrow that they left Jerusalem in the afternoon to go to a little village called Emmaus. As they went they talked over all that had happened since Friday, but stopped short on finding that a stranger had suddenly joined them. He saw they were in trouble and said kindly:

"What are these discourses that you hold one with another as you walk, and are sad?"

One of them, whose name was Cleophas, answered:

"Art thou only a stranger in Jerusalem, and hast not known the things that have been done there in these days?"

To whom He said: "What things?"

And they said: "Concerning Jesus of Nazareth, who was a Prophet mighty in work and word before God and all the people; and how our chief priests and princes delivered Him to be condemned to death and crucified Him. But we hoped that it was He that should have redeemed Israel; and now, besides all this, to-day is the third day since these things were done. Yea, and certain women also of our company affrighted us, who before it was light were at the Sepulchre, and, not finding His Body, came saying that they had also seen a vision of Angels who say that He is alive. And some of our people went to the Sepulchre and found it so as the women had said, but Him they found not."

The Stranger listened quietly to the end of their story. Then He said:

"O foolish and slow of heart to believe in all things which the prophets have spoken. Ought not Christ to have suffered these things, and so to enter into His glory?"

And beginning at Moses He showed them from all the prophets that He who was to come was to be a suffering Messiah, not the founder of an earthly kingdom as the Jews expected. So far, then, from being cast down by what had befallen their Master, they ought to take comfort from it, seeing how exactly all the prophecies had been fulfilled in Him. Moreover, if suffering was the way by which the Messiah was to redeem the world, it was not to last for ever. For Him and for all His followers the cross was to lead to the crown.

The disciples listened with rapt attention. Here was a new light thrown upon that shameful death of

On the Way to Emmaus

*"Ought not Christ to have suffered these things,
and so to enter into his glory?"*
(Luke 24:26)

their dear Master which had seemed to be the end of all their hopes. The cloud upon their hearts began to lift. A strange peace and joy seemed to flow to them, not from the words alone, but from the very Presence of the Stranger. They could not bear to part from Him; He had made all the difference in their lives.

They drew nigh to the town whither they were going, and He made as though He would have gone farther, but they constrained Him, saying:

"Stay with us, because it is towards evening and the day is now far spent."

And He went in with them.

And while He was at table with them, He took bread, and blessed, and broke and gave to them. And their eyes were opened and they knew Him, and He vanished out of their sight.

Here, then, was the explanation of that happy afternoon. And they said one to the other:

"Was not our heart burning within us whilst He spoke in the way and opened to us the Scriptures?"

And rising up the same hour, they went back to Jerusalem, and they found the Eleven gathered together, and those that were with them. Before they could speak they were welcomed with the glad cry:

"The Lord is risen, indeed, and hath appeared to Simon!"

They looked around. How different the state of things in the Upper Chamber from what they had left a few hours ago! Joy on every face. Peter's a sight never to be forgotten; such peace there, such deep content. No word of what had passed between him and his Master escaping him, as if his secret were too sweet to be broken by a word, but the certainty of the Resurrection so strong within him that on his simple assurance the rest believed: "The Lord has risen indeed, and has appeared to Simon." He is confirming his brethren according to our Lord's words at the Supper.

At last Cleophas and his companion get a hearing and tell their story of the wondrous walk that afternoon, and Who went with them, and how they did not know Him till the breaking of bread. Those who had not yet seen our Lord listened with beating hearts; they believed, but oh, that they too might see Him!

A stir; a startled cry! For there He stood in their midst—Himself, the very same; the face, the look, the smile they knew so well.

"Peace be to you; it is I, fear not," He said.

But they being troubled and affrighted supposed that they saw a spirit.

And He said to them: "Why are you troubled, and why do thoughts arise in your hearts? See My hands and feet, that it is I Myself; handle and see, for a spirit hath not flesh and bones as you see Me to have."

And, when He had said this, He showed them His hands and His feet. The disciples, therefore, were glad when they saw the Lord. But while they yet believed not and wondered for joy, He said:

"Have you here anything to eat?"

JESUS APPEARS TO THE DISCIPLES

"Peace be to you. As the Father hath sent me, I also send you."
(John 20:21)

And they offered Him a piece of broiled fish and a honeycomb. And when He had eaten before them, taking the remains, He gave to them.

Then He said to them again: "Peace be to you. As the Father hath sent Me, I also send you."

When He had said this He breathed on them, and He said to them: "Receive ye the Holy Ghost; whose sins you shall forgive, they are forgiven them; and whose sins you shall retain, they are retained."

The third Sacrament instituted in the Upper Chamber. The Thursday before, the Blessed Sacrament had been instituted there; the Apostles had been made priests, and received the awful power to consecrate. And now, reserved for the evening of this glad Easter Day, when His word again and again is "Peace," He institutes and leaves in His Church for ever the blessed Sacrament of forgiveness, the Sacrament of Peace.

How grand is our Lord's generosity in this first meeting with His poor disciples! How completely He sweeps away all fear that their desertion of Him is to make any difference in His feeling towards them! Even if the women's tale were true and the Lord was risen indeed, He would look out now for followers more worthy of Him. So they must have thought. He knew this and set Himself to reassure and comfort them in every way that loving Heart of His could devise. Before His Passion it was their suffering, rather than His own, that troubled Him. In His Risen Life, what is due to Himself seems forgotten in His concern for them. One would think He had to make amends to them for what they had borne for His sake. And so He hastens here and there, from one group to another, bringing brightness and happiness to all. Before His Passion they were "friends," now they are "brethren." His one thought this Easter Day is to bring joy to all who love Him. Not so much as a hint at any need of forgiveness.

Oh, what a beautiful character is our dearest Lord's! At the Last Supper it seemed as if self-forgetting love could go no further. But when He comes back from the grave, and the weight that all His life long had pressed upon His Sacred Heart is gone, there is a gladness, almost playfulness, about Him as He appears and disappears and hides, that takes us by surprise, and discloses depths of tenderness we had not known before.

One alone of the Eleven, Thomas, was still in trouble because in unbelief. He was not with them when Jesus came. On his return the rest exclaimed joyfully:

"We have seen the Lord!"

But he said to them: "Except I shall see in His hands the print of the nails, and put my finger into the place of the nails, and put my hand into His side, I will not believe."

Poor St. Thomas! few among the Apostles loved the Master better than he. It was the very depth of his affection that made him hesitate to believe what seemed too good to be true. Perhaps, too, he was a little jealous of the others. Why had he missed what had made them so joyful! His mind worked slowly. He did not jump at conclusions. The impulsiveness of Peter, James, and John was something of a trial to him. He rather prided himself on the prudence of his resolve not to believe like them till he had seen like them. And so he remained aloof, wretched and miserable, a trial to them all. But they saw how he was suffering, and they were patient with him and kind. And their charity was rewarded. He had no right, it is true, to lay down the conditions on which he would believe, and to get himself into such a state that nothing but a miracle could bring him round. But if faith and hope had gone, love remained, and our Lord had pity on him and humoured him and gave him the proofs he required.

After eight days again the disciples were within, and Thomas with them. Jesus came, the doors being shut, and stood in the midst and said:

"Peace be to you."

Then He said to Thomas: "Put in thy finger hither, and see My hands, and bring hither thy hand and put it into My side, and be not faithless, but believing."

Thomas answered and said to Him: "My Lord and my God!"

Jesus said to him: "Because thou hast seen Me, Thomas, thou hast believed; blessed are they that have not seen and have believed."

Our Lord's Appearances after His Resurrection were for His friends alone. His enemies had abundant proof that He was risen, but they did not see Him again. They had had their day of grace, and His visible presence on earth was no longer for them. He had told them shortly before His Passion that if they believed not Moses and the Prophets, neither would they believe if one should rise from the dead. These words were fulfilled now, for the awful "signs" of Friday afternoon and Sunday morning left them hardened as before.

When the guards at the Sepulchre, who, at the presence of the Angel, were struck with terror and became as dead men, had come to themselves, they went into the City and told the chief priests all things that had been done. And they being assembled together, taking counsel, gave a great sum of money to the soldiers, saying. "Say you: 'His disciples came by night and stole Him away when we were asleep.' And if the Governor shall hear of this, we will persuade him and secure you." So they, taking the money, did as they were taught. "And this word was spread abroad among the Jews even unto this day," says St. Matthew.

"Spread abroad," it might be, but not believed. That the disciples of Jesus—simple, timid men, who had all taken flight when He was seized in the Garden, and had not dared to show themselves since—could have attempted such a thing, or that Roman soldiers, trained up under strict military discipline, and placed there only the evening before, should be all asleep at the same time, and should sleep so soundly and so long as not to be awakened either by the rolling away of the stone or the carrying off of the body—this was a story too ridiculous to deceive any. But the soldiers, who had nothing to lose and much to gain by spreading it abroad, did as they were told. It was no concern of theirs that people asked: if they were asleep how could they see the theft of the body? If they did not see it how were they witnesses?

"He that sitteth in the heavens shall laugh at them," says Holy Scripture, speaking of the plots of the wicked. These words come to mind as we see the priests carefully sealing the stone and setting their guards on that Sabbath afternoon. These guards were the first witnesses to the Resurrection, and that seal was its surest sign. God allowed it so to be for the confirmation of our faith. He knew that everything about our Divine Lord would be attacked by unbelievers, that the day would come when the Mystery which is the very foundation of our faith in Him would be assailed.

That day has come. Because they cannot understand how Christ rose again, men are saying that the Resurrection is an impossibility, and this they try to prove in books and papers that are read by men, women and children of every class, in every country, of every shade of religious belief.

As children of the Catholic Church, we must be on our guard against the unbelief of the day in every shape. But most of all must we fear and fly from anything that would shake our faith in the Resurrection of Jesus Christ. If that goes, all must go. If that goes, we are no longer Christians, for it is our faith in the Resurrection that makes us followers of Christ. We are not disciples of a dead but of a living Man, the God Man Jesus Christ, yesterday, to-day, and for ever.

We believe in this wonderful Mystery because the Holy Scripture, which is the word of God, affirms it, and because the Church of God has taught it from the beginning. But we may strengthen our faith and meet the objections of those who try to shake it by considering two points about the Resurrection:

Men are to be found now who say that our Lord was not really dead upon the cross, and, therefore, could not rise again.

Now, both pagan and Jewish writers declare that Jesus Christ was put to death by Pontius Pilate in the reign of Tiberias Cæsar. The piercing of the sacred Side proves His death; so do the words of the centurion to Pilate, and Pilate's gift of the body to Joseph of Arimathea, whilst the precautions of the priests make both His Death and Resurrection as clear as day to all but such as will not see.

Again, the wonderful change in the Apostles proves the truth of the Resurrection. They never so much as dreamed of their Master rising again. After His death they were utterly disconsolate and hopeless, hiding away within barred doors, afraid to show themselves abroad. A few weeks later these cowardly men were proclaiming the Resurrection boldly. No fear of their rulers nor of torments nor of death could silence them:

"Jesus of Nazareth, whom you by the hands of wicked men have crucified and slain—this Jesus hath

God raised again, whereof all we are witnesses," said Peter in his first sermon to the Jews.

Standing a little later before Annas and Caiaphas to answer for his boldness in healing a cripple in the Name of Jesus, he said:

"Ye princes of the people and ancients, hear. Be it known to you all and to all the people of Israel, that by the Name of our Lord Jesus Christ of Nazareth whom you crucified, whom God hath raised from the dead, even by Him, this man standeth before you whole."

Think of Peter, poor, trembling Peter, who at the first word of a servant girl had denied his Master, speaking in this strain before the dreaded Sanhedrin! How he insists. How little he cares what they do to him. And when he and John are forbidden to teach any more in the Name of Jesus, their only answer to the Council is:

"If it be just to hear you rather than God, judge ye. For we cannot but speak the things which we have seen and heard."[1]

To witness to this truth, and preach to all men Jesus crucified and risen again, the Apostles gave up friends and country, embraced a life of hardship and suffering, and at length joyfully laid down their lives. Would they have done this had the Resurrection been a fable?

Our faith is built upon the Resurrection; that is, it rests upon this great truth as a house on its foundation. Take away the foundation and the building falls to the ground. Give up faith in the Resurrection and belief in all other articles of the Creed breaks down.

---

[1] Acts 4.

The Apostles

"And with great power did the apostles give testimony of the resurrection of Jesus Christ our Lord; and great grace was in them all."
(Acts 4:33)

We believe them on the word of Jesus, and we believe in Jesus because of the Resurrection. The Gospel is sometimes called "the preaching of the Resurrection of Jesus Christ." This was the proof He gave to friends and enemies that He was God. It was this wonderful fact that made the first Christians by bringing such multitudes into the Church at Pentecost. It was to commemorate Christ's rising from the dead that the first day of the week, Sunday, the Lord's Day, was appointed by the Apostles to take the place of the Jewish Sabbath.

Many men have worked miracles in His Name and have even raised the dead to life. But no mere man has ever raised himself to life. This God alone could do. Jesus Christ alone could say: "I have power to lay down My life, and I have power to take it up again." His Resurrection, then, proves Him to be God. If He is God, then all He has taught is true. We must believe in Him and we must do all He has commanded us.

There is no article of our Creed that we should say with more triumph and joy than this: "The third day He rose again from the dead." And with more hope. For it is because of the Resurrection of our Head that we, the members, look for our own and say: "I believe in the Resurrection of the body and life everlasting. Amen."

But we must go back to the Appearances of our Lord to His disciples, by which He confirmed their faith in this astounding Mystery. When during forty days they saw Him, touched Him, heard Him, ate with Him, they could no longer doubt the reality of the Resurrection. He was as real a person to them as Peter or John; He might be looked for at any moment; they could put their questions and difficulties to Him as before.

About a week after the Resurrection the Eleven left Judea for Galilee. They were glad to go north. Jerusalem had few happy memories for them. There the Lord had suffered and died. His enemies were there and more infuriated than ever since His Resurrection from the dead. It was by the simple folk of Galilee that He had been most followed and loved. Everything there—the mountains, the fields, the highways—spoke to them of Him. And above all, the Lake. On its beach they had received their call to follow Him and become fishers of men. There He had spoken the first parables and worked many of His deeds of mercy. He had stilled its storms and come to them across its waters. What wonder that they were glad to find themselves once more on the shores of that dear Lake!

It was strange to go back to nets and fishing after that marvellous Passover; but they were poor men, and had to live by their labour. And so when Peter said one evening:

"I go a-fishing," six of them answered:

"We also come with thee."

One of them was Thomas. He had learned his lesson; he was not going to lose a chance again by separating himself from the rest.

They put to sea and laboured all night, but caught

nothing. The sun was rising next morning when, through the light mist, they saw a Figure standing on the shore, and heard a Voice calling:

"Children, have you any meat?"

The weary men answered: "No."

"Cast the net on the right side of the ship," said the Voice, "and you shall find."

They obeyed, suspecting nothing. But when the net sank heavily, and they were scarcely able to draw it for the multitude of fishes, John said to Peter:

"It is the Lord!"

In an instant Peter was over the side of the boat and making for land with all his might. The six came up presently in the boat dragging the net with fishes.

As soon as they came to land, they saw hot coals lying, and a fish laid thereon, and bread.

Jesus said to them: "Bring hither of the fishes which you have now caught."

Simon Peter went up and drew the net to land full of great fishes, one hundred and fifty-three; and, although there were so many, the net was not broken.

Jesus said to them: "Come and dine."

Tired and hungry, they stretched themselves on the beach. And He went in and out among them giving them fish and bread. They looked at Him in silent wonder; looked at the Wounds in His feet and hands. They listened to Him, took food from His hands, touched Him as He went past. And when He came and sat down amongst them as in the old days, and the fresh morning breeze stirred His hair, and there were the sweet words and ways that belonged to Him alone, revealing Him every moment—what more could they want to convince them of the truth of His own words on the Day of the Resurrection: "It is I Myself?" St. John, who was there, tells us that "none of them who were at meat durst ask Him: 'Who art Thou?'" knowing that it was the Lord. He goes on to tell us what happened after that early dinner.

When they had dined Jesus said to Simon Peter:

"Simon, son of John, lovest thou Me more than these?"

He said to Him: "Yea, Lord, Thou knowest that I love Thee."

He said to him: "Feed My lambs."

He said to him again: "Simon, son of John, lovest thou Me?"

He said to Him: "Yea, Lord, Thou knowest that I love Thee."

He said to him: "Feed My lambs."

He said to him the third time: "Simon, son of John, lovest thou Me?"

Peter was grieved because He had said to him the third time: "Lovest thou Me?" and he said to Him: "Lord, Thou knowest all things; Thou knowest that I love Thee."

He said to him: "Feed My sheep."

Our Lord would give Peter the opportunity of making reparation by three professions of love for his three denials. And He asked him for a greater love than the rest, because of the greater trust that was to be committed to him—the charge of the whole flock.

The Church, as you will remember, consists of two classes: the Teaching and the taught. The taught are the simple faithful, whom our Lord calls the lambs; the sheep who look after the lambs are the bishops; they make up the Church teaching. Over all Peter is set as Shepherd. Teachers as well as taught, bishops and priests as well as the simple laity, are to look for guidance to Peter and his successors. As in the East a flock is kept together by following the shepherd, who walks on in front and leads it, so the flock of Christ is to be kept united by obeying its chief Shepherd the Pope; who is the successor of Peter and the Vicar of Christ.

"Go, tell His disciples and Peter," the Angel said to the women at the Sepulchre. Why "and Peter?" Was he not one of the disciples? Yes, but the first among them, who had charge of the rest and had to confirm them. This he did on the very Day of the Resurrection. And with wonderful success. What was an "idle tale," when told by the women, was the truth indeed when it came from Peter: "The Lord is risen indeed and hath appeared to Simon."

We must not think that the Gospels give us all the Appearances of our Lord to the Apostles after His Resurrection. St. John tells us expressly:

"Many other signs did Jesus in the sight of His disciples which are not written in this book. But these are written that you may believe that Jesus is the Christ the Son of God, and that believing you may have life

The Great Commission

*"Going therefore, teach ye all nations; baptizing them
in the name of the Father, and of the Son, and of the Holy Ghost."*
(Mt 28:19)

in His Name." St. Luke says: "He showed Himself alive after His Passion by many proofs, for forty days appearing to His disciples and speaking to them of the Kingdom of God," that is, the Church, which our Lord often called by this name.

In one of these Appearances He was seen by more than five hundred disciples at once. This Appearance on the mountain was the only one of which the time and place were known beforehand. Here our Lord was to meet His own by appointment. From all parts—Jerusalem, Judea, Galilee—they flocked to the spot, full of joyful expectation. And there, in presence of this large number of believers, He gave to the Apostles the solemn commission to teach the whole world.

And Jesus coming spoke to them, saying:

"All power is given to Me in Heaven and in earth. Going, therefore, teach ye all nations, baptising them in the Name of the Father, and of the Son, and of the Holy Ghost. Teaching them to observe all things whatsoever I have commanded you, and behold I am with you all days even to the consummation of the world."

XLI.

"This Jesus shall so come as you have seen Him going into Heaven."

And now His work on earth was done; the day was come for Him to return to the Father.

The Eleven were again in Jerusalem, in the Upper Chamber sanctified by so many mysteries. St. Luke tells us that He appeared to them as they were at table. And eating together with them, He commanded them that they should not depart from Jerusalem, but should wait for the promise of the Father, which "you have heard," saith He, "by My mouth; for John indeed baptised with water, but you shall be baptised with the Holy Ghost not many days hence."

And He led them out as far as Bethania.

How they must have thought as they followed Him up the slope of Olivet, of that night six weeks ago when He had led them from the Supper Room through the streets of Jerusalem to the scene of His lonely Agony, the beginning of His Passion. Now His sufferings are over, and He is going up Olivet to mount thence to His Throne.

They pass Gethsemane. The glory of the noonday sun is on the olive trees beneath whose shade He prayed that awful night. Here is the path down which they came on the day of palms when He wept over poor Jerusalem. Higher and higher they go, and now they stand on the summit.

He looks around. To the north is Galilee and Nazareth and the Lake. Six miles to the south, Bethlehem and the Cave. At His feet Jerusalem; and over there, Calvary and the Sepulchre. He thinks of all the glory to His Father, all the treasure for us, the three and thirty years of His Life on earth have won, and His Heart is full of joy. "It is finished," was His last thought on Calvary; it is His last on Olivet.

The time is come for Him to leave the earth, but He is long in bidding it farewell. His Mother is close to Him, and, pressing round, are His dear disciples, glad now, because they love Him, that He is going to the Father. For each He has a last word, the word He knows will reach the heart and meet the needs of each, and keep up faith and hope and love unto the end.

And He said to them:

"Go ye into the whole world and preach the Gospel to every creature. He that believeth and is baptised shall be saved, but He that believeth not shall be condemned. And these signs shall follow them that believe: In My Name they shall cast out devils; they shall speak with new tongues; they shall take up serpents; and if they shall drink any deadly thing, it shall not hurt them; they shall lay hands on the sick, and they shall recover."[1]

---
1 Mark 16.

And after He had spoken to them, lifting up His hands, He blessed them. And, whilst He blessed them, He was raised up, and a cloud received Him out of their sight. And, while they were beholding Him, going up to Heaven, two men stood by them in white garments who said:

"Ye men of Galilee, why stand you looking up to Heaven? This Jesus, who is taken up from you into Heaven, shall so come as you have seen Him going into Heaven."

"And they adoring went back into Jerusalem with great joy."[1] "And going forth they preached everywhere, the Lord working withal, and confirming the word with signs that followed."[2]

We began this story of Jesus of Nazareth with the question of the persecutor Saul: "Who art Thou, Lord?" We end it with the cry of the heathen centurion, as, sore afraid, he stood in the noonday darkness beside the Cross:

"Indeed this Man was the Son of God!"

This is the testimony borne by Heaven and earth and Hell itself to Jesus Christ. By the Angels singing in the midnight sky over Bethlehem. By the star that led wise men to His feet. By the Voice at His Baptism. By the winds and the waves of the stormy sea. By the earth that gave up its dead at His word and shuddered beneath His Cross. It is the

---
1 Luke 24.
2 Mark 16.

The Ascension

"Ye men of Galilee, why stand you looking up to Heaven?"
(Acts 1:11)

testimony of type and of prophecy, of His teaching, of His miracles, of His Resurrection and Ascension, of His divinely beautiful Character. It is the testimony of those who hated Him unto death and of the very devils themselves, as well as of those who in every age have loved Him and laid down their lives for Him with joy. It is the testimony of His Church to the end of time, of all who have eyes to see and ears to hear:

"Indeed this Man was the Son of God!"

Writing to his converts at Ephesus, St. Paul bade them hold fast the faith they had received, and beware of the false teachers who were come among them. As the soldiers of his time warded off an enemy's arrows by a shield that covered them from head to foot, so were these new Christians to "take the shield of faith wherewith to extinguish all the fiery darts of the most wicked one."[1]

To you, the children of this twentieth century, the great Apostle would give the same solemn charge. There are men in these days who are trying to undo all that Jesus Christ has done, who deny whatever in His Life they cannot understand, and teach children that such facts as His Resurrection and Ascension could not have happened because they do not see how they happened. It is very wrong and very cruel thus to rob the little ones of their faith in Him who died to save them from sin and hell.

---

1 Ephesians. 6.

Do not listen to such teaching. When men or women, companions, books or newspapers, would shake your faith in Jesus Christ—up, then, with the shield of faith: "I believe in God the Father Almighty, Creator of Heaven and earth. And in Jesus Christ His only Son, our Lord."

Cling to Jesus Christ. Let no one—let no thing—separate you from Him. He alone, by His Precious Blood, can wash away your sins. He alone can comfort you when you are poor, or sick, or desolate. He alone can give you courage in the hour of trial, victory in temptation, and help in the awful hour of death. When all desert you then, He will stand by you and keep you from harm if you have clung to Him all your life through as your Saviour and your Friend.

Cover yourselves, then, with the shield of faith when danger threatens. Be glad that as children of the Holy Catholic Church you are preserved from the ignorance and the disbelief which is taking Jesus Christ out of the hearts and the lives of so many who are outside. Say to Him joyfully with Peter and with Martha: "Thou art Christ the Son of the living God."

And be not afraid to profess your faith boldly:

> Jesus is God! if on the earth
> This blessed faith decays,
> More tender must our love become,
> More plentiful our praise.[1]

By your reverence in His Presence, by the frequency and the fervour of your Communions, by the observance

---
1 Faber.

of His Commandments and of the precepts of His Church, profess your faith in Him.

And if at times it costs, as it most certainly will, to show yourselves the followers of Jesus Christ, look forward to that Day when He in His turn will confess you before the whole world. Remember that this Jesus, who has been taken up from us into Heaven, is to come again. Look forward to meeting Him with joy at His Second Coming, to being owned by Him then for one of His, according to His promise: "He that shall confess Me before men, I will also confess him before My Father who is in Heaven and before the Angels of God."[1]

---

1   Matthew 10; Luke 12.

Additional titles available from

St. Augustine Academy Press
Books for the Traditional Catholic

Titles by Mother Mary Loyola:
Blessed are they that Mourn
Confession and Communion
Coram Sanctissimo (Before the Most Holy)
First Communion
First Confession
Forgive us our Trespasses
Hail! Full of Grace
Heavenwards
Home for Good
Jesus of Nazareth: The Story of His Life Written for Children
Questions on First Communion
The Child of God: What comes of our Baptism
The Children's Charter
The Little Children's Prayer Book
The Soldier of Christ: Talks before Confirmation
Trust
Welcome! Holy Communion Before and After
With the Church

Titles by Father Lasance:
The Catholic Girl's Guide
The Young Man's Guide

Tales of the Saints:
A Child's Book of Saints by William Canton
A Child's Book of Warriors by William Canton
Legends & Stories of Italy by Amy Steedman
Mary, Help of Christians by Rev. Bonaventure Hammer
Page, Esquire and Knight by Marion Florence Lansing
The Book of Saints and Heroes by Leonora Lang
Saint Patrick: Apostle of Ireland
The Story of St. Elizabeth of Hungary by William Canton

Check our Website for more:

www.staugustineacademypress.com

www.ingramcontent.com/pod-product-compliance
Lightning Source LLC
Chambersburg PA
CBHW021916180426
43199CB00031B/38